I0138408

GO

A Memoir
of Movement

GO

A Memoir
of Movement

JESSE O'REILLY-CONLIN

IGUANA

Copyright © 2023 Jesse O'Reilly-Conlin
Published by Iguana Books
720 Bathurst Street, Suite 410
Toronto, ON M5S 2R4

All rights reserved. No part of this publication may be reproduced, stored
in a retrieval system or transmitted, in any form or by any means,
electronic, mechanical, recording or otherwise (except brief passages for
purposes of review) without the prior permission of the author.

Publisher: Cheryl Hawley
Front cover design: Jonathan Relph

ISBN 978-1-77180-628-2 (hardcover)
ISBN 978-1-77180-606-0 (paperback)
ISBN 978-1-77180-605-3 (epub)

This is an original print edition of *Go: A Memoir of Movement*.

A Note on Names

With the exception of Hasan Hasanović, a survivor of the Srebrenica genocide, I have changed the names of all the people I encounter in this memoir to protect and safeguard their privacy and anonymity.

Introduction

It's April 2019, and my mother and I are sitting in the back seat of a car cruising along the smooth asphalt of the A7 connecting Casablanca and Marrakech. The driver asks if we wish to stop for anything at the approaching gas station. We politely say, "No, thank you."

I am thirty-four, and she is fifty-eight.

Morocco is the one hundredth country I have had the privilege of visiting, and I thought it would be fitting to visit it with my mother, the person who introduced me to travelling all those years ago.

She is reading Lonely Planet's guide to Morocco and tells me that our *riad* in Marrakech is close to Jemaa el-Fnaa, the city's famous central square and market. After she flips through a few more pages detailing Marrakech's array of attractions, she says, "I think the city will be a bit more touristy than Fès." And I agree.

In 2017, Marrakech welcomed over two million tourists for the first time in its history, helped by an increased number of European visitors, particularly from Germany, Spain, Italy, and France. A mere hop from Europe, Marrakech seduces its guests to enter its fabled souks, endless alleyways selling any conceivable kind of pottery, metalwork, or textile; the city dares them to wander through the square and be enticed and cowed by the snake charmers, henna artists, food vendors, and street performers. For Europe, Marrakech, and Morocco more generally, offers a slice of the exotic right at its front door.

Moroccans, and other travellers from sub-Saharan Africa, have tried to visit Europe but with vastly less success than Europeans have had visiting Morocco. In the first half of 2018, Moroccan authorities, with Spanish blessings, raided known migrant-hosting neighbourhoods of Tangiers, Nador, and Tétouan—cities close to the border of the Spanish enclaves Ceuta and Melilla. These crackdowns have led to the apprehension of thousands of migrants, asylum seekers, and refugees from throughout Africa who travelled to Morocco in hopes of seeking safety, opportunity, or both in Europe. Some of those apprehended were then bused to the Algerian desert and left to survive under the Saharan sun. Further to the east, along Libya's shorelines, more displaced people climb into decrepit dinghies, sail into the Mediterranean's vast blueness, and then drown. In 2018, over two thousand died on their way to Europe. The ones who survive must navigate the tangled web of European migration and refugee laws and confront citizens who are hostile to their presence on their coasts and amid their cities

In an attempt to bring some order to global migration, on December 11 and 12, 2018, the world met in Marrakech, and the United Nations General Assembly adopted the Global Compact for Safe, Orderly, and Regular Migration—the Marrakech Compact on Migration—as a framework to manage the lawful movement of the world's more than 250 million migrants. The guidelines are not legally binding, nor do they burden states with additional obligations; they prioritize state sovereignty as well as state cooperation in strengthening legal migration pathways, curbing irregular migration, and protecting the human rights of migrants. Despite the state-centric language and state-friendly provisions, twenty-nine states did not sign the compact in Marrakech, including Italy, Australia, and the United States.

However, in Jemaa el-Fnaa, the compact and its significance seem far from everyone's minds. The place is as kinetic as its reputation. It's a world unto itself, full of motion and unparalleled buzz. Despite the number of tourists, the market still holds the energy of exchange, of people from different corners of the globe meeting in a shared or communal space to buy or sell or trade. The snake charmers charm, the street performers perform, and the henna drawers draw. Men stand elevated behind their carts of fruits—a colourful collage of mangos and bananas and kiwis—waiting for customers to come and request a specific drink, to grab a handful of fruit, toss it in the blender, and create something delectable. They shout and motion for my mother and me to come and choose from their endless variety, just as restaurant touts shove menus under our noses and promise they serve the best tagines, the most delicious of mint teas, the perfect couscous. And we both reply in unison, "Non, merci." Craftspeople spot my mother's silver jewelry hanging from her wrists, the dozens of bracelets she has collected over the years from different countries, and they motion for her to come and pursue their goods. "Madame, ici." "Madame, ici." "Madame, ici." I cool my anxiety.

Crowds of locals gather around performers, four or five people deep, and despite my standing on tiptoes, I cannot see what the men do, only hear their voices as they tantalize and intrigue the onlookers, who stand in rapt silence. Above us, patrons watch the scene from restaurant balconies, sipping teas or coffees as the sun gently sets and the minarets gently glow. And more and more tourists stop to have their pictures taken with heavy DSLR cameras or light iPhones, posing with the energy as the background, the undeniable power of people in motion. Among the sellers, I wonder if any are migrants. Do they call Marrakech home, or does their final destination lie further away? I wonder how many actually have the legal right to work and live in Morocco. And I wonder still how many rely on movement for their very survival, and how many have had their right to movement scrutinized and eventually stopped. "Let's walk around the square one more time," my mother says.

I have never met a border I could not eventually cross. For people in the West, the world opens itself for discovery. According to the United Nations World Tourism Organization, the tourism industry is one of the great cogs of the world economy—in 2016 alone, it produced 7.6 trillion US dollars. The industry affects and influences many segments of a national economy, including hospitality, transportation, and entertainment. In terms of tourists themselves, their numbers increased from 528 million in 2005 to 1.19 billion in 2015. Europe receives the most international tourists while also producing the most—635 million in 2017. For the same year, the Middle East and Africa sent the fewest tourists, 42.1 and 39.8 million, respectively. And despite the lingering effects of the pandemic, tourism shows no signs of slowing. For a certain portion of the world's population, travel has never been easier; for the other, much larger pool, however, it has never been fraught with so many obstacles.

I am of the privileged portion. I find it rather curious when people call me adventurous or independent or courageous for simply travelling. I have the ability to do these things through no great effort of my own. I have the financial means. I have the time. And, most importantly, I have the passport. Whenever I cross a border, I am rarely met with derision or suspicion. Whenever I hand over my passport to immigration agents, whether in a polished airport or a decrepit building at a land crossing, I feel no great trepidation when they rifle through my passport pages filled with stamps and multicoloured visas, or when they check my details against what appears on their computer screen, or when they compare my passport photo with the actual human standing before them. I experience no great anxiety under this silent interrogation, no great fear from being pinned down and analyzed under a microscope's hot light, because I know I belong. I know, for me, a border is a mere administrative hurdle, something requiring a little patience, a bit of resolve—it is certainly nothing dangerous. For the border guards, my Canadian passport humanizes me more than my words, thoughts, and experiences. I need prove nothing to them other than my birthplace. My Canadian passport speaks for me. It grants me access to the world; it gives me the privilege to move.

I have seen others with more unfamiliar passports experience the border in different ways. On a shared taxi ride between Yerevan and Tbilisi, I sat beside an Iranian man while we drove over the undulating hills of northern Armenia. At the Georgian border, though, he disappeared somewhere within the Georgian immigration building and never returned to his seat next to me, which sat unoccupied all the way to Tbilisi. On a bus journeying the ten kilometres between Bethlehem and Jerusalem, I watched Palestinian commuters disembark at the border, form a line in the rain, and wait patiently to have their documents checked by young Israeli soldiers holding automatic weapons; and I continued to watch them, the Palestinians, wait outside the bus, wait to have their dignity approved by armed military personnel, when another Israeli soldier, much younger than I, with a machine gun draped over his shoulder, entered the bus, asked for my passport, and nonchalantly glanced at it before moving on his way. On the border between Ghana and Togo, I followed my Togolese guide as he approached a Ghanaian official, showed his identification, and was promptly asked for a bribe to return to his country of birth. But when the official realized my guide had no such money and saw me—tall and white—standing behind him and waiting, he motioned for me to pass. It was only when I said the Togolese man was my guide that the Ghanaian official did his duty and allowed both of us to leave his country.

I have seen and heard stories of others who have tried to travel to my country—or the nation-state on whose land I had the particular fortune of being born—and have had great difficulty accessing the land of the red maple leaf. Checking in and boarding Canada-bound flights from Bogotá or Addis Ababa, I have witnessed people, who usually do not look like me, have their documents scrutinized, their stories checked, and their credibility judged. In the customs areas of Toronto Pearson International Airport, I have witnessed Spanish-speaking families ordered to unpack their suitcases and answer a litany of questions about their purpose for travelling to Canada and where they intend to stay. I have read about those travellers who have had their asylum claims rejected or have committed a crime and are then imprisoned in detention facilities for years because the Canada Border Services Agency cannot organize their deportation with their country of birth. These men and women must then sit and wait, wait and sit, behind bars and within cells, and they grow so desperate and distraught that many have taken their own lives. I have read about the Canada Border Services Agency's desire to increase deportations of failed asylum claimants and other undesirables by 35 per cent, which would amount to around ten thousand people removed per year. I have read about the recent attempt by the Canadian Liberal government to reduce the number of asylum claimants in the country by amending the Immigration and Refugee Protection Act to disqualify any asylum seeker who has made a refugee claim in any other country. And I have read about the populist resurgence in Canada, mainly among its white citizens, who fear the country's growing diversity, and who desire more walls and more border security and more respect for traditional Canadian values, whatever those may be.

Yet this book is not about the inequities of the tourist industry, the global refugee crisis, or the privilege of those who get to call themselves travellers, although these issues do pepper the following pages. This book is far more modest in its goals. In the following stories, I explore my evolving relationship to travel and what it has meant to me over the years. I wish to talk about why, after one hundred countries and at the age of thirty-six, I have as strong a desire to leave as I did when I was eighteen and took my first international trip alone to New Zealand and Australia. What have been my motivations? What, if anything, have I learned about myself or the world? Why must I continue to depart again and again?

I remember the first time I travelled beyond North America. It was July 1998, it was to Norway, and it was with my mother. I was fourteen. Months before, she had asked if I wanted to join her on a trip to that fabled land of fjords and mountains, where in the summer months the sun never sets. I remember she asked me in dramatic fashion. It was a quiet Saturday morning—my sisters and father were still asleep—and she sat me down on our florid couch underneath one of her many hanging plants. She held a piece of white computer paper in one hand and a black pen in the other. I watched her hand float above the white, tracing out big letters to form even bigger words. Her mouth curved into a smile while she wrote as if she could sense my excitement building and blossoming and beckoning her to reveal the motive behind such a curious ritual as well as the words emerging on the page. At long last, she sat the pen aside and held the paper to my eyes: "Would you like to go to Norway?" I remember the exhilaration rush through me, filling me up with great delight and wonder, until I felt as a big as a blimp ready to float away. I was ready to speak, to shout, *Yes!* and to then ask a million questions about when, where, how, why. My mom simply put a finger to her mouth, imploring my silence, and with her eyes told me that for now, Norway would be our little secret.

What I remember most of our three-week trip through the Land of the Midnight Sun was how everything felt so new to me, so wonderfully different. The landscape was more undulating and unpredictable, a far cry from the flat farmlands of southern Ontario. The cars appeared smaller; their licence plates had a different design. At restaurants, the tip was already included in the bill, and my mom once accidently tipped our waiter over fifty dollars. The language was gloriously impenetrable, so different from English or French. I learned to say "thank you," or "*takk*," in Norwegian and used it whenever I could in the naive hope that the recipient would think I was a native speaker despite my brownish curls, which stood out among the heads of blond and straight hair.

With an old film camera, I took pictures of everything and exhausted dozens of rolls of film, much to my mother's chagrin, because of the cost. We sailed on the Hurtigruten ferry between Kirkenes and Bergen and drifted between tiny fishing towns sitting below mountains, at the sea's edge, in the belly of the fjords. For each community we stopped at, no matter how small, I had to buy a postcard from the ferry cafeteria, again much to my mother's chagrin. I had to prove I was there. I had to use every piece of evidence I could, any scrap of proof—a coin, a brochure, a ticket stub. I had to somehow document all the amazing things I had seen while floating down the Norwegian coast, as if I could somehow absorb each colourful house, each strip of serene coastline, each scene of beauty. Because I loved it, as much as a fourteen-year-old boy understood the verb or could, indeed, love anything. I loved the movement and travel, and I did not want to lose that sensation of drifting through difference and strangeness. I loved the newness of every morning, the fresh sea breeze, and the ever-changing landscape. Movement was exciting. And I knew on some level that Norway would not be the end of my journey but only the beginning. I knew I would move again and again, and I did—to Costa Rica, Türkiye, New Zealand, Australia, Indonesia, Denmark, etc.—just as I knew that Canada, which came to represent in my mind a static and sedentary idea, would never satisfy me in the same way again.

As I visited one country after another, my mom would joke that she did not get her first passport until she was thirty, as she was too busy raising three children, with the help of my father, and completing her dissertation and PhD. She would tease me over email or phone, when I was gallivanting across Europe or South America, that when she was my age, she was breastfeeding an infant while reading Simone de Beauvoir, Adrienne Rich, or Toni Morrison. And it was her own experience, as well as her playful ribbing, that always relativized for me certain adjectives often used to describe travellers. Indeed, I could never understand how travelling overland from Mexico City to Panama City could be deemed more challenging, or even more adventurous, than having and raising children while pursuing schooling at any level. Yet she never dissuaded me from travelling, never discouraged me from jumping on a plane, train, or bus, even after I had my backpack and passport stolen from an Auckland hostel when I was just eighteen; even when I had another bag stolen—this time with a laptop included—from a bus station in Trujillo, Peru; and even when I was mugged by some guys in Johannesburg's Central Business District. She was there with a supportive ear or with a plan of action. She worried, as did my father, but never let her concerns or even fears warp her approach to my travelling. And although at times I felt her concern overbearing or blown out of proportion, I now appreciate those sentiments for what they were: love. But it was not a love that squeezes and then suffocates a child's ambitions, that closes doors or forestalls movement out of some misguided sense of duty or protection. It was a love that allowed both self-discovery and failure, but wrapped in a blanket of concern, thought, and empathy.

My father was more of a homebody who, not unjustifiably, reasoned that one could spend one's entire life exploring an Ontario county without ever becoming bored or uninspired. His county of choice was Hastings. When my mother did force him to travel—heroically dragging him to the airport and then onto the airplane—it was generally to a place she knew he would like or, at least, tolerate. Being a descendant of Irish emigrants fleeing the Great Hunger, he loved the Emerald Isle, and he also adored Newfoundland and Labrador because they're Newfoundland and Labrador. But he seemed just as comfortable learning about a place through the written word, through the stories and tales and legends that had come to symbolize a region or community. He travelled through novels and non-fiction. As much as I respected his approach and could appreciate how a well-assembled sentence could transport a reader to a different place and reveal the intimate details about a community, culture, and way of being, I much preferred to visit those places in the flesh.

I never really questioned why I had this manic need to travel. If you had asked me, I would have said travelling enriches life. Travel's effect on people lies not so much in its physical bridging of different people and cultures but in its psychological connecting of disparate parts: how it engenders a particular way of thinking about other people. Travel encourages a mode of thought transcending nationalism's provincial concerns—a method of empathy prioritizing the inherent value of all and of seeking commonalities through our differences.

I still believe this about travel's potential, but my initial desire to travel did not have such lofty ambitions. I travelled to get away, simply to go. I would depart and return home, depart and return home. And then I would do it again. My eyes were always studying maps; my mind was always making mental itineraries of all the places I would visit on my next sojourn and was always making calculations about how much money I would need for a month, or two, or three of travel. I stayed both in hostel dormitories with ten other people and in hotel rooms with all the space I needed and more. I slept on trains and on buses. I camped. I got drunk by myself and, sometimes, with other people. I watched with a certain amount of pride my passport fill with colourful stamps and visas, and I would flip through it, smiling, as if reading a book I had just published. I took thousands of photographs and posted them, at various times, on Facebook, Instagram, and Flickr. I watched the upload bar with rapt attention, eagerly anticipating the moment when the photos would become visible online, and my friends would scroll through them with hot jealousy. And this online photo exhibition of famous cities and landmarks became my way of showing the world I had done special and remarkable things with my life. For a boy who had done relatively little of note, travel became my way to prove to the world that I had not wasted the time given to me. Travel came to define and validate me. I was special.

Travel, however, at least my conception of it, began to deceive me. I became so enamoured with the idea of movement and seeing and doing everything I could that I grew oblivious to the movement of my friends, family, and romantic others who remained in Canada. Travel, paradoxically, fostered a type of binary thinking in which travel birthed personal revolutions and engendered the greatest of epiphanies, whereas a sedentary lifestyle—a lifetime emplaced in a single community—and its monotonous routines and brutal sameness resulted only in a sort of pathetic acquiescence to the status quo. Yet whenever I returned home, I soon noticed that my friends, family, and romantic others had not merely stayed encamped in a single space or mode of thinking; they, too, had changed. They had travelled greatly without crossing any physical border, and they had grown tired of waiting for me.

It's summer 2008. I am sitting on a patio drinking a pint of Carlsberg with my ex-girlfriend, who is Turkish-Canadian. We had broken up a few months earlier on a cold day in March—over MSN Messenger. She had lost patience with my distance, both emotional and physical. She had become too frustrated with my plans of leaving and returning, of planning a future without her. She had waited for me when I studied abroad in Copenhagen for a year, even though I gave her no assurance that we were, in fact, in a long-distance relationship. And when I returned, she wanted something concrete from me, something tangible, something she could hold. So, when I could not promise her a future together, we decided not to postpone the inevitable.

We remained friends, though, and on this lovely evening, we are talking as freely and naturally as we once did. After two or three pints, I grow bold and tell her why I must always leave. "Life for me has always existed outside Canada," I say. "It's always been something I travel to rather than something I experience in the here and now." She lights a cigarette and then offers me one. She has always been generous with her cigarettes. The nicotine helps settle my thoughts and cut away the fat, leaving only the essential. "Being stationary has always felt like a kind of prison," I say, looking at my hands. She smiles and says, "It's no way to live." My blank expression signals to her I do not understand. "Well, if you cannot find peace or purpose wherever you are, travelling won't change that. You follow yourself wherever you go. You can't run from yourself. Whether in Toronto or Tehran, you are you." She takes a sip of her beer and then touches my hand. "And if you do feel the need to leave, don't promise yourself to another person."

Within a month, she had moved back to Türkiye, and I would not see her again for five years—until her wedding. After she left, I worked on finishing my master's thesis, dedicating an untold number of hours towards its completion, and during that time spent reading at a library cubicle or typing away at my computer in my room, I motivated myself by imagining what I would do once I had submitted my thesis, once I was freed from the responsibilities of my master's degree. Travel was on my mind, since I hadn't left Canada for over two years and had begun to feel that unrelenting itch to throw some clothes in a bag and jump on a plane. My country total had sat at thirty for a while, and I so desperately wanted to move to thirty-one and beyond. I kept to myself, locked away in a room with a computer and my notes, and finally submitted my thesis in November 2008.

Excitement followed relief, and in those weeks following my master's completion, I scoured the internet looking for potential places to visit. Teaching English in East Asia had always piqued my curiosity, especially given the many attractive benefits those jobs offered. But my passion did not belong to East Asia, at least not then; South America had already captured my heart. The continent had always intrigued me ever since my aunt had visited Uruguay when I was a boy. I asked my mom where Uruguay was, and when she said South America, I went to my globe and traced my finger around the southern part of the United States; I saw Georgia, Alabama, Mississippi, even Florida, but no Uruguay. My mother told me my error, and although I felt a little embarrassed, the gaffe made me want to learn more about this massive continent called South America. I took courses in university and became fascinated by the history, which only furthered my resolve to visit the continent once I had finished my master's. And even though my thesis was about the religious practices of enslaved Africans in Jamaica during the trans-Atlantic slave trade, South America and its cultures and landscapes called me more than that Caribbean island.

I completed a TEFL course, and whereas most of my colleagues had their sights on South Korea, Japan, or Taiwan, I was searching the internet for teaching posts in Peru, Brazil, and Argentina. These positions did not pay as well as the East Asian ones, but I did not care because my interest laid not in making money but in visiting places I had always dreamed about. I found a six-month volunteer program teaching English to kids in Chile: volunteers received a monthly stipend, lived with a Chilean family, and taught English at a local school twenty hours a week. The application involved organizing transcripts and letters of reference as well as answering a series of personal questions in essay format. I recently revisited what I had written.

What personal goals are you hoping to achieve as a teacher in a Chilean school?

First and foremost, I strongly believe that living abroad and immersing yourself in a different culture can be one of the most rewarding experiences in life. Removing yourself from your safety zone and delving into an unfamiliar culture can have the effect of deepening and expanding your personal outlook on life while, simultaneously, increasing your awareness and appreciation of the sheer and amazing diversity on this planet. Likewise, such an experience forces you to grow and mature, emotionally and psychologically; it compels you to engage in discussions that you might not normally partake in at home.

More specifically, I hope to learn Spanish during my sojourn in Chile. Recently, I have given more thought to completing a PhD in some facet of South American history, and a workable knowledge of Spanish is a definite must. Throughout my undergraduate and master's degrees, I took several courses in Latin American history. Whether it was studying Peruvian, Chilean, or Argentinean history, I was continuously fascinated by the enormous complexity of the region; grappling with the dizzying array of interactions (sometimes violent) between culturally diverse peoples, whether indigenous, Spanish, or sometimes African, throughout the colonial period and beyond proved to be a tremendously worthwhile experience. Throughout my academic experience, though, I always felt a pronounced disconnect between what I was reading in a book and the actual physical place that was being described. Because I had not experienced these cultures and places firsthand, I sensed that I could never fully appreciate their histories. It is my hope, therefore, that living and working in Chile will deepen my understanding of the amazingly rich culture and history of the region.

What perceptions do you have of Chile: the people, the culture, the school system, etc.?

What first comes to mind when I think of Chile is its intense geographical diversity. From the deserts and geysers in the north to the radiant blue glaciers and snow-capped mountains of the majestic Patagonia region to the south, with the towering peaks of the Andes and the sparkling waters of the Lake District comprising the centre, the dramatic landscape of Chile has always captured my imagination.

Although not as culturally diverse as its neighbours to the north, the population of Chile has, nonetheless, always struck me as cosmopolitan. Chile's people are mostly of Spanish ancestry dating back to the colonial period. After the colonial period, however, Chile was flooded by a wave of European migration, including Germans, Italians, Croats, and some English and French people. Chile, though, is by no means an artificial mirror of European culture; many different Indigenous peoples still live in various parts of the country. The northern Andean foothills, for example, are home to around twenty thousand Aymara and Atacameño peoples. The cultural landscape of Chile, in my mind at least, is a blend of European and Indigenous elements, with the former encompassing large segments of the urban population, and the latter comprising mostly the rural areas.

After only brief searching, it has come to my attention that Chile also has a vibrant arts (film and theatre) scene and a rich literary legacy. I am eager to delve into the works of the Nobel Prize–winning poet Gabriela Mistral as well as the literature of Isabel Allende. As well, I would very much like to attend a season production of a play in a town in the Lake District during one of its cultural festivals.

How do you feel you will adapt to living and working in a developing country? Give examples of how you have adapted to different lifestyles and circumstances.

I have extensive experience living, studying, and working abroad where I had to adapt to meet new and pressing challenges. In 2003, when I was eighteen, I embarked on a five-month journey to work in New Zealand and Australia. Upon my arrival in Auckland, New Zealand, my backpack was stolen from my hostel room; my passport, airplane tickets, and clothes were all taken. Consequently, I spent the next several weeks visiting various police stations, Canadian consulates/embassies, and travel agencies in hoping to recover or replace my stolen documents and possessions. In the end, I had to be issued a new passport; I was given replacement tickets; and I purchased new clothes. Obviously, this experience taught me how to cope in difficult situations and persevere in the face of daunting challenges. Without the comfort and security of my home, I was presented with a stark choice: adapt or go home. Luckily, I maintained my composure and refused to let the selfishness of a single individual ruin what would become a life-altering experience.

During the third year of my undergraduate degree, I participated in a ten-month exchange program to Copenhagen, Denmark. I lived with a Danish family, attended the University of Copenhagen, and familiarized myself with the intricacies of Danish culture. Each day presented a new yet rewarding challenge. Whether it was trying to overcome language barriers or wrapping my head around Copenhagen's dizzying and frantic bicycle lanes, I strove to meet each challenge with a touch of sensitivity and patience.

I believe these experiences and life lessons serve to greatly enhance my ability to effectively adapt to living and working in Chile. I have learned that to successfully adjust to a new country (developing or not) it is of the utmost importance to face each new situation with an air of serenity: what seems like an inconvenience or an annoyance one day may prove to be the most worthwhile of experiences. The willingness to learn, grow, and persevere from each inevitable difficulty is the foundation for a successful and worthwhile living-abroad experience.

Looking back, I see those words were a mixture of truths and lies. I wanted to visit Chile, of course, but I also knew what those recruiters wanted to hear. I have never read anything by Mistral or Allende, and I am no longer convinced that travel automatically leads to personal growth; rather, it has the real possibility to engender a life of narcissism and selfishness. To make oneself an island.

While writing those sentences, I remember, vividly, that an MSN notification flashed at the bottom of my screen—a message from a young woman I had met just after I'd handed in my thesis. She wanted to know how the writing was coming and what time I would be at her place on Friday. We had plans to go out. She and I had met through a mutual friend, and I liked her. She and I became close. She and I shared things beyond the realm of friendship. And even though I knew I was leaving soon, I still pursued her because I wanted her. I wanted everything—the girl and the world. I did not realize then that a life of movement is about making choices. It's about making sacrifices and compromises to ensure that you can look yourself in the mirror without being overcome by feelings of revulsion and self-hatred. If this collection of stories is about anything, it's about how I came to appreciate the road alone and how I made peace with my choices. When I left for Chile and South America in June 2009, I thought the trip would change me, and it did, but in unexpected ways; yet what I mostly thought was that everyone else would stay the same. I thought I was the main character in everyone else's stories. Yet travel is not a precondition for movement. Sometimes people take the biggest steps simply by standing still. The world waits for no one, and this memoir is my story of that realization.

This collection of stories ranging from 2009 to the present day is about my maturation as a traveller—a traveller's *Bildungsroman* if you like. It recounts my journey to adopting an identity of movement and what choices that involved—which doors closed as others opened and upon which events did my focus lie at the expense of others. What kind of person did I become with travel? And as much as this memoir is about my going to other countries and situating myself within them, it is also about leaving. What did I leave behind? What, ultimately, did I lose?

In these stories, I am so many different people—some likeable, others not so much. But they are all variants of me in all my imperfections and anxieties. Throughout the decade, as I travel again and again, I make more and more peace with my decision to leave. I accept the consequences and slowly understand that other people do not orbit me but I them. They are the sun, and I am a planet. In these stories, I gradually move from seeing travel, the world, only as medication—escitalopram, a serotonin booster, a little white pill to cure me from my obsessive and anxiety-riddled thoughts. I slowly put me aside, as much as possible, and move to understanding the world as existing outside myself, a world full of people and their stories. For me, travel becomes so much more than only escape. It is my melancholic way of life.

I have checked in for my flight to Santiago and am now waiting in the departures lounge. I rest my boarding pass and passport on the free seat beside me, open my laptop, and connect to the airport's Wi-Fi. Around me, travellers busy themselves with the art of waiting: they have a pint, or grab something to eat, or pick something up from the duty-free shop. I wonder where they are going. Are they going somewhere more exciting than I am? Or they doing something bigger, better, bolder?

At the bottom of my computer screen, her MSN name flashes in orange. I click on her, and her message says how sorry she is for the awkward, subdued goodbye, as she could have cried a lot there in the bus station but did not want to make a scene, did not want to be overcome by emotion, but, she says, she will miss me very, very much. She says to please send her regular updates and to please let her know how I'm settling in and how everything is going. She asks me not to forget about her.

I tell her I could never forget her. I promise to message her when I arrive and then the day after and then the day after that and then the day after that…

Part I

South America
2008–2010

1
Stay

Toronto, Iquique

2008-2009

There exists a picture of her and me floating somewhere in the tangled circuits of social media, kept in some server farm deep in the pine forests of northern Norway. In Madison's pub in Toronto, on a late May evening in 2009, she and I sit at a table encircled by my smiling friends. My hair falls to my shoulders, and I wear that ugly striped shirt she was gracious enough to say looked nice. A smirk has formed on my face, and my shining eyes stay focused on hers. In a grey hoodie, she leans towards me. Her head tilts slightly, and her slender fingers that I know so well touch a pint of Moosehead. Yet her face remains hidden, only a cheek and its dimple visible. Is she smiling in the photo? A few days later, I would depart for Chile and not see her again for close to a year.

And in my uglier moments now, back home in my parents' basement, surrounded by old video cassettes and dusty picture frames, I say she smiled at me in that Toronto pub. I sometimes forget the little things; my mind is often focused on other more important and grander matters. Memories are imperfect, of course, and after much time, they grow into different shapes and become infused with strange meanings. Like her. I can write to her now, for I know she will never care to read this. In a sense, I write only for me. In a sense, she ceased being real a long time ago. Yet how visceral she, the picture, remains for me; how deep her memories still burrow. Her smell lingers. Her taste loiters. Her touch lasts. She is forever in me. Closure is an invention of mental health entrepreneurs. Nothing ever goes away. I say these lines not to make sense of things but to relive them again and again and again. They remind me of a person I no longer am. And sometimes I do mourn for him. I speak freely now because my audience is largely ghosts. Something I never told her is that I am at my most honest when there are no consequences, my most heartfelt when alone among drywall and shadows, my most alive while running away.

Her name is Lovely—not her real name, of course, but a pet name I took to calling her. We meet on Halloween, 2008. She is the roommate of a friend of mine, Genevieve, and they, along with Samantha, the third roommate, are hosting a costume party. I knock on the door of their Junction-neighbourhood apartment, and I see Lovely come bounding down the stairs with her subversive smile spread across her face—a soft, pleasing grin that hides some subterranean force. She is dressed as a ladybug, and I have come dressed only in a simple suit. And when Lovely asks me who I am supposed to be, I tell her I am Patrick Bateman, Ellis's American Psycho, and she only nods and smiles, leading me up a flight of stairs to the festivities.

The party is full of youthful energy. The conversations are happy, the costumes silly. Genevieve's brother comes dressed as a sumo wrestler. The night is warm for late-October Toronto, and we sit on her deck, underneath a mammoth maple and above the downtrodden Junction streets, before the condominiums and Starbucks and A&Ws invade. Lovely is reserved and reflective. But not cold. She drinks Peroni, and I get drunk on Havana Club. She appears sullen, hiding some recent tragedy, and I watch her with a piqued curiosity. When she later asks me, in the kitchen, towards the end of the night, whether she could steal a shot of my rum, I say, "Of course." But I also debate asking her what's wrong, and I do, high on my sense of entitlement, as she would later state, and she says, "Oh nothing," and takes a sip of cheap wine before washing the dishes. In the night, I still hear her in the kitchen and then a loud crash, a dish falling maybe, and I come running but trip over my drunkenness and fall on my face. Thank goodness she didn't see me in that state, all vulnerable and unmanly.

In the next weeks, I add her to Facebook. I look through her photos, ones of her making tie-dye T-shirts at a summer camp for kids with multiple sclerosis, of her getting kissed on the cheek by a girlfriend, of her making silly faces amid some drunken escapade, of her standing with her ex-boyfriend, with whom she has just broken up. She likes one of my status updates. I check her few musical likes and send her YouTube links of the latest band making waves in the indie circle. There is nothing quite as magical as sharing something you love. She likes some. I drop hints of upcoming shows at Lee's or the Horseshoe, but she only replies with her guarded adjectives, declaring how "neat" and "exciting" it all is. She is cagey and addictive. She sends me videos of goats jumping over cedar-rail fences, of donkeys with long ears and toothy grins. Her favourite film is *Air Bud*. Her favourite food is cheese.

We chat for hours on MSN. Her status is always "away." I tell her my stupid, silly stories, trying to sound experienced and clever. I tell her funny tales about my year in Copenhagen, my adventures. I am a global citizen after all. She laughs in degrees of lettering and initialisms: "HAHAHA" for a polite chuckle, "HAHAHAHA" for a good giggle, and the classic "LOL" for a deep and lasting belly laugh. She speaks in emojis, each yellow face or broken heart representing a great gamut of emotions and feelings. I learn to speak her language, and she tells me things, too. About her parents' marital troubles, about her father's poor health, about her family's money woes, and how those struggles have inspired her to do social work, to help the marginalized, to fight social injustice, and to bring a slice of sun, an empathetic ear, to Toronto's homeless and addicted. She is applying for a master's degree in social work and asks me to look over her statement of interest. I like her sentence variety but feel some run a little too wild and advise a few semicolons and a conjunctive adverb or two ("moreover" being my sexy favourite, as she would recall) for breath and rest, adding a little calm to her rhetorical winds. In return, she promises to let me borrow her copy of *It Takes Two*. She tells me about her placement at an organization helping people express themselves through untraditional mediums, less oppressive storytelling formats. I tell her about my plans to teach English in Chile next year.

I visit her in early December for her birthday. I talk with Genevieve in the kitchen while eating cucumber slices and waiting for Lovely to arrive home from her job at the MS Society. And when I finally hear the door open and see her walking up the stairs, the grin is there, but I find it so odd to again put a human form to internet typographies. I have bought her People for Audio's new album as a birthday gift, and I hand it to her by the fridge. My voice quivers a bit as I explain how I want to give this CD to her now in case I forget later. There are too many unnecessary words flowing from my mouth, too much explanation, but she thanks me all the same. Yet everything is a little more difficult and a lot more real, and I feel uneasy and anxious, unsure what I am responsible for or what I may be guilty of. But we drink and the words come easy. The atmosphere grows warm and fuzzy, sentences fly unguarded, inhibitions flow over rotting palisades. I joke that she and Samantha resemble Danny DeVito and Arnold Schwarzenegger from the film *Twins*, and it goes over kind of well. Later in Margaret's, the most hipster shoebox club in the Junction, the DJ drops Underworld's "Born Slippy," and I hit the dance floor, orchestrating my own violent, flaying interpretive dance, which generates gasps and raises eyebrows, but I don't mind. And then, sitting at the table with Lovely, around a dozen bottles and glasses, the candle wick dancing, I admit my fondness for her, take her hand, and gently kiss it. I can't remember what she does.

I still feel ashamed for such an inappropriate gesture, such an invasion of her space, such a violation of her autonomy. The next day, she tells me over MSN that it's fine and not to apologize, but when I am shovelling the driveway back home in Bradford, listening to Lykke Li, I feel that shame grip me and squeeze me, draining me of my resolve, pride, and strength. And I should have left it there and stopped my chase of her. I should have dropped the pursuit and concentrated on my trip to Chile and the world. But later that week, I ask her on a date by joking that we could put to rest the historic and illusionary animosities between Port Perry and Bradford, our respective hometowns, if we simply got to know each other a little better. She says no and I say okay, but we continue to talk well into the morning about everything—embarrassment, heartbreak, fear, Chile. No matter what happens, I tell myself, life is better with her in it, no matter the form, shape, or texture the relationship takes. You see, I have always prided myself on being above the pettiness of romance, the scratches that irritate the more insecure, the less sure-footed. Friends are what matter. Allies and alliances. Yet when she calls me later in the month, upset about one of her encroaching calamities, I sing a Modest Mouse song to her (ridiculous, I know) about life's roughness, its unshakeable hardness, and she's quiet on the other end, and I still find it remarkable that I don't register the lurking suspicion that this is not in fact right, that this is not okay.

Over the next weeks, we stay so close. At New Year's, we go with Genevieve to her boyfriend's house party and, on the staircase, Lovely tells me in a not-so-low voice (uncommon for her) that she thinks he's a jerk and Genevieve could do so much better, but then Genevieve comes bursting in to inform us that everyone in the kitchen can hear our talking. A few hours later, after Lovely's had one too many drinks, she throws up in the washroom but remains so ladylike when someone comes knocking on the door. She replies, "Just a minute," in a tone that is somehow both mousy and threatening.

In the new year, on a wind-torn Wednesday in January, I visit Lovely at her placement on Queen Street West, right across from Dangerous Dan's infamous burgers, and she shows me her shared office space hidden deep in the building's bowels, very dungeonesque, and she lightly slanders some of her co-workers, shows me the work she does, and we go for something to eat at the Green Room on Bloor. What we talk about I can't recall, but I see Lovely dip her fork into the lettuce and cherry tomatoes, take them to her mouth and chew in that indescribably cute way—jaw circling, eyes cast away, with delicate and fragile little swallows. She eats slowly. She savours. But I rush and empty my plate with the rashness of a toddler. I recognize the music they play and name the band. She merely nods, remaining passive yet also somehow prepared to pounce on any nearby threat. She is an iceberg, and part of me fears what lies beneath the still waters. Yet there amid the low light, cheap pho, and Creemore pints, among the university students finding their voices and fighting for their futures, I fall for her. No, sorry. I choose to pursue her. And then in Spadina Station, standing in a stream of people, we hug awkwardly, unsure where to put our hands or for how long to hold the embrace. As I leave, I turn to see Lovely disappear down the stairs. Some of my clearest memories are of her walking away.

In Shoxs sports bar, deep in the heart of the Junction, Genevieve and I watch Lovely cry. Her parents have separated. Her eyes are bloodshot. She sips a pint. Genevieve offers warm words, and we listen to Lovely's sad ones. Every few minutes, she turns to me, but I can offer only a tired grin or a platitude or silence. I drink my orange juice and feel that anxiety come again, stifling and accusing, settling under my collar, reminding me of something that I already know but refuse to see because of her face, because of Lovely. Later, outside of Dundas West Station, in front of a busy McDonald's, beside a Toronto Sun newspaper box, we see our breath twirling in the black February sky, and I try to tell her how sorry I am and that it will be alright, as there is nothing else to say, right? What can you say other than tomorrow may be better? What else can you do but hug someone and just be there for her? If she trusts you that much to disclose her secrets, then you stay, and you listen. You don't yet go.

The next weekend, I visit Lovely when her roommates are out of town. I bring her a block of cheddar, which she warmly accepts, and a bottle of rum, which we don't drink. We go for dinner and talk of pleasant things. Later at night, after making top-ten lists of our favourite things, she sits on the sofa and I on the rocking chair. We watch *WALL-E*. And I ask for permission to sit next to her, and she consents. On the screen, WALL-E collects trash on an abandoned Earth, and Lovely's feet are curled on my lap. WALL-E meets Eva, and Lovely's face has come close to mine. Her cheek sways across mine. I say how nervous I am, shaking, and she tells me to kiss her, and I obey. Later, WALL-E stays with Eva when she powers down, and he follows her through whatever turmoil and disorder come. Lying on Lovely's bed in her room, among a marked copy of *Mrs. Dalloway*, a biography of Debord, walls with squashed spiders, and a shelf carrying an old television set, I tell Lovely that I will still leave in three and a half months, and it is best not to define this as anything concrete, and she says okay. In the mirror, she plays with my brown hair; my touch travels along her skin.

The next months are full of laughter and silence. She visits my Bradford home, my parents, and my pets. We play drunken Trivial Pursuit and soak in the hot tub. We go for walks in nearby cedar groves, their branches fat with snow, watching chickadees and red-headed woodpeckers swoop in the air. In the city, I take her to see Mamet's *Glengarry Glen Ross* and Harrower's *Blackbird* at Soulpepper Theatre, and we talk about the personal temblors both plays evoke, the quiet, horrible memories that shape and guide us. At the Phoenix Concert Theatre, she leans back on me, and I rest my chin on her shoulders, my arms coating her, while we absorb Mogwai's devastatingly beautiful set, the long instrumentals invoking such prodigious sensations in me that she shakes her head when I stare down some fool who dares to speak during one of the band's epic ten-minute songs.

One late April afternoon, we cross a bridge over the Don Valley Parkway, holding hands as we enter Corktown and move through the downtown core into Queen Street West, stopping every now and then to shop for Genevieve's birthday and sample gourmet pizza, sip margaritas. And when I say I hope to do a PhD in England someday, she smiles and says nothing. Across the street, we see the parade of Tamil protestors, red flags with tiger faces waving in the wind, march down University Avenue, protesting the interminable civil war in Sri Lanka and the ceaseless atrocities committed against Tamils in Jaffna, the top tip of India's teardrop, and we admire the activism of their diaspora, the determination, despite the distance, to defy silences and to defend the sanctity of both their homes.

Over the closing weeks, whether sipping cocktails in Ossington's raucous bars, perusing African history titles in Dundas's used bookstores, or kicking soccer balls on sunny May afternoons, listening to Sufjan Stevens in bed on warm nights, I try not to rest my eyes too long on hers, try not to talk too long about the deadline or what happens after. I only mention mechanically, as if on autopilot, that this is a great opportunity, yes very great, and I would regret forever not going to Chile to teach English, not sampling each experience there, not tasting each gilded opportunity. She nods and says nothing, and then I say nothing. And when Lovely is accepted into the University of Toronto, I feel better, knowing perhaps that she is less likely to make me stay, that now she too has that reason to go on, a spark that pushes her towards great things—albeit closer to home.

My final Saturday, that night at Madison's when our photo was taken, I get drunk, and later at her place, after a final cigarette, I vomit over her second-floor deck into her eavestrough, and I apologize, and she takes me to bed. The next day, my head is glass, my stomach eviscerated, and we crawl to the subway to begin our journey to my house, where we spend our last time together hungover and tired. Lying in bed, Lovely jokingly tells me that she hates me, hates me very much, and a coolness falls over us, and we fall asleep in silence after I switch off the lights.

The next afternoon, I drop her at the Newmarket GO Bus Terminal. Saying our goodbyes, we hug and, on the bus, through dirtied glass, Lovely waves to me until the bus moves, brakes, and pulls out of sight. Driving back home, I stare at the empty seat beside me and behind those flashes of sadness, pricks of regret, a sensation of relief comes to me, I'm sorry to say, and when it settles, I should realize that she does not go so gently into the past, does not holiday so well in memory.

My city of Iquique, Chile, is the stuff of science-fiction writers, a figment of some feverish imagination, since the city simply should not be. Along Chile's northern coast, the Pacific's waves are unmerciful and beat the shoreline. Amid the sand, dust, and salt of the world's driest desert, the Atacama, there crouches Iquique, swathed in sand, its apartment blocks standing as monoliths, bravely repelling the encroaching dunes and volcanoes and mountains. The city was born in the second half of the nineteenth century with the discovery of sodium nitrate nearby, and it ravenously sprouted, growing along the coast and up the dunes, attracting both money and men, creating an outpost at the world's end, a tavern at the desert's terminus, a real mirage, bountiful and full of riches. Now, after decades of booms and busts, the city barely remembers its treasures. Along Arturo Prat Avenue—the martyr who gave his life in the War of the Pacific, helping bring about the victory over Bolivia and Peru, that gave Chile this city, this coastline—crews water patches of grass and douse fledgling palms with liquid, protecting this splash of colour at all costs, a tiny shield against brown's ubiquity. Across the streets, Playa Brava stretches towards the distant dunes, and over its drifting sands, young families fly kites, barefoot kids kick footballs, and tanned surfers ruffle by, boards underarm, daring themselves not to test Brava's murderous breaks. The city streets are windswept. Slivers of sand sneak under the doors and through the windows of the colourful, fragile homes standing in neat lines along *Calles* O'Higgins and Allende and others, and they ache and creek under the slightest wind or tremor, shiver at the thought of a tsunami rising over the Pacific, of which, perched as they are on the dunes' slope, they would have the perfect view. Iquique is vulnerability writ large.

Lovely writes me daily, long Facebook messages, full of Toronto details, of the lives and routines that I left. She airs her frustrations with her friends, her difficulties with student loan repayments, the troubles with her family. She finds long hairs in her bed and laments that she no longer has me to talk to; she feels, in some strange way, as if she were going through a breakup, and she hopes I will be kind enough to tell her whenever I fall for any other girls. Honestly, she insists, she wouldn't get mad. I laugh at her insecurities and tell her that there are no girls and that I miss talking to her, too. Lovely is jealous of my meeting new people, of my experiencing new things. And I can hear the first murmurings of resentment, the solidifying of a particular narrative, one that I can hardly blame her for adopting.

I tell Lovely some things about my new school, my new Chilean host family, my new life in this sandy corner of Chile, but not all.

Coated in light beige, my house is utilitarian and unromantic. Teetering halfway up Dragon Dune, it stands midway along the city's socio-economic spectrum, the dwellings getting flimsier, the people poorer, the higher the sands. My host mother wears blue blouses and glasses and spends hours on the computer talking to friends when she's not teasing me for my limp Spanish; hers sputters as manically as a trader's. She makes wonderfully thick soups full of meat and vegetables, and when we sit alone at the table in silence, she makes me read the condiment ingredients in Spanish, and I flush and falter over the strange sounds, the double consonants, the devilishly silent *h*, but it is the struggle that makes the mundane memorable. My host sister teaches English at my school; she is affable and approachable, going to great lengths to make my stay as comfortable as possible. My host brother is a young ruffian, early twenties, with a kid in hand. He's a child of the mines, often venturing to the mountains for days on end and labouring in their dark pits for hours upon hours without respite or fresh air or sunlight. His gear and helmets, heavy pants, and coats often lie scattered across the living room, where he sits on his rest days watching American television shows with Spanish subtitles, which is how he became fluent in English. The father has been in the mines for months, and not much else is said about him.

We all smoke. On weekends, with the smell of eggs and bread mixing with tobacco, the house has a wonderful diner vibe, and we all lounge in the dining room or in the backyard—a poor man's courtyard full of sand, a washing machine, and clotheslines—on lumpy sofas and smoke and talk nonsense through translation. It never rains here, they tell me, and in the night, in the desert, it can get cold, and I brush away their threats of *frio* and reply confidently, "*Soy de Canadá.*" We grow familiar and jokes come easier, and I tell my brother that I hope to visit Argentina and wonder if I should send his thanks to the country, given, of course, that without the brave San Martín and his heroic crossing of the Andes, Chile would still be Spain. His mouth widens into his smile—wide, wild, and whimsical—and he stares at me, dumbfounded, doubting that I could have said such a blasphemous remark. He replies in kind that Canada looks beautiful as America's top hat, and I laugh and love that we can joke about something as inane as nationalism, things as inconsequential as borders, that to love a country would be, to paraphrase Vonnegut, as silly as hating one. But after we finish speaking, he leaves and visits his toddler before returning to the mines, my sister plans for her sixty-hour workweek paid in a pittance, and my mother retreats to her computer screen. Nothing appears as simple as it did a few seconds earlier, for I cannot shake the privilege that sticks to me like sap.

In the hubbub of Iquique's Wild West downtown, at the intersection of two sand-covered, forlorn-looking streets, stands my school, three-stories strong, full of children and teenagers from ages seven to seventeen. Outside, the school appears as a reformatory prison for wayward children, the walls grey and menacing and unwelcoming, and the security ever present and omnipotent. Inside, the ground screams with colour—large swashes of blue, red, and orange—and the sky and sun are visible, since no roof covers the institute; instead, there is a courtyard full of ping-pong tables and seating areas, while the classrooms ring every floor, each providing a lookout over the space, the ideal spot for a watchman, inspired maybe by Bentham's panopticon, to spy on advancing Peruvians over the rolling dunes or loitering teenagers looking for cigarettes or worse. Part public and part private, the school exudes upper-middle-class intentions; the teachers wear quasi lab coats adorned with the school's logo, while the students meander in rather perfunctory uniforms, dyed a dull blue. The school is a lesson in hierarchy.

My third-floor English classroom—with its finicky door, strewn desks, and cheap wipe boards—houses the school's English library, full of widely read authors, mostly male Europeans, who have been translated into English—Saramago, Camus, Dostoevsky—the perfect texts for language learning. In the first weeks, my co-teachers bring their students to visit me there, and introductions are done, and they all look at me skeptically, a mixture of curiosity and derision, as if I were a green alien—a novelty, sure, but one that will soon be intruding upon their lives. The girls ask me if I have a girlfriend, and I say no; the boys are busy bashing one another and throwing garbage and take my co-teacher's threats only half seriously. I then follow them to their classrooms and survey my co-teachers' classes to get a flavour for their structure, the pedagogy, the approach. I am amazed when I see my native tongue broken down into bits, dissected like a bullfrog's bladder, and ruthlessly analyzed, and I know that each flowery sentence, each strand of my prose, says less about me the person, the writer, the speaker, and more about how language operates and shapes and controls. The grammatical codes are foreign to me, and when the teacher asks a question, I know the right answer but not why, not how, powerless to explain why one word works better than the other. Luckily, I don't instruct grammar; I am there to get them talking and listening. I am the celebrity peacock.

The morning Lovely screams at me through email is the morning I am bitten by a dog. Every morning outside my house, a pack of fluffy dogs roams, and it must be my exotic smell that attracts them for they bother few others and take to me like bees to nectar. And this morning, an aggrieved bearded collie nips at my calf, and I feel its fangs sink into my skin before I kick it loose and make threatening overtures to the others. Yet in the colectivo, squashed between two other riders, on my way to school, my thoughts are less on the bite and the risk of rabies, and more on Lovely, her words and accusations. She writes that I treated her as a stepping stone, a mere bridge between the completion of my master's degree and my leaving for Chile. She says that for me, she was just something that kept me occupied, busy, and entertained until I was ready to move on to the important thing. She was my clown, jester, buffoon. She asks me in a desperate, pleading tone just what the fuck we were thinking, what the fuck we were doing, spending all that time together, becoming so close and intimate, only to rip it from our skin, soak it in gas, toss a match, and watch it burn. She says it was going so well, so why? Why leave? Or why, she wants to know, did I even pursue her. She says I used her. She says I saw her only as a safe bet, a pleasing, rent-a-girlfriend that I could dispose of at a moment's notice. Toss away. Discard and ditch and dump. She says I used her. She says that I used her.

Outside my school stands a shack that sells instant coffee in paper cups and twenty-cent confectionary. And on that morning, after reading Lovely's accusations, I sip my coffee at a picnic table, light a cigarette, and think about her. I watch the students streak into the school and try to hide my smoke from disapproving teachers who haunt the environs. In the distance, trucks climb over the dunes on lonely lanes of asphalt that follow the fallow coastline for hundreds of miles through abandoned mining towns and hills, full of Pinochet victims, to Arica and finally to Peru's border. Iquique is a city of ghosts. One hundred years ago, striking miners marched along this street, Thompson, to Baquedano—the old mining heart of the city, flush with new nitrate money that built the famous wooden clock tower and municipal theatre, which hosted gaudy plays and operas and balls for the well-fed crowds. The miners and other tradesmen, ten thousand of them, had descended from the nearby hills and towns to protest their hellish working conditions, the pauper wages, the obscene company store prices, and they brought northern Chile's economy to a standstill. Five thousand workers occupied the Santa Maria School for over a week, and when General Silva Renard, on orders from President Montt, ordered the workers to vacate and they refused, Silva gave the command, and his soldiers launched volley after volley of bullets into the school, shattering windows, puncturing doors, and killing over two thousand men. Their bodies were littered in a hole somewhere in the desert, unremarked upon for decades. I try to put this all together, sitting there on my chair, with her, the city, the atrocities, but it doesn't fit, no enlightenment comes. And when I enter the school, the philosophy teacher wants to talk to me about de Beauvoir, and soon both Lovely and the dog bite have faded from my mind. On the drive home, the colectivo driver asks me if I have a girlfriend, and I say no. Perplexed, he wants to know why. There is no time, I say.

I respond to her email in curt sentences. I am angry. I defend myself. I pepper my prose with such words as "audacity" and "cognizance" and "agency." I never lied to you, I write. I never misled you. I told you from the beginning that I would leave, that I would do this. You knew. You entered this relationship under your free will. You chose. You acted. You decided. I never forced your hand. I told you I have to do this and that if I didn't, I would regret it forever, and

I would hate you for making me stay. It is a once in a lifetime opportunity. I have to visit these places. I must go.

Later that afternoon, I am running along Playa Brava, dodging the waves crashing upon the shore, ducking the kite lines flown by families, sidestepping the sandcastles and the children with their little yellow shovels, and the sun shines hot on my glistening face, and I know I have lied to her, in a sense. This is not a once in a lifetime; this is what I do. I leave. I exit. To leave is to be reborn. To encounter the unfamiliar is to be enriched. To travel is to be reincarnated every day. Every day is an epiphany. Every day is Stephen Dedalus on the beach. Every day is full of infinite possibilities, endless beginnings, fields of potential. Home is the place that sucks the spirit dry, ensnares you in routine and responsibility, makes the mundane seem marvellous. Home is four walls. Home is a shack on ice in mid-April. Yet as I quicken my pace, that image of Lovely, eating lettuce leaves, illuminated by a bending candle wick, doesn't shift, doesn't flee. And the more I see her, the picture, the more I want to believe that both worlds are possible, that I can have my cake and savour it too, that I can have her and this beach, that I can have it all. I do not let her go. But when she apologizes for her outburst, I sense her letting me go, pushing me out to sea. In her rehearsed, businesslike words, I sense her wish to move on, to distance herself little by little from me, from my words, my look. Her words beat with a soft subtext of partition, with an unspoken promise to never confide in me again.

In the next weeks and months, we talk more or less regularly, with little noiseless spells. She tells me about her first weeks of graduate school, the maddening schedule, and the ruthless workload. One night, she is working at Robarts Library and tells me she is going home soon, and when after a few hours, she appears back online, I say I was about to go bed, and she chastises me for considering sleeping without knowing if she was okay. I apologize but argue there was not much I could have done if something had happened. Her silence confirms something.

I tell her about teaching, about the struggle to instill some order in my chaotic classroom, about the girls who look at me and coolly deny my authority, about the boys who rearrange the desks and talk freely and look flabbergasted when I intrude and tell them to please be quiet and sit down. I am an authority figure, and it feels odd. And most of the time, I despise the little monsters.

There are moments though, brief respites, sitting at my desk correcting paragraphs or preparing a lesson, when I look at the walls and see my students' work taped there, and I feel a small sense of satisfaction. These are children after all, undoubtedly full of secret grief and confusion, and I should be sympathetic. So when a little hellion, ten maybe, refuses to listen and races around the classroom, shattering the small tranquility I had mustered, I send him back to his classroom, to his English teacher, amid his cries of *"una broma, una broma,"* and I tell him I don't care if it was a joke. Yet when my co-teacher tells me that as punishment, he has been suspended from the football team, my heart seizes, and I can see his little face rumple, and I plead with her to reconsider, that the punishment surely outweighs the crime. Or when one of the Grade 9 twin girls thieves a bag of candy from the classroom—I always reward participation with sugar—I fly into a rage and demand restitution, and I tell Lovely, and she says just to listen to them, understand the why before you punish the how, and I grow angrier and angrier at her nonchalant condescendence, her haughty moral relativism. When the guilty do ask for forgiveness, I hate myself for the outburst, my childish temper tantrum, and I hate Lovely for being right, for being better. Because as the weeks unwind, and I stay longer and longer, the stakes become that much higher but so do the rewards, the riches of watching something struggle yet persevere, yet grow in desolation, a forest in the sands with trees stretching to the light.

At my house, we all adopt a routine. My mornings consist of chilly showers, pieces of bread, first cigarettes under morning's twilight, and agile movement to avoid the morning melee of many people crowding together in a small space. Mostly, I like the early-morning quiet, the soft split between night and morning, the stillness, the hush. After school, I struggle to communicate with my host mother without the help of translators and always feel guilty and self-reproachful for not learning more Spanish, not making more of an effort. But we do talk strategically through the words we do know, and she takes her revenge when she sticks olives into my sandwich after I kindly explain that I would prefer baked sand to the awful bitterness of that pitted glob. She always laughs at my distorted face. The weekends are full of rum and hangovers, Facebook rants, and music sharing. On Saturday nights, I post songs on Lovely's Facebook wall and imagine her pressing play for the first time and becoming consumed by the strings, the notes, the synthesizers, falling under their spell, succumbing to the hazy delight, its emotional pull, feeling that space it now fills, and wondering how she ever survived without it. I see her falling in love with them. But every time I share a song, she takes longer and longer to like it, to comment on it, and I admonish myself for such selfish thoughts. She has a life. She has friends. She has passions. And to quell my growing anxieties, I pour myself a drink and light another cigarette.

The father has returned from the mines and has cast a pall over the house. The dinners pulse with unspoken tension; husband and wife do not speak; daughter and son offer the shortest and simplest of sentences to the father. The conversations run brief and cold. His ruddy and rough complexion, his stocky and compact frame, bespeak a military man, one obsessed with ritual and routine, discipline and punishment. However, he is not from the army but from the mines, another profession that demands allegiance to order, position, and rank. He is conservative. He intimidates there at the table, sipping his soup and tearing his chicken. He is a hard, unflinching man. And when he turns his attention to me, his questions coming in short, swift bursts, I become redder and feel the pricks of perspiration. He wants to know about Toronto, its population and ethnic composition. I say it is one of the most multicultural cities in the world, but problems of racism, exclusion, and marginalization still exist, and he scoffs at the suggestion and makes some offhand joke about Black people and how the Mapuche, an Indigenous group in southern Chile, need to adjust to the modern times. I eat my meal, head down in angered reticence, thinking about how much silence I owe as a guest. I imagine again San Martín's army crossing the Andes to help O'Higgins free Chile from the shackles of Spanish enslavement, his infantry largely made up of emancipated Black Africans, who know more than most that slavery is more than metaphor.

The father stares at me, his eyes holding my anxious and fraught posture, and asks in boyish glee, making no effort to hide the joyful countenance draped over his whiskered mouth, whether Pinochet was a president or a dictator. "*¿Presidente o dictador?*" He knows such a question has steep consequences, layered in political explosives, and has divided not only his own country but the world. I already know what he thinks of old Augusto, am already playing the arguments internally. The general did what was necessary. On that afternoon on September 11, 1973, he saved Chile from itself, rescued it from an avowed Marxist, Allende, and restored order, restored balance, restored prosperity. He hacked the economy from socialist hands, planted the seeds of neoliberal reform, and watched the riches fall on certain segments of the population. Labour unrest was quelled. The ornery remarks of dissidents were shushed. The poison of communism was sucked and spat out. Chile was inoculated.

I sit and wait for the lecture to die, for his smug smile to dissipate, for the translation to end. I think instead of a village just north of here, Pisagua, a hamlet of old mining lore, now full of abandoned hospitals and army barracks, a ghostly town to which parents threaten misbehaving children with exile. Twenty years ago, twenty bodies were found there buried in the sand, whose minerals preserved the cadavers in perfect form: clothing, bandages, flesh, slashes, and bullet holes, all visible, all mummified by the sand, all there. In the early days of Pinochet, the town transformed into a concentration camp where critics were tortured and killed, thrown to the sands, others to the Pacific. Atacama became a mass grave for the three thousand people who disappeared under the general's watch, with a sandy graveyard being discovered every few years. In the lonely communities of the Atacama, in some parts that have never seen a drop of rain, old women walk with shovels, stopping periodically to dig and hope, for closure, for a sense of peace, for the remains of their beloved. One found her husband's shoe and nothing more. Amid the unmarked graves, deep in the desert, stand observatories. With their giant antennas and slick radio dishes, they resemble rhinoceros beetles standing upright on a pair of legs, their heads reaching to the heavens. The telescope can pinpoint golf balls fifteen kilometres away. With its high altitude, thin atmosphere, low humidity, and lack of rain, the Atacama is the world's best place to peer into the universe and rummage in its further galaxies and darkest corners, probe gas clouds and watch stars, planets, and worlds form through mingling waves of incandescence.

Towards the end of the semester, we prepare for English Week, in which schools from all over Iquique gather at Plaza Prat to perform English songs and other English-related acts. Most of my classes have chosen to perform English songs, and I must practise with each class to work on pronunciation and enunciation. One class rehearses Michael Jackson's "We Are the World" and its trite lyrics. Pacing the classroom floor, I lose myself in the monotony, the repetition of the same lyric over and over, and I often order, "Again!" before they have even finished. Each rendition kills me a little, and seeing my students' lacklustre and bloodless faces, I sense they are dying a little too. Another class practises Placebo's "The Bitter End," a teenaged angsty rock song full of references to "winter days," "suicide," and "broken bones." From its opening chords, it accelerates with a rapid beat and tempo, Brian Molko's androgynous vocals, and his barely decipherable lyrics. And when the students try to keep up and trip and stumble over words like "anesthetized," they begin to sound less like distinguishable words and more like cacophonous shrieks, formless noise that cracks and croaks without meaning or harmony. Other groups research English-speaking countries, their cultural practices, and one group of twelfth graders asks me what a typical example of Canadian cuisine might be, and I ramble about how there is no prototypical dish, no one meal that typifies the vast range of Canadian eating practices. They look at me blankly and sulk away with heavy disappointment. Later, when Lovely tells me over email I should have just said poutine, I respond I would rather have them present an empty bowl as an example of Canadian cuisine than French fries drizzled with diarrhea-esque gravy.

Despite the uninspired vocals, tedious rehearsing, and overall humdrum of the music classes, a little light has broken through the grey. During some lunch hours, while the rest of the children lounge in the courtyard with arms draped over one another's shoulders, the school drowning in a chorus of laughter, I sit with a girl, eleven maybe, in the quiet confines of my classroom and sing Toni Braxton. Throughout the semester, this girl has always been shy but conscientious, a diligent worker lacking the confidence of the better English orators among her peers. When requested to speak in class, she always says each word deliberately, her fingers slowly moving over the line, with her mouth patiently forming each odd sound until the word coalesces. The results are impersonal and cold, but the effort is beyond reproach. Yet now, sitting beside her, my larger frame undoubtedly causing her some form of anxiety, she sheds her automaton skin whenever I press play and "Un-Break My Heart" stirs to life on the CD player. When the first string and piano notes shimmer, she forgets I am there and transforms before my eyes from timid girl into thundering diva. Her tiny frame begins to shudder; her minute hands curl into fists and become locked to her chest. In the power ballad's first seconds, she shakes and stirs and sways, her eyes closing, her lips preparing. And then she drops the first prefix in a low note, a deep baritone; I am stunned by her power and resonance, the sheer drama shot from her vocal cords. She follows Braxton's range and imitates the pain and torment lodged in each lyric to such effect that I believe her. She holds and commands each note, stretching and pounding consonants to their breaking point. She rocks over the bridge and lets the slow tempo gently move and nudge her body. Yet it is only the calm before the denouement, the crashing climax, and when the song reaches its feverish top, the hurt, the tears, the goodbyes forming into an unbearable apogee, she flails her arms in the air, careens her neck, and matches the song's muscle word for word.

In the coming days, I practise with her more and more. In between songs, I ask questions about what she thinks the song is about and the meaning of certain words and phrases, and it becomes clear that she doesn't know most, can't explain the significance of the majority of verbs and nouns. Yet when I go to the wipe board and attempt to draw the meaning of *unbreak* through a series of messy lines and x's, I see boredom fall across her face and realize that I am draining the magic. For to distill the definition of each word is to miss the point. She doesn't need translation; she doesn't need explanation. Despite her young age, her limited time here on the sandy coast of Chile, she knows what the song is about. She can feel its meaning through the music. And when she sings, she tells me the song is about survival. She tells me the song is about resurrection. She tells me the song is about taking the past, honouring it, and moving forward. And what is even more important is what she has already done, long before I arrived. She has said yes. She has decided that she can. She can bare her soul in front of some gringo. She can work until those words sound from her as naturally as they do from Braxton. She has the confidence and audacity to sing, to see something through to the end, no matter the embarrassment, the stares and giggles of *no you can't*. She endures here in the desert. She is a spring. She is an oasis. And when she sings again, so full of passion and devotion, amid the bones and bodies of miners and dissidents, the femurs and fibulas that won't rot, won't go away, that stay and linger and remind, I know that it takes far more strength to stay than it does to leave.

In front of the municipal theatre, draped in the colours of the Chilean flag, the children of Iquique perform a medley of English songs under Atacama twilight. There are hits and misses, triumphs and failures, but as I watch some of my students perform, looking unrecognizable without their blue tracksuits, a feeling of pride again begins to circulate within me, and I clap with enthusiasm. The twelfth graders are busy doling out baskets of poutine—I decided to impart that hallowed recipe of Canadiana to them after Lovely's relentless ribbing— and they offer me one covered in cheese curds and soupy gravy, but I politely decline. I stand with the other English teachers, and we discuss the event, the pageantry, our students, the challenges and joys of living here in Iquique, when the event's coordinator points to us and requests that we join him onstage. I stand on the stage in front of rows and rows of proud parents sitting in white plastic chairs and am asked to talk about my time in Iquique, my school, my family, in Spanish if possible. The coordinator beckons me forward. Swallowing my mounting anxiety and fear, I creep to the microphone and look upon the city of the Atacama, Iquique—the outcast—as well as upon the eyes of its citizens—the hardy and brave. In the dusk, the stars are not yet visible, but the dunes tower before me and roll like waves in the dying light. The lamps of Plaza Prat are lit, and the few sprinkles of green appear healthy, as do the half dozen palm trees. Children chase one another around the fountain, over the bridge, and past the water jets, with the wind gently ruffling the Chilean flag atop the glowing clock tower. Old-timers sit on benches near the old tramlines waiting with pronounced curiosity as to what this strangely accented man will say.

My sentences are short, simple things. I construct curt declarations with my limited verbs and conjugate them carefully. I say I like my students and that my school "*es el mejor de Iquique*," which generates whoops and claps from its students standing and sitting in the creeping night. I say I like my family and the people and the city, especially Playa Brava. I say I like the food, which gets a few chuckles. Soon I run out of words, yet I want to say so much more. I want to say that Iquique is unconquerable. I want to say that through the earthquakes and massacres, the tsunamis and recessions, your city has remained defiant, has won existence from an ocean of sand, has tamed the advancing dunes with an unrelenting ferocity. I want to say that whenever I think of Iquique, I will see my mother sweeping sand from the kitchen. I will see that boy who sits on the lip of a dune, amid fine sand ripples, staring at the trash, tiendas, traffic of his city below, the beauty of buildings meeting sky and sea, the Pacific unfurling beyond his eyes, the boy who sees his home crystallized among the ever-present dangers, the threats that make each day precious, the work that gives the city its hope. Yet on the stage, all I can say is *gracias* and all I can do is give a sheepish wave, a thankful smile.

When I leave Iquique after six months, in December, I don't go home. I don't return. I travel for five more. And when I tell Lovely, she takes a few days to respond and then say only how exciting it all is, how very neat. The goodbyes are hard, as they always are. My co-teachers get me a lovely card signed by every teacher at the school thanking me and wishing me well. I have my picture taken with the students, their energy still as palpable and destructive as ever. When the airport van collects me in the early-morning blackness, our street lights the only glow, my family helps me carry my luggage and situate it in the back, and I hug each member, even my father, and thank them for everything, thank them for hosting a stranger and making him feel a son. But when the van turns on Castro Avenue and merges with the highway sandwiched between the dunes and ocean, Iquique's lights twinkling in the rear-view mirror, another volunteer teacher turns to me and says, "The whole family was there to see you off," and I reply, "Yes, but they are probably celebrating now." We laugh and that warm sense of relief fills me, the satisfaction of having completed something, the release of being finished, and now I can see it through whichever lens I choose. I have done it. I am free to go. But there, too, a little deeper, creeps a melancholy that says I could have done so much more. It's an odd sensation to fully experience things only once they have passed.

It's a few weeks later in Chiloé, Chile's haunted archipelago, that I think I see her for the first time. It's a foggy December morning, and across the Rio Chacao, I watch her walk among the sodden jade hills with a bucket full of mussels in one hand a stack of rhubarb in the other. Her jean shorts reveal her bare thighs, which are as strong as Patagonian cypress. An elastic holds her brown hair in a bun. Her arms are stringy and rippled, her eyes the shade of sandstone. At the shoreline, she crouches beside her bonfire, which she fans with the giant rhubarb leaves. The smoke floats past poplars before dissolving into the ashen sky. And before long, she too has disappeared along with her smoke signals. My eyes become heavy with memory. In Chiloé, the uncanny rises with the fishermen every morning, and trolls and warlocks and dwarfs reveal strange, hidden things.

Meaning "place of seagulls" in the Huilliche language, one of the island's earliest tongues, Chiloé has always found more solace in the sea than on the ground. A land apart, full of hidden coves and thick forests, Chilotes formed solidarity in their solitude. And solitude breeds myths and myths make legends and legends long for characters. The Incas feared the lands stretching from their borders, places where birds were as big as men and the bluest water turned to blackest mud and men succumbed to the salty whispers of forest succubi. Rumours of skeletons the size of longboats, of bones as sharp as shale, and of beasts with scales for skin wafted through Cuzco corridors. The Spanish, too, thought best to leave the island alone.

The Sunday morning I see her is a long morning, a morning not uncommon to sleepy seaside fishing communities like Castro. No one strolls its bloodless streets. They lie barren under a sky the colour of sharkskin. Clouds are a constant canopy of wet wool in soggy coastal Chile. They flatten into long chrome fields that fall onto the verdant grasses.

Sedated, the town sinks in a warm bath. The houses are hardy boxes with colourful facades and roofs of sheeted tin that sound like machine gun fire in the rain. No rain has fallen yet, and I hear nothing on the perpendicular streets, whose shops remain closed and whose wooden churches stay boarded. The wind rebels only for a moment. Heavy with drink, fishermen still lie cocooned somewhere in warm blankets. Two hours earlier, Castro might have been rough. Now, a vicious calm strangles the asphalt, tumbling in eerie reverence towards the inlet. I take the sidewalk, the last man alive, as the road moves from pavement to gravel to stone to sea.

Castro does not sit on the sea, rather on a sheltered bay along the archipelago's eastern seaboard facing the mainland. The geography here is mangled, with each little island resembling a piece of ripped paper floating through the turquoise waters, its sides worn and ragged. The tide has fled leaving only a sliver of sea, which passes through muddy embanks littered with cardboard and kindling of rotten alerce. At Castro's harbour, water levels can rise and fall as much as twenty feet. And standing on the moist grounds, I see the effects of such a pendulum: half a dozen rowboats lie tilted on the riverbed, beached like bass. A yellow one sits untied among the mossy rocks. The winds and sea and sun have chipped its stern and peeled back the paint to expose old hardwood cut in measured planks. Its seats go unmanned, no oars in the rowing station, no bags of clams. The ship's belly has fasted for days, which curves into the mouth of a sei whale. Behind the old boatyard rise fields of sage.

I struggle across the spongy floor past sunken logs and dead trees. Across the stream, the land bends into farms the shade of tweed, shielded by rows of conifers. Up ahead at the end, my eyes fasten onto a bloated beast lying prostrate in the milky puddles. Chiloé tickles me just under my chin, and my imagination flares and snorts and yelps. And goes to work. I see a fallen proboscidean, a mammoth maybe, rotting under a swarm of black flies. Its belly decays amid the puma bite marks; its hairy skin withers into pools of bloody mucus. Soon only curls of costae the colour of cartilage will remain, rounding into a flimsy carapace, which, I notice upon approach, has become a boat's shell, a deep-sea hull built to blast through the Pacific's worst weather.

Tentacles of rope fire from the water and seize the ship's stem, holding it in place until the river rises. Across the bulkhead, a playful sailor has written "*Tonina*," a Chilean dolphin. This hunk of old wood does not remind one of the grace and agility of a dolphin, those silvery bullets shooting over swells. But maybe that is the point. Old sea folk are old-time storytellers who love spinning silky yarns. Sorting through his netting, his hands fat with calluses, his face reddened by rum, the fisherman talks in garbled, half-thought sentences, cigarette hanging from his mouth, about the time he and his crew fought through fifty-foot waves before they were corkscrewed and thrown fifty miles off course and then saved by a pod of fifty dolphins, who led them, each flipper raised heavenwards, back home.

Now, disenchantment washes over the ancient boat grounded there in the muck. The deck stays dry. The tire fenders hanging from the sides no longer touch new quays and instead wait for bored teenagers to puncture them with steely jackknives. The boat will rip and rot under the sun and die as a piece of offal licked and chewed and carried away by some predator once used to the texture of whale blubber.

Beyond the boats aestivating in the mid-morning mist, the *palafitos* extend their backsides over the estuaries. These homes stand on legs of timber like a cast of crustaceans crawling and stumbling on its claws to the sea. Some stilts stand in the jade shallows while others are freed from waters but sheathed in algae. The skinny stakes protect the steel-sided and low-pitch-roofed homes from the tides and vermin that feed on worms and molluscs among the sands and scrub. The windows are big and face the lagoons. They are the windows of the brave who confront floods with the stoicism of a soldier. Iridescent hues wash the homes the colour of hope. Hopeful that loved ones return from the sea's clenched jaw. Hopeful that loved ones return with enough hake to sustain the family. Hopeful that loved ones return with a sense that life, however hard, however punishing, is worth the toil because love exists in the spaces between the stakes stabbed through the banks. Even in the foggiest of mornings, planks painted in pinks guide even the surliest and stingiest of sailors home.

Bruce Chatwin did not think much of Chiloé—islands of fish and farms, of beauty, sure, but also of beggary, where the men are lazy and irresponsible and the women as cutthroat and spry as the weather. The green lands shelter *brujos*, murderous warlocks, who prey on souls bent over in their potato patches, trousers peat stained and torn. They dash flecks of mayhem on the lives of the hardy and hard working. They spread disease. They steal property. They suck the fingers of village women. They shear the skin of Christians and sew waistcoats, which glow from holy sweat and light paths in the black nights. In the darkest cave, they hide their secrets protected by a disjointed boy, the *invunche*, who can count and lick his vertebrae notches. The islands are untrustworthy and tempestuous, where men are not men but things.

Of course, Chatwin never visited Chiloé, at least not in his famous narrative, *In Patagonia*. In the loud winds of southern Patagonia, Chatwin cut the barest and grandest sentences from the greyest granite. His prose was chiselled opal. He was an expert on roofs and faces. Yet he rarely ventured far from his European brethren, his depiction of Indians a master's thesis in waiting for a post-colonialist. The Chilotes he met in the Argentine latifundia, estancias, and ranches of expatriates from the old continent were migrant workers, rebels, or suicides. They either died on the pampas or absconded home poorer than when they left. For Chatwin, Chiloé and its people were defeat personified.

Gazing at the elevated houses along Castro's shores, I suddenly feel at home in Chiloé. The palafitos yawn, stretch, and rise. I hear the first voices of the morning, joyous cries ringing from the interior of one of them. Two young brothers break from the rear door and clamour down the slimy wooden ladder to the puddles. The older boy wears a cherry-red sweater, and the younger runs through the rocks in torn track pants. The clouds have broken and have lightened into cumulus bundles of cotton spooling along emerging streaks of cyan. The sun has survived. Their mother hips her way through the door yelling warnings in furious Spanish, arms filled with mauve sheets. The boys respond with a half-hearted "*sí, Mamá,*" already focused on hunting clams with birch twigs. She shakes her head and begins to clip the sheets to the line in flashes of perfected movement. The boys hopscotch through thrown tires. The town blinks and wipes away the tired.

Ungrounded boats lurch towards deeper water. Teams of men in orange overalls sort through nets, ropes, and lines. They work in intense silence, hoping that some watery goddess may reward them with a bounty of cod. The boat's hull slinks in colours the same as the sky. It is worn and weary and wrecked. A film of fine light slants over Castro's colours.

And then in the distance, I see her again, Lovely, and it is nice. I hope she stays a little longer this time. She is again working among the rocks on the other side of the stream in a background of green. Her fire is thick and confident. The smoke wafts over her face as the flames crackle. She stares at the fire lost in her thoughts, which do not include me. I know not what she thinks, and it is better that way. It is safer that way.

Away from the fire, she claws through the soil with her long, uncut nails. She digs and wipes the sweat away, leaving scratches of black along her forehead. A pit sits in front of her.

She wets a cloth, selects two smouldering stones, and drops them in the pit. She repeats this until the stones line the pit's bottom, releasing lazy streams of smoke until they hiss and sizzle and scream. She retrieves her bucket of mussels, shy little shells of succulent fish, and places them along the stones. *Let them fry*, her eye cool eyes say.

On the mussels, she throws chunks of pork, hunks of chicken, cuts of sausage, slices of mutton, and a dozen dumplings. She covers the pit with her rhubarb and listens to the food cook. As the mussels heat, their shells open, and their juices spill over the hot rocks and steam the meats. Her chin rests on her knees. She removes her elastic, and her long brown hair falls over her flannel shirt. She is quiet and waits to eat.

For a second, I think she sees me, and even though I know it is not possible, I still wave and shout her name. My voice has no effect on her. It cannot seem to reach her. She just waits for her meal to finish cooking. The more I scream her name, the more she stares at the fire, losing herself further in the smoke and flames. And just as I run towards her along the beach, screaming her name and waving my arms, she stands, grabs a piece of meat from the fire, and takes a large bite from it. She sees me then, I know it. A satisfied look appears on her face. She wipes the juices from her mouth, turns her back to me, and disappears into the air.

2
Little Children

Cuzco, Peru

January 6, 2010

At Sacsahuamán, the Inca fortress-temple lying two kilometres north of Cuzco, I find shelter under an archway made from boulders. The low, lazy clouds have already drizzled enough to dampen my cotton shirt underneath my counterfeit rain jacket. Underneath the massive stone balanced precariously atop two others, I see rows of shacks climb the green mountains in the distant haze. Many of the communities on Cuzco's periphery and in the Sacred Valley—Ollantaytambo, Pisaq, and Pikillaqta—survive on subsistence farming. In the available pasture, they grow maize, potatoes, and quinoa. They raise llamas and alpacas and harvest their fur for textiles. They rear guinea pigs and sell them to local restaurants as *cuy*, a local delicacy.

Fed by two rivers, Saphi and Tullumayo, the lush, verdant valleys have nourished Andean peoples for centuries, long before the Incas rose to prominence, long before the Spanish marched through Cuzco dressed in steel. They lived in ayllus, organizations of families descended from a common ancestor, and farmed and grazed on small plots of land. Economic and moral obligations existed between ayllus. Groups worked together. If one group needed extra help harvesting their crop, another provided it. If a child lost their parents, if a wife lost her husband, if a person lost the ability to work, the ayllu took them all in. They shared what they had and thanked the same deities for it. But as it often is the case in unforgiving places, where wealth is limited and poverty always beckons, resources became scarcer, and competition grew over land and water. Ayllus developed a more militaristic, parochial personality.

I walk around the site and marvel at its architecture. Boulders sit atop other boulders and form three terraces receding backwards like steps. No mortar holds them together. Instead, they have been sanded and shaped by hand, pieced together as if a puzzle. Beautifully intricate, the work of true genius, the fortress was built by thousands of forced labourers, workers plucked from vanquished ethnic groups forced to send their strongest to build Inca temples, a form of tribute or *mit'a*. The complex blends wonderfully into the landscape as I gaze past the stones and into the valley winding towards the horizon.

The rugged Andes were not only obstacles but pathways. The steep valleys and canyons cutting through the mountains served as trails running north and south for thousands of kilometres. These natural roadways linked far-flung places and the Incas added their own to the growing network. Relay runners, called *chasquis*, navigated these unobstructed paths, often jogging for days at a time—the best could reach Quito in less a week—to relay messages or to pass quipus, knotted strings whose colours revealed secret messages. Soon the Incas built garrisons along the roads to serve as storage space for food and as shelter for their armies. And their armies came quickly and furiously over and through the mountains. In less than a century, from 1438 to 1525, from Sapa Pachacuti to Sapa Huayna Capac, the Incas seized a large swath of South America, from Chile to Ecuador. They called their empire Tahuantinsuyu, Land of the Four Quarters. The Inca rulers centralized power in Cuzco, eroded local autonomy, and ended the spirit of social equality once existing in these parts of the Andes. The ruling elite became further separated from the masses of Indigenous peoples toiling in the fields or crafting lovely textiles. The Inca rulers, or *Sapa*, claimed descent from Inti, the sun god, and with each victory, they built temples praising the sun's brilliance.

I climb down from Sacsahuamán, through back flooded passageways and muddied embankments, and from above, Cuzco's red-tiled roofs resemble a field of fallen maple leaves. The city enthralls me, the one I have always dreamt about. I take photos everywhere. I visit Korikancha, an old Inca temple to the sun once covered in gold sheets and sheltering all kinds of golden statues, which the Spanish melted soon after their arrival.

The temple also housed the mummified bodies of past rulers, an act representing the continuity of Inca power. Skilled anatomists removed their organs, tanned their skins, and embalmed their bodies using ethanol. To honour the past ancestors and to guarantee future fortunes, the Incas revered these mummified bodies with great aplomb. They dressed them in fine clothing and decorated them with golden trinkets. At times of celebration, the mummies were brought from their lavish chambers and placed in a ring around Cuzco's main plaza. Each had a special interpreter who announced the messages to anxious onlookers. They gave advice about marriage, harvesting, and battle. And after each had finished his proclamation, the thankful placed offerings at their shrivelled feet. They were the link between the past and present, between the living and the ancestors. The temple is now called the Church of Santo Domingo, and a man takes a photo from where these mummies were once kept.

I sit on one of the plaza's benches and watch people scurry about. I have an hour before my orientation at an organization for which I will volunteer for the next month. The sun has fought its way through the clouds. It is a pleasant afternoon. Amanda expects me home for lunch at four. A woman named Jackie moves in today. A kitten brushes up against my leg and purrs. I see a couple of stray dogs bound up a flight of stairs in an alleyway. I have read about local campaigns fighting to protect these animals from slaughter, about the necessity for neutering them to stop them spreading, to control the numbers. I nudge the cat away while another dog almost gets hit by a car. I hear another meow and then another longer cry and sense claw marks on my skin, light at first, and then deeper, more forceful scratches breaking the skin, and I smell and then feel the blood dripping over my pale flesh.

I look up and all the people, the Indigenous men and women, have stopped moving. They are emplaced, stuck in their last motion, a leg elevated or a hand extended. Their eyes stay open, their bodies dressed in welts, blisters, bruises, and scars. I have done it. I have placed and posed them. They smile at me for only a few Peruvian soles. Puppies and kittens dance around them, stopping every now and then to sniff at them, to gawk at them, and to study them. A few hiss, a few bark. They fill themselves on llama and alpaca meat. They lick their lips and lounge on the plaza's grounds.

A noise startles them as some shadowy figures run through the plaza and into the temple. They know, from terrified runners and messengers, that a stranger has strangled Atahualpa, the Sapa, to death by wire in Cajamarca. Garrotted, they call it. The invaders have garrotted a living god, and now they are just steps away from Cuzco. I watch the figures emerge a few minutes later; each has what appears to be a little child wrapped in white sheets slung over their shoulders. But children usually cry; children usually struggle. These bodies do not move; they stay stiff, cradled in these men's arms. Each has now separated, fled down a separate corridor, and taken refuge in an abandoned home.

Soon the animals scatter as Spanish soldiers and Dominican friars march into the plaza. A soldier holds one of the shadowy figures by the neck. He is bloodied and shaking, and he points to a nearby building. A few soldiers return minutes later with one of the mysterious bundles. They unwrap the dirtied rags and step back in shock. There lies what appears to be a little child whose skin has yellowed and withered. His arms cross over his chest; his hair falls past his shoulders. He looks alive. A few soldiers jokingly ask him questions, but he does not answer. The friars condemn the barbarous act as they cross themselves. They point to the corpse and ask the shadowy figure what its name was, but this time he says nothing and only looks away. The friars notice though that the decaying child wears little golden rings and necklaces, and one reaches down and removes the pieces, careful to cover his face, and places them in his pocket. A soldier carrying a torch lights the bundle and, as it burns, the Indigenous men and women, stuck as they are, nonetheless wail and cry as a child might. The smoke floats to a cloudless sky, and the sun shines on a gutted and ruined and burning Cuzco. The shadowy figure smiles though because he knows the visitors have not found all the bundles. They stay hidden in caves, along mountaintops, under the earth, and wait.

On the glass door to the volunteer organization, someone has etched a map of the world next to Visa, MasterCard, and American Express stickers. More carvings promote TEFL certification, homestays, and Spanish language classes. A large sign sells Machu Picchu treks and white-water rafting adventures. The door swings open, and two young women in jean shorts gallop past me onto Avenida El Sol and turn left towards the historic centre.

I walk through the partition towards a lone man wearing a blue cardigan and leaning on a wooden countertop. He gazes into a computer screen. Behind him, promotional brochures are displayed on shelves, the tops of which exhibit little flags of Canada, the United States, Australia, Ireland, and Peru. A map indicates the organization has offices in Guatemala and Costa Rica as well. Above him, a television screen shows repeat footage of their volunteers at work. A young white woman writes lessons on a chalkboard in front of rows of silent children. A man coats a wall with plaster. A young woman spoon feeds a child sitting in a highchair. A man crouches over a child writing in the notebook and says something to the boy. The boy nods and writes. Nods and writes. Nods and writes.

"Welcome," the man says. "How can I help you?"

"I am here for orientation."

"Name."

I give it.

"Very good. We are about to begin. Follow me."

I trail behind him as he explains the organization's various volunteer programs and support services. The site is large and already I feel lost, disoriented, unable to retrace my steps if asked. We enter a raucous room full of people speaking at once. Two people, one local and one foreign, sit at each table and speak at one another in Spanish and then in English.

"This is our tandem program," my guide says. "We pair up Spanish and English native speakers who wish to learn the other's language. Each session is an hour. The first half is in English, the second in Spanish."

I watch a Peruvian man struggle to express himself in English while his partner gently coaxes and encourages him with hand signals and body language, helpful little hints, and soon he has formed his sentence, and they both laugh at the difficulty of speaking in the other's tongue.

"We find this program to be very successful," the man says. "It's a great avenue towards intercultural exchange, learning about each other's culture. You make friends, maybe a date or two," the man says with a grin.

The action unfolds before me. The room is packed; people sit at every table practising new words and phrases. In the back, women sell baked goods and coffee. I overhear some volunteers discuss their projects. Jungle conservation. Construction. Animal care. Teaching. Medicine. They speak with such confidence and zeal, rambling about plans, intentions, and goals. They have the passion of a missionary and possess that unconquerable desire to set the world right. They have the appetite, craving, and thirst to help. I see them as an army, a grand military of teenagers and young men and women ready to beat back the darkness threatening to cover Peru in everlasting destitution.

"Pretty impressive, isn't it?"

"Yes. Yes, it is."

The man deposits me in a classroom with other newcomers, and I take a seat. My guide drops a welcome folder in front of me. Before I have a chance to read it, a woman materializes in front of us. Her shirt and pants are perfunctory, dull, the clothes of labour and toil. She has tied her blond hair up. She has a confidence I find aggressive, as if she expects admiration and attention for simply being, as if she has become used to receiving it. She seems to revel in the aura of an audience. She is perfect in front of a crowd.

"My name is Brenda, and I help coordinate the various volunteer programs here. I have travelled and worked and volunteered throughout the world—everywhere from Cambodia to Mozambique—and I always get super excited when I see so many new faces ready to embark on a rewarding yet challenging experience."

She takes a moment to ready the seriousness of the next line.

"I can honestly say that throughout my travels, I've had no greater experience than helping others. There's something so rewarding about engaging with the community you visit, working with them, communicating with them, building those relationships of trust. It is a life-changing experience, and it will stay with you for the rest of your life. I believe when travelling you have a responsibility to give something back. So congratulations on taking the plunge, on wanting to dedicate your time and money to worthwhile causes, to wanting to help those in need."

Some clap, others smile. We all listen and absorb her words.

"I know everyone is eager to learn more about their programs and what specifically they will be doing in this fabulous city of Cuzco. But first, I want to talk briefly about a few issues that may help you settle into your new environments more seamlessly."

Some ready their pens.

"We ask you all to be patient. The value of patience cannot be overstated. Things will never go as planned. Conflicts will inevitably arise. Between you and your project managers. Between you and your host family. And even between you and this city and its different ways of doing things. But please remember that anger gets us and you nowhere. It accomplishes nothing. If you have a problem, take a deep breath and come talk to us. Phone us. Stop by to chat. That's why we are here. We are the mediators in a way. We have a foot in both worlds. Every problem has a solution. We must talk with one another, not against one another. We must be goal oriented."

Some scribble a few notes; others mumble sounds of agreement.

"The second value flows from the first: Have an open mind. Develop flexibility. This is not America, Australia, or Canada. We cannot expect to find the same amenities, enjoy the same level of comfort, the same degree of routine. We have tried to accommodate your living and dietary needs, and we have tried to offer compromises to those who have other issues. But this is Peru. Peru is a developing country and may not offer all the services we have come to expect in the West. Poverty exists, and many Peruvians struggle to survive."

She glances down at her notes.

"Despite three per cent growth to the economy in 2009, for example, over two million Peruvians still live on less than $1.25 a day. Forty per cent of the population are said to live in extreme poverty. Unemployment remains high, as many Peruvians work in the underground economy. Great disparities in wealth exist between countryside and city, between Indigenous and non-Indigenous. The government cannot afford many basic services and cannot afford to pay professionals a decent salary."

She has become sombre and pleading.

"This is why we need to be flexible. This is why our work is so important. We need to understand that life here is difficult, and we need to accommodate ourselves to those realities. For those of you volunteering in an orphanage, for example, you might find some of the work troubling. You will be spending time with kids with no families, no support networks, with very little love in their lives. We are here to offer that attention and assistance. Proper childhood development requires love and devotion. To become functioning, emotionally mature adults, they need that love, and they are not receiving it. You are here to improve their quality of life. You are a role model. Play with them. Have fun with them. Show them they are valued. Show them they do matter. Show them love exists in this world."

Brenda speaks for a few more minutes and outlines other potential sources of conflict. She briefly discusses the other programs. For the professionals in the crowd, the young teachers and doctors, she reminds them that their Peruvian counterparts can learn so much from their expertise. She talks about health concerns, what to do if you get sick; she gives us advice about how to safely navigate Cuzco's nightlife. She gives recommendations for restaurants and tourist attractions. She tells us to have a wonderful time. It will be life altering, she promises. It will open our eyes.

After Brenda finishes, another woman ushers us to a room containing about thirty computers. She tells us we are free to check email and update our social media accounts, but we should be aware of others who may be waiting. I walk past the computers and sneak glances at their screens. The local Peruvians play video games mostly; others type out messages in some kind of chat room. The volunteers scroll through their Facebook accounts. They update their statuses with colourful adjectives and exclamation points. They upload photos of themselves in front of nameless ruins. They upload photos of themselves holding cocktails and beer bottles. They upload photos of themselves carrying animals or children. They are always smiling. Smiling.

January 9

Along Avenida Grau, just past the well-packed Avenida del Ejército, we stop at an austere white structure with a gated oval doorway. Above the entrance juts an elaborate balcony, in the baroque style, its metal railing adorned with four crucifixes. The facade is otherwise bare except for a half dozen barred windows, which, from the inside, must squeeze the outside world into mere colourful chunks, pieces of people and places, as if one had glaucoma. An outside world visible but not seen. Next to me, Lyanna, another volunteer, waves to an elderly man sitting on a stool past the partition.

"*Perdóname, somos voluntarios con la organización,*" she says.

The man shuffles to the gate, inspects us with a disquieting eye, before unlocking the gate and motioning us in. Lyanna leads us past the courtyard, where groups of children spy us suspiciously, and into the administrators' offices. Three sombre-looking women work at desks or sort through boxes of bureaucratic documents outlining biosocial information on each of their charges: history of abuse, medical ailments, mental illnesses.

"These women are the orphanage's heart and soul," Lyanna says, waving to one smartly dressed woman rising from her paperwork. She robotically extends her hand, and Lyanna warmly embraces it.

"*¿Cómo estás, Clara?*"

"*Todo bien.*"

Her body stays rigid, her voice monotone.

"*¡Qué bueno! Pero pienso que están ocupados todos los días. Trabajando. Trabajando. Trabajando.*"

Clara remains unaffected by Lyanna's enthusiasm.

"They are so super busy here," Lyanna explains to me.

"*Sí, Lyanna, estamos trabajando mucho.*"

Clara examines me for a moment, noting my khaki pants, cotton T-shirt, bedraggled backpack, before shifting her study back to Lyanna.

"*¿Cuantos voluntarios?*"

"*Solo uno, un hombre de…* Where are you from again?"

"Canada," I say.

"*Sí, uno hombre de Canadá, y va a trabajar acá para uno mes.*"

"*Uno mes,*" Clara repeats.

"*Sí* … you're here for one month, right?" Lyanna asks, turning to me.

I nod.

"*Me llamo Jesse,*" I say, shooting my hand forward. Clara shakes my fingertips once, twice, and then drops them. She seems to hold something back, some urge that she has long practised repressing. Her compact frame appears wound, wrapped in a tight coil, ready to spring and snap.

"*Bienvenido a casa, Jesse. Buena suerte.*"

Before I can say thank you, she has returned to her work rummaging through paper stacks and sorting files. One woman in a grey skirt removes a half dozen binders from rickety shelves and flips through their contents. She makes notes and compares information. The third woman rifles through filing cabinets and grabs folders in a blur of action as if she were plucking fish from a lake. I hear the subtle sounds of pages turning, of pen on ink, and of fingers on keyboards. They say nothing more. The sound is of work.

I follow Lyanna towards the children huddled together gossiping near the teeter-totters. The roofs are of rusted terra cotta, which slope at a forty-five-degree angle, and ring the grassy courtyard. In the

Andean sky, they strike one as fields of clay, rich in metal oxides and organic matter, each gooey handful ready to be shaped and modelled into a work of art. Along the lawn, an assemblage of red tiles forms a crucifix, guiding the boys to the north and south, east and west wings.

The children devour us. They pull at Lyanna's pant leg; they inspect my watch and search my pant pockets. They want to be lifted, chased, watched, adored. I give a few high-fives, but most flock to Lyanna. They do not yet trust me.

"*¿Cómo están, niños?*" Lyanna shrieks in her childish voice. The boys scream "*bien*" in unison. She lifts one in her arms while two others wrap themselves around each of her legs. Three boys shout questions at her. Two others compete for her attention, pushing and shoving each other, until it escalates into a wrestling match.

"*¡Basta!*" Lyanna yells, and the two pugilists comply.

"They are starved for attention," she says, patting one on his unkempt hair. "But eventually they will grow fond of you."

"*¡Regalos!*" one boy screams.

"Gifts," Lyanna says. "They always want gifts."

She sticks her tongue out and makes funny faces to the boys on her lap. One rests his hand on her cheek and glides his fingers down her skin.

"What's my role here?" I ask.

"Oh, it's very unstructured. You can give them some informal English lessons if you want or make up games for them to play. The important thing is that you show them attention and affection. They need all the love in the world."

"But there won't be any classes?"

"No, no. It's winter break, which is why we all need to have fun," she says, pinching her lap-held boy right on his cheek. He gasps in surprise.

"They are so adorable, aren't they? I wish I could take them all home with me."

She tickles the boy under his arms and neck, and he succumbs to a torrent of laughter. His eyes are wild; saliva drips from the side of his mouth.

"I leave at the end of the week, so this is one of my last chances to visit the boys."

She places the boys on the ground, stands, and wipes any residue from her jeans.

"Let me show you the facility."

We walk along the tiles followed by the chorus of boys. Yellow benches line each side as does a series of ferns, planted at even intervals, that seem to struggle in the January cold. Blue and red plastic tables sit scattered throughout the yard. A derelict desk leans under the drooping branches of a deciduous tree. A few pink flowers struggle through a forgotten garden. We come to the orphanage's centre, where a bust of a head stands covered in water droplets.

"Who is he?" I ask.

"Orphanage's founder, maybe, not sure."

We peer into the kitchen where a team of women chop vegetables and negotiate a stove full of pots and pans. We watch a handful of children play a game of marbles under the sloping roofs. I study a boy flick one and watch it carom off the pole and into the gutter, a thin strip of ground running between the lawn and walkway. He reaches into the sludge to retrieve it, and Lyanna reprimands him with a tsk tsk. The boy ignores her, tosses the marble to his friend, and wipes his hands on his pants.

"They stress hygiene, here," Lyanna explains. "It's incredibly important."

The classrooms are spare, economical spaces: A few books stand on the shelves. Pictures adorn the walls. A few children play board games, and controversy erupts after each move. Lyanna only smiles.

"Boys will be boys."

Along a series of green bars, teenagers challenge each other to pull-up competitions. Their biceps bulge with each pull; their lat muscles flex through blue long-sleeved shirts. The winning boy does fifteen, and sweat glistens on his forehead. He claps hands with the other boys, who recognize his superiority, and he looks at us without waving before kicking a football at the wall.

"He leaves the orphanage next month," Lyanna says.

"Why?"

"He will turn eighteen. No longer a child. Time for him to face the world."

"And do what?"

"Look for work."

The younger boys gravitate towards him, and he ruffles their heads and lets them feel his arms. He picks up one and mocks throwing him in the classroom. Everyone laughs.

"It is difficult to imagine being in here for eighteen years."

"Better than starving on the street or worse," Lyanna assures me.

A young boy takes my hand and walks next to me.

"See, how quickly they become accustomed to you."

With his free hand, he retrieves a piece of grimy meat and gives it to me. In a flash, Lyanna intercepts it and gives it back to him.

"No," she says, waving her finger at him.

"If you don't want to be sick for a week, I wouldn't eat anything offered here."

I watch the boy skip into a classroom.

"Also, try not to let them wipe their snot on you."

I am not really listening to Lyanna anymore. Instead, I marvel at the orphanage's logic. Keep them alive, no matter what. Keep them alive until they are no longer your responsibility. The boys shuffle from one corner to the next, from one activity to the next. They begin to appear indistinguishable and move in predictable ways, as if one has wound a key in their backs, tightening their gears, and now has released it, prompting them to step and then step again and again, in a twitchy, shaky fashion as they circle the orphanage around and around. A house of moving mannequins.

"I will miss them," Lyanna says.

A team of white men in white coats appears in the doorway, and the children scatter in every direction.

"Dentist time," Lyanna says. "We should go."

As the dentists arrange their equipment and lay out their tools, we pass them and nod silently at one another. The children keep a safe distance from the men in white coats, with whom I am sure they associate pain and discomfort. At the entrance, the gatekeeper blocks the flood of children with outstretched, ensnarling arms, and we wave goodbye as he locks the door. I hear their voices as we saunter away, little words and phrases in an innocent register, until the honking and braking cars drown them.

Cuzco flexes in the afternoon sun. The sky is a cyan blue with small etches of cloud. At this height, the sunrays are merciless, and the Andes' shapes are razor sharp. Lyanna marches in long strides, and I have difficulty keeping up. I feel the lack of oxygen in the air. The entire city sits in its mountain bowl as we step towards it. There is something so perfect about the scene; it's the one I have seen countless times in pictures. History has been preserved here. It's a living museum. Soon I can see the lines of tourists circumventing the cathedral and slinking and sliding through the city's side streets. Most are on vacation, it would seem, and wear colourful, carefree clothing. They try on wool sweaters, select postcards, study paintings, flip through books. I watch beggars approach them with hands outstretched, and the tourists ignore them, as I would.

Lyanna is saying something.

"What?" I ask.

Lyanna wears her perpetual smile that seemingly stretches around her face.

"I asked if you had any plans tonight."

"None."

"Well, you should drop by the office and see what's on. There may be a pub crawl."

Without saying goodbye, Lyanna disappears, and I, too, wish to vanish within the crowds.

January 10

I sit in a chair in the living room; the phone rests under my shoulder. A voice.

"Hello?"

"Lovely?" I ask, easily recognizing her voice after all these months.

"Jesse? My goodness, is that you?"

"It is. I managed to get your cell number from Genevieve."

"Oh, very tricky. Where are you now? I can never keep track."

"Cuzco, Peru. Volunteering at an orphanage for a month."

"Oh right. And how is it?"

"Fine. It's fine. Umm. Yeah. The children seem to find me amusing. I like the people I live with. The city's beautiful. But how are you, though? Placement and school still kicking your butt?"

"Yes, yes they are. Not much of a life outside of the two. But it should lead to a job afterward."

"Well, it will be well-deserved."

In the kitchen, my host mother, Amanda, prepares lunch, and I want to cry. Everything around me suddenly feels so fake, fictious. On the television set, two basketball teams play. One man hacks the ball from another, and shoving ensues. The referee blows the whistle.

The tablecloths are stainless. I count three golden candle holders.

I hear Amanda open the fridge and arrange her wares.

"*Jesse, ¿estás viendo la televisión?*" she screams at me.

"*No, Amanda.*"

I flick off the television.

"Sorry about that."

"No problem."

"I wanted to ask. I called you yesterday, and it went to your voice mail. And your voice said to leave a message for you and Brent. I was wondering, then, if you two had gotten back together."

"No, no. He's only looking for jobs and is using my number for employers."

I feel relieved.

"There's nothing to worry about, Jesse."

"Okay."

"When are you coming back?"

"I don't know. I don't know."

"See, Jesse, there's nothing to worry about."

"I miss you."

"Okay."

"I do."

"And I'll be thinking of you, too."

"Keep in touch."

"Oh, there's very little to update here. But you enjoy your adventures."

"I'll call again."

"I'm sure you will."

In the kitchen, Amanda chops potatoes. With the blade in her right hand, she slices the vegetables in half. She secures one on her cutting board, flat side down, and cups her left hand, dropping her fingernails along the potato. At a forty-five-degree angle, she lowers the steel towards the peeled spud and slices a thick strip. And another and another, until she turns the bisected mound and cuts the other way. With every flick of her wrist, the blade almost touches her knuckles but never does, and with each assured slit, she moves those pointy bones further left until no potato remains, only its chunks.

To her right, a pot sits on a burner. With every potato cut, she groups each bit into her hands and dumps them into a bowl of water. She then grabs another potato and begins again. Little bottles of spices line her shelves; in front of her, bunches of herbs wait to be sorted and diced. The smells of garlic and onion mingle and pronounce themselves. From the pot's bottom, they must sauté.

The rhythmic sounds of her slicing soothe. Repetition has always calmed me, the peace in knowing what comes next. Not the rain, though. The certainty of rain never settles me.

Lost in the sound, the art of her labours, I watch her work, her back to me. Her brown, slinky hair tumbles past her shoulders. She is older, fifty maybe, but moves with an elegance only experience provides. She wears a white blouse, dark pants. Her skin is lighter, whiter than the orphaned children I supervise in the city's outskirts, away from the tourists' gaze. Near her, a calendar is open to January 2010. My eye rests on the thirteenth, about three more weeks to go.

"*Estoy preparando pollo y sopa*," Amanda says, sensing my presence behind her.

"*Qué lindo*," I reply.

"*Me gusta su comida*," I continue in my childish Spanish.

I reach for the handle to the door leading to the veranda, to the ashtray I so desperately want to fill, when I hear her words I always dread.

"*No deberías fumar.*"

I nod in obedience but still retreat into the outside grey.

No, I should not smoke, I tell myself, lighting a Marlboro and letting its sedative effect subdue me. I already feel better. My mind has awoken. I release the first bit of ash into the tray hanging from a brick wall, which protects me from the outside world. I can hear Cuzco but cannot see it. The prattle of daily living sounds from nearby alleys. Somewhere a dog barks. From the wall's top, shards of glass stab the air. They resemble a child's art project, a reimagining of what the back of an early reptile might look like. I doubt anyone has ever jumped the wall or has ever tried to rattle this fortress. I understand her fears. She's a single woman, and she lives a life of plenty amid an ocean of paucity. The surrounding mountains, though, are not nearly as unforgiving as they were just a few years ago. The Shining Path no longer hunts the Andes, transforming every peasant, by word or gun, into a Maoist guerilla revolutionary primed to rip the wealth and power from the usurpers, the land barons and business tycoons, to restore a sense of pride to the long-degraded Indian, to reinstate a balance between land and people. I only support leftist armed uprisings from the comforts of university libraries, and I enjoy imagining the mud-covered rebels executing a ragtag of western gringos in their Guevara T-shirts who sympathize with their cause and who look an awful lot like me. Lined up under another gorgeous mountain, the snow powdery and sparkling, the air crisp and fresh, the valleys beautiful and endless, the Peru of their dreams, the Westerners see the row of rifles aimed at them, and before the explosions, before the bullets rip through their skin and cut them down, they must think that they only came to help, only wanted to aid those with whom they felt some affinity.

Amanda's husband died of lung cancer, a lifetime smoker. When I smoke on her veranda, she never speaks to me, never pops her head out to see how I am doing. And when I watch my smoke dissolve into the night sky, I wonder what she thinks about when she smells a tray full of old butts sitting just outside her kitchen, what must she feel when she dumps them into a trash bin. When she does glance through her kitchen window and sees the red cherry glowing and the hazy grey lines wafting into the night, does she momentarily mistake me for her late husband? Does she have to stop herself from racing outside and yelling at me, shouting at me to think of his health, their future? It's easy to notice the past in the present. I know I should not smoke, but I still do.

Amanda has two or three volunteers staying with her at any given time, mostly young, mostly white, mostly from English-speaking countries. Her house can easily accommodate the number of guests. It is grandiose, opulent, cultured. Her bathroom gleams spotless, the bathtub a curved porcelain beauty. Her bookshelves contain the latest Pulitzer Prize winners. A piano sits in a corner. Sofas and coffee tables decorate the living room, and the effect is of a tea room or a young girl's dollhouse. A chandelier hovers above the oval kitchen table made of fine wood, oak maybe. Photographs, whose details I do not bother with, linger on the walls. Mostly, the house is silent. Mostly, it feels like a museum.

Later, lunch nears, and the cooking food has almost become a meal. The pot steams and hisses. The rice has fluffed. Amanda busies herself around the dining table, laying the cutlery, placing the plates and bowls. A jug of water sits in the centre. A few flowers wilt in a vase. She gestures for me to sit while she rolls away the television set. She moves to keep herself from thinking, I want to conclude. She fills her house with strangers to keep herself from feeling. I pour a glass of water and stare at where the television was. Amanda scurries back and forth while the water refreshes me.

Jackie bursts into the room, flushed and beaming, as she always is, and greets us in her frantically friendly way, which exhausts simply from its proximity. I like Jackie, early twenties, Californian. She is someone in between things—between university and real life, between boyfriends, between countries. She is from the buffet generation, a little of this and a little of that, never completely satisfying herself on one particular entrée, one particular dessert. I should know. I fatten myself from the same trough. Experience, we all come to Peru for experience.

"*Buenas tardes*," she says, plopping herself on a chair.

Plaster and concrete stain her jeans; her blond hair unfurls in wonderful disarray. She has grey streaks along her white arms, which hang exposed from her tank top.

"We laid the foundation of a house today," she says to me. "I love shovelling and hammering shit."

She grits her teeth and flexes her biceps; little doughy lumps of muscle protrude through her soft skin.

"I'm getting huge," she says.

Amanda serves the plates of steaming rice and chicken.

"*Qué rico*," we both say together, and Amanda smiles before racing back into the kitchen.

"I'm so glad I changed my volunteer project," Jackie says, a lump of rice perched delicately on her fork. "I despise children."

I nudge my chicken with the fork.

"When do you leave for the orphanage?"

"Soon," I reply, glancing at the afternoon clouds accumulating over Cuzco.

"Better hurry. You know how the rains come every afternoon."

"Well," I say in my sardonic way, "at least I have a fancy new poncho."

"Indeed, you do," Jackie says, grinning, a dimple forming on her left cheek.

Wearing oven mitts, Amanda re-emerges carrying a large soup bowl and sits it on the table. A ladle leans against the glass edge.

"*Cuidado*," Amanda says. "*La sopa es muy caliente.*"

Yesterday, Jackie dragged me through Cuzco's back-alley markets. Away from the ornate cathedrals and charming streets, the tourist clubs, and artsy craft shops, these *mercados* act as miniature cities themselves. They are living, breathing entities. The atmosphere electrifies and pulsates, waves of people pushing helpless shoppers past each stall, under every umbrella, through every passageway, a network of commerce, a labyrinth of underground exchange. Women in bowler hats and wide, colourful skirts relax beside baskets of bananas, limes, and oranges. Textiles of every shape and shade dangle from metal pulls. Mounds of alpaca yarn rest on carpets. A man in a leather jacket sorts through a table full of used running shoes. Counterfeit adventure goods—The North Face, Patagonia, Nike—lie folded on shelves. Rain gear drops from the tent liners. The vendors shout their deals in an orchestra of languages.

I let Jackie choose a poncho for me; she artfully haggles and speaks Spanish for these moments. It is serviceable, practical. She knows her numbers, an accountant's translator, and bargains with a sly grin and a playful naivety. I try a poncho on and she shrugs her shoulders in her attractive, condescending way. She and the merchant settle on a price, and I stuff the glorified trash bag into my backpack.

She weaves through the crowds, a catfish after larvae, her golden hair my lighthouse through the bodies. Her right hand trails behind, and I imagine myself catching it, being pulled along, a child, a little terrified child. She stops at a blue-tarped stall with shelves of bootlegged DVDs, all the Oscar-nominated films: *Inglourious Basterds, District 9, Avatar, Up in the Air, The Hurt Locker, Up*. But Jackie scans the tables for something far more specific.

"*¿Tienes* Dexter?" she asks the man surveying her with a mild interest, while her face folds and tightens into tough lines of anxiety.

He hands her a few cases emblazoned with a man's coy face sprinkled with blood.

"Season Four is supposed to be the best," she says, studying the discs in her hands. "Jesse, you will love it."

Her brown eyes shine on me. I like when she says my name. A woman pushes past us wearing a cape from cloth as vibrant as a rainbow. I follow as its pinkish hues fade into the black stalls full of suitcases and stereos and other manufactured goods.

"*¿Cómo te fue a su proyecto?*" Amanda asks Jackie, who chews a tough piece of chicken.

"*Todo bien, todo bien*," she responds after swallowing. "*Estamos construyendo casas*," she elaborates, struggling over the syllables in the gerund form of *to construct*.

Amanda sips from a spoonful of soup. "*Qué bueno*," she says to herself. She dips her silver spoon back into the yellowy liquid, swirls it around, before scooping a piece of potato and lifting it to her lips. Her mouth circles, her jaws and teeth slowly punishing the chunk into bits. And when she finally ingests it, she relaxes, her shoulders slumping, her arms falling to the table. The process seems to exhaust her, as if she were chewing a stone not a spud.

"*Y Jesse, ¿a qué hora te vas para el orfanato?*"

I glance at my watch and then at the thick, determined clouds outside. "*Muy pronto*," I say.

Amanda lifts another spoonful. "*Qué bueno*," she says. "*Qué bueno*." She then drops her spoon in the bowl; a few splashes land on the tablecloth.

"*Algo paso in Haiti ayer, ¿no?*" Amanda asks. She leaves the soup for a moment and skillfully severs a chicken slice, scarring its white breast.

"*Sí, un…*" I turn to Jackie, "How do you say earthquake?"

"*Terremoto*," Amanda automatically says.

"*Sí, un terremoto.*

"*¿Y cuantos muertos?*" Amanda wants to know the number dead.

"*Miles*," Jackie says.

"Thousands and thousands dead," Amanda repeats in English. "*Qué horrible.*"

An uneasy silence falls on the table.

I remember seeing it on the television.

Families sit huddled in mountains of wreckage. Every few minutes, another ripped corpse is pulled from the collapsed metal and cement. Babies wearing oxygen masks lie on stretchers. Houses tilt. Scarred children sit on tires and wait. Cameras in their faces. Haiti, the birthplace of freedom. I hear the words devastation and courage. Haitians are asked about the end of their livelihoods, the lost ones, the gone. Cameras in their faces. Piles of bodies. Cameras in their faces. NGO employees in professional attire discuss the rescue mission. They speak in monotone authority, direct and confident. They use the language of expertise, and whenever a Haitian woman appears, she wails, arms punching the sky. Cameras in her face.

I gulp my water.

"*Me voy*," I say, standing and pushing the chair in. "*Gracias por la comida.*"

Amanda nods.

"*Dexter* tonight," Jackie whispers to me.

Amanda glares at me.

"Jesse, do not spend all morning watching television," she barks in English. "Cuzco is full of cultural treasures waiting to be discovered. Don't waste your time in here. Go outside. Do something."

Jackie raises her eyebrows and looks away, trying not to laugh.

"Don't forget your plates."

I take them to the kitchen sink.

At night, Jackie and I pull two chairs close to the television. In between them sits a bag of Lay's salt and vinegar chips, a cylinder of Pringles, and some bottles of soda. Jackie summarizes the first seasons in long-winded sentences while she rips the discs from their case.

"Basically, he's a serial killer who hunts other serial killers as a way to control the darkness within him," she concludes.

She inserts the first disc.

"Now, shut up. If you have any questions, save them until the end."

The first episodes are mildly entertaining. The predicaments Dexter gets himself into are amusing. Every murder has a creative ritualistic element. Very elaborate. The suspense is ripe, the characters dynamic, for the most part. I do find it odd to cheer for a serial killer, but I suppose that is the show's appeal. You root for the anti-hero. You applaud a killer, a bad man. You get that ambivalent feeling, the soft breath on your neck, hinting at the immorality of it all, yet you eagerly anticipate the next episode and the next. Charismatic Dexter. Vigilante. Righter of wrongs. Righteous Dexter. You do not ask questions. What would be the point? You watch to escape. You watch to feel something.

Every now and then, I sneak a peek at Jackie. She cradles her knees, pulling them to her chest, and both her bare feet rest on the chair. The show has engulfed her. She hardly blinks or moves. She nibbles on an occasional chip. At a particularly brutal scene, she might gasp or cringe but beyond that, her eyes follow the plot with no regard for the things around her.

Dexter has taped a man to a table, and when he plunges his knife into his victim's heart, the man shrieks, and I ask Jackie if she could turn down the volume because Amanda may be sleeping. Jackie does so without speaking, and we watch Dexter carve up the man into little bits and shove them into garbage bags. Amazingly, Dexter avoids capture each time, as if his actions were preordained, natural, existing without reason or cause, outside of history and effect. He just does without consequence.

Despite my best efforts, I point out a few plot conveniences, and Jackie rebukes my nitpicking.

"Can't you fucking simply enjoy something? I'm surprised you even leave your room in the morning."

"It's fine," I say. "Just teasing."

I shut my mouth and watch Dexter torture a few more bad guys.

Outside, the sky thunders. Before I go to bed, I have one last cigarette and watch Cuzco through lightning flashes. I wonder what I will do with the children tomorrow. Remember not to ask too many questions, I remind myself. Like watching *Dexter*. It spoils the fun if you overanalyze it. It is meant to be experienced in the present. Stay with us in the present, Jesse. Remember not to think too much, Jesse. It ruins everyone's good time. Especially yours.

January 13

A muddied football slows atop a wet patch of grass. It has ceased rotating and sits there, plump and tantalizing. Then, two boys descend upon it, legs kicking and thrashing, their arms entangled, their frustrated shouts and grunts reverberating through the orphanage. They stomp at the ball, missing it mostly, more focused on pushing and grabbing and hacking each other than moving the ball forward. The other boys stand and watch, waiting for the matter to resolve itself. The ball squirts free and another boy has it on his foot, and he dribbles towards the goaltender standing between a blue plastic table and a tree with a trunk painted white. The goaltender rushes forward to cut the angle, but his movement leaves him vulnerable to a ground shot, and the boy simply side foots the ball, which slithers along the grass. The goaltender still moving forwards cannot get low fast enough, and the ball sneaks underneath him, through the makeshift goal, over a garden, before bouncing off a classroom wall. Some boys cheer, others hang their heads. Not wanting to play favourites, I offer a half-hearted clap from a nearby bench.

A boy in a second-hand sports jacket plops down on the bench and nudges a yellow plastic ball in my direction. I bought the ball for fifty cents after the volunteer coordinators told me to try and incorporate physical games into my extracurricular activities. I grab it, and the boy scampers to an open grassy plot, accustomed to the routine. The sun has squeaked through the rolls of dark clouds, and I must squint when I gaze to the sky, judging where to toss the ball. Because the courtyard is so compact, and such little space exists to sprint and run, I must throw it as vertically as possible—any slight angle or forward propulsion to gather speed and distance would cause the ball to land on the roof or onto the neighbouring streets.

The boy has folded his arms and taps his foot. He waits, and his patience evaporates like the puddles around him.

"*Rapido,*" he demands.

I bend my knees, draw my right arm back, and fire the yellow orb. I immediately lose it in the sun, but the boy still tracks it, sliding back and forth, side to side, studying its descent from the heavens, his left hand shielding his eyes, and when the ball reappears just above the roof, the boy forms a basket with his hands, and he catches it as delicately as if it were an egg dropped by a passing condor. He grins and rolls the ball back to me.

"*¡Otra vez!*" he screams in delight.

Soon another boy has joined him waiting in the grass, and the first boy eyes him with suspicion. I heave the ball again, but this time

I misjudge the trajectory, and the ball angles across the sky and descends above the roof. Below, however, the boys do not seem concerned about the ball's fate as they wrestle and spar with each other for position, blocking, checking, and pulling for any advantage. With fingers on each other's collars, they look skyward to see where the ball might fall. It hits the terra cotta roof, bounces several times, and starts to roll to the edge. Seeing the ball spin towards them only increases the shoving and battling for space, and when it falls to the red tiles and bounces innocently only metres away, the boys unhook from each other and race towards it. Fingers outstretched, legs and arms flexed in sprint, the boys are side by side, but then the boy in the sports jacket plunges and reaches for the ball, and it lands in his hand.

The boy is outraged as he watches the other boy flee with the ball raised in triumph. He barks accusations and wags his finger at him.

"*¡Tramposo!*" he yells. Cheater.

Muttering threats under his breath, he marches towards me, takes my hands, and pulls me to one of the rooms, as if to say to his foe, *You may have the ball, but I have the thrower.*

We sit on the carpeted floor. He grabs my notebook, which I left on a desk, and opens it to the last page we worked on. On it, I have written out questions to get the boys practising their English, rudimentary ones asking about their likes and dislikes. The social workers have warned me, though, not to ask any questions about their history, about how they became orphaned, about lost parents or siblings, about their future hopes once outside these white walls. Nothing about dreams. "Do not ask them their birthdays either," one woman told me, "for we do not know most of them." I respect their rules, but for an English-language volunteer who uses these subjects as talking points, as segues into short, improvised conversations, the number of tabooed topics leaves precious little to talk about. I read over my hand-written questions again and find them less than useless. The boy stares at me with a soured expression as he waits to be entertained by this long-haired stranger. I decide to resort to a time-tested game that appears to have cross-cultural appeal: hangman.

"*Este juego se llama* hangman," I say.

I draw a gallows pole, scribble the English alphabet, and scratch out five solitary lines separated by a small space.

"*Esta palabra es una ciudad de Perú,*" I say, passing my pen across the lines. I further explain the instructions in Spanish and English. He must choose a letter for the mysterious word, but if it has no such letter, a body part emerges on the pole.

"*Cada cuerpo tiene una cabeza, un cuello, dos brazos, y dos piernas,*" I tell him. "*Y después, ¡estás muerto!*"

I strangle my throat and mimic choking sounds, which excites him greatly. The macabre has an extensive appeal among the young.

He scrutinizes the letters, moving his finger over each, before he stops on *e*.

"*No hay un* e."

I draw a sphere for the head, three dots for the eyes and nose, and a frown.

"Your head," I say in English. "Very pretty, no?"

The boy falls back in playful anguish and squeals in delight. He returns to the letters and studies each again. This time, his finger lands on the *o*.

"Yes, there is an *o*."

I write an *o* atop the last line, and he stares at the remaining spaces, undoubtedly arranging letters and forming an unending series of words in his mind.

He points to *t*. No *t*. I scrawl out a long, scrawny neck, and the boy gently scolds himself. The game has turned serious.

He taps *s*. Yes, an *s*. I write the letter on the third line.

He presses his finger on *r*. No *r*. I draw a flimsy, muscleless, boneless arm. He pounds the carpet with his fist and utters a few indecipherable curses.

He analyzes the lines again, and his eyes dart back and forth between them and the letters. Back and forth. Back and forth. He glances at me for neither help nor guidance. It is he and the letters, the word. Nothing else matters.

He decides on *m*. I draw a second formless arm. He runs his hands through his hair, his face tormented and frustrated, and I wonder if this was such a good idea. I know nothing about this child, about his personality, disposition, disorders. I am neither a psychologist nor a social worker; I am only the entertainment, the drunken jester stumbling around the king's court, summoned to amuse the morose children whose parents have vanished.

I watch him steadily. He does not seem ready to stop. No. He glares at the letters as if trying to burn them with his retinas. He is now a vision of concentration, a temple of focus. He sits on one knee, chin resting on the other, and thinks.

"U." And I nod. I write the letter on the second space, and he claps his hands. I can see he has almost grasped it, and the word lies there below his consciousness, only under his tongue, just behind his breath.

But instead he points to *n*. I shake my head and create the first gaunt leg, but I reassure him in my insecure Spanish that he can have as many body parts as it takes.

"*No te preocupes*," I say. Do not worry.

He ignores my coddling and fixates on the remaining letters. I sense he cares not for my gentle comfort, and has grown tired of the sympathetic words of white-skinned temps. He must despise how we come here with cheery dispositions and photographed smiles; he must hate the head pats and tickles as if he were only some fluffy animal existing for our amusement, as if he were only a mouth to feed or a toy to hug. He must loathe our optimism, our platitudes and slogans, and envy our ability to gorge ourselves on his culture, despite our ignorance of its history and realities, while he sits and stares at the walls imprisoning him in his country.

The boy looks at the letters. His finger circles the letters and orbits each one. His eyes again flash from his hanging body to the last unoccupied lines as he matches each to the last spaces. A subtle smirk expands across his lips. He knows. He must know it. And, yes, his finger decidedly drops on the *c*, and I fill the last two spots: Cusco.

"Your city," I say.

He seems unfazed by his victory, and I cannot explain his reluctance to celebrate. He won, yet he stays reserved and muted, allowing himself only the most modest of smiles.

Then, he grabs my pen and turns to a fresh page in the notebook. He rewrites the alphabet, draws the gallows pole, and strikes nine spaces across the white space.

"*¿Una ciudad o un país?*" I ask.

"*País.*"

"*¿Sudamérica?*"

"*Sí.*"

Judging from the length of the word, I know it can only be one of two countries.

"A."

He runs the pen across the spaces, spelling the word out in his mind, and writes an *a* on the last line. He taps the pen on the paper. I know the country. The game is over, but I play along to give my competitor the illusion of control.

"I."

He smiles and wags his finger at me. He draws a big circle with matted hair and a frowny face drooping to my chin.

"M."

Again, his index finger rises to my eyes, and it wags back and forth. And now I have a neck, a long one, a body almost, emaciated, stretching to the page's bottom edge. He taps the pen, waiting, waiting.

"R."

He cackles and savours my misfortune. He draws my first arm slowly, deliberately, to ensure I see it extending to the heavens, as if my hanging torso were waving to God. He even gives me stubby little fingers. His smile is sly. He loves it. I will give him a little more before I take it all back.

"O."

He clicks his tongue and wags his finger, but this time towards the floor. He does not look at me, embarrassed maybe, maybe feeling guilty that he has chosen a country so beyond my comprehension, maybe thinking it was unfair of him to expect the entertainment to know anything more than hugs and games, as if the clown should know anything about the continent he visits. He draws my second arm shorter than the first. I begin to feel annoyed.

"T."

He sighs and snorts. And here comes my leg, looking thin and untoned, unworked, an office-working leg, one designed to sit and command others to move around. Lethargic. My body atrophies before my eyes. It hangs there ugly and undignified. The boy giggles and giggles. His last, I promise myself.

"L."

The boy gives a heartless clap and signs an *l* right before the *a*. I play the part, looking concerned, appearing perplexed by the remaining letters. I rub my forehead, scrunch my face, take deep breaths. The boy enjoys my torment.

"N."

He nods and puts it on the third space. His mood has become less celebratory, less assured. I wonder if he has begun to second guess his choice of country. It has too many letters; it gives me too many chances. His body tightens, becoming still, and changes into a little bronze statue mounted on a podium. He kneels in reflection, a symbol of thought.

"U."

He writes the letter fourth from the end. He checks the letters and remaining spaces, calculating his chances, which have dwindled considerably in the last few seconds. He still possesses that stoic bravery as if kneeling for a general or father, awaiting instructions. Our eyes meet and he wonders if I have it. *Do you have it?* His brown eyes ask, twinkling and sparkling in anticipation and anxiety.

"E."

He traces his pen over the spaces and makes sure he puts the three *e*'s in their correct place. Only two spaces remain, and he looks forlorn, resigned to the inevitable. Yet he still kneels, his gaze away from mine, fastened instead to the notebook and all it holds. His intensity is photogenic and begs to be captured for posterity. His resiliency. His courage. Every day, I hide my camera in my backpack and debate the ethics of photographing orphans. With one hand, I unzip my backpack and feel the camera in my fingers, with the other, I point to *v*.

He writes it on the first space and sighs. One space remains. He sees my body hanging there, one leg short; just one more letter and I am dead, and he has won. The camera is in my hand, and I imagine how I could frame the photograph, the boy hunched over a notebook, pen in hand, in his shabby clothes, surrounded by a bare room. What are the underlying themes? A boy works towards education. A boy works towards a future. A boy practises his English with a volunteer. I will capture his determined face, flexed in focus, and post it on my Facebook wall. And every day, I will look at it and marvel at all the things I have done. I went to Peru. I volunteered in an orphanage. I already see the lauding comments. Every day, he will appear before my world, my friends and family, eyes frozen in concentration, a bronze statue, unknown except for his ripped clothing, staring at a borrowed notebook, unknown except for the caption I provide.

Before I reveal the camera, I point to *z*. The boy pauses for a second and examines exactly where my finger lands. "*¿Sí?*" he asks. And I nod and prepare my mock celebrations. But something curious happens— he takes the pen and draws my second leg, and there I am hanging to death, my body complete and asphyxiated, choked, dead, swaying in the breeze. In the last space, he writes *s*, before he overcomes his surprise at the turn of events, leaps to his feet and wags his finger directly in my face. "*¡Estas muerto!*" he shouts. "*¡Estas muerto!*" I strangle my desire to argue, drop the camera, and merely smile. I watch him race around the room, arms reaching to the ceiling, screaming a Spanish I do not understand. He growls and curls his fingers into fists. And in a flash, he has disappeared from the room and has joined his friends back on the soccer pitch. I am alone in the room, the notebook open, the pen rolling from the opened page to the floor.

January 17

I am a stray kitten. A calico. I am cute, cuddly, but dumb. Very dumb. I need shelter, sustenance, something to play with. Outside your door, in a thin strip of sunlight, I lie, lounge, and stretch. I eat moths, pursue butterflies, chase beetles. When you open the door and see me sunbathing on your porch, you stop in your tracks, and when I meow and rub my fur against your leg, you fall in love. You scoop me in your arms. I purr and rub my whiskers against your cheek. You take me inside, set out a saucer of milk, place a plate of tuna. You give me my own bed. On the weekends, your grandchildren pet and scratch me. You put a collar and leash around my scruffy neck, and in the afternoons, you walk me around Cuzco's back streets. We stop at a children's home, and the gatekeeper lets us pass. I prance up the steps into a courtyard covered in sunlight, my tail pointing to the sky. The boys see me and scamper towards the ball of fluff stretching and yawning in the corridor. Their fingers scratch under my neck, and pet and massage my rumpled fur. They pass me around, and each boy grins and says strange words in falsetto squeals, but I don't understand their language. They look deep in my eyes and reveal themselves in ways they generally keep guarded, hidden. Flickers of futures dance across their irises: futures of fun, futures of afternoons beyond the plastered palisades, futures of families, friends, lovers. But I am a cat, and cats need not worry about such alien matters. Because when I leave the children, I do not look back, do not pause at their shrunken faces, do not reflect on their stunted childhoods; I only gallop forth into the afternoon sun. And soon, maybe, I will grow tired of my mother here in Cuzco, maybe become bored of the language, the same dreary routine, and maybe I will go to Africa. I hear they like cats in Africa.

Before long, though, cats clog Cuzco's roads. I see them scampering everywhere; their silky, checkered coats contrast with the ashen sky. I bound from my mother's porch and join the colourful clowder parading down Avenida El Sol. We chase pigeons on a whim and playfully hiss at one another. We tumble and bumble along the asphalt, indifferent to the cars honking at us, unfazed by the shouts of recrimination thrown our way for … for what? Eating where we shouldn't? Licking milk that doesn't belong to us? Defecating and spraying where it is prohibited? Mating and frisking where we please? We are cats. We know no better. We have grown up among the cooing and sighing. We have learned to expect everything. Everything in our lives has confirmed this for us. We are special. We are the ones. The world waits for us.

There is comfort in seeing yourself in strange places. I feel stronger among other cats. I feel I belong. No longer do I sense that vulnerability of a new country with strange customs and difficult beliefs, for something wonderful happens when you travel together as cats. Even in large numbers, the place begins to welcome you. It warms to you. Sprinting through Plaza Tupac Amaru and into the historic centre, ensconced in my brethren—the bobtails, shorthairs, Burmese, and Burmillas—I see shops marketing to cats. Pictures of cats racing up the Inca Trail stick to windows. Organizations encourage cats to volunteer in the jungle or at construction sites. Hotels and hostels welcome cats with special rates and discounts. Bookshops sell cat-written books about Cuzco and its history. The citizens have become kind to me and my brothers. Whenever I pass the locals, they kneel and lay their fingers on my back and under my neck. I purr and rub myself against them. I like the attention. I do not look my scratchers in their eyes, but I know they must like it to satisfy me like this, to appreciate me like this. How could they not? I am a cat.

January 17

Jackie pushes her way through throngs of people amassing on a Cuzco Saturday night.

"I'm pretty sure it's this way," she says.

The sun has set behind the mountains, but now clouds have gathered overhead. The city lights wash the city in a hypnotic glow. We stroll along Portal de Comercio, the left wing of Plaza de Armas. To my right, among tourists in chullos taking photographs, stands a statue of Pachacuti, the great Inca emperor, pointing to the mountains. His axe is as tall as he; his cape flows past his boots. He rises from a two-storeyed fountain spouting water around him; green and purple lighting brightens the waters, the fountains, and him, the Great Earth Shaker. He appears invincible, a man of the sky, a mover of mountains. Behind him, the cathedral stands in rusted opulence.

The lights cast it in a golden hue. Hauntingly beautiful, its body was made from pilfered Inca stone nearly five hundred years ago.

We continue along Calle Plateros and admire its green street lamps and blue balconies. Trekking agencies selling Machu Picchu have closed for the day. A few touts still linger about offering the best prices for the best treks. Near Fuego Burgers & Barbecue, women in makeup dispense fliers advertising live bands at the hottest clubs. Happy hour specials adorn the windows of adobe-built bars. Free drink tickets blow in the evening wind.

"We are getting closer," Jackie says.

"Who are we meeting again?" I ask.

"Jocelyn. I met her at yoga. She's an anthropologist."

At Calle Tigre, we turn right, and the street dead ends at the entrance to Los Perros bar.

"Don't be scared," Jackie teases, motioning me into the darkened space.

Cylinder-shaped lampshades drop from the ceiling and dim the lightbulbs, neutering the potency of the red and yellow walls where half a dozen abstract dog paintings hang. Someone has written the day's specials in English beside the bar and its rows of liquor bottles. Ambient music plays for the few patrons lounging on sofas sipping mojitos and nibbling Thai-style won tons over wobbly candles.

From one couch, a larger woman in her thirties waves to us, and Jackie rushes over to embrace her. She wears an alpaca sweater tightening around her shoulders and torso. She has dressed in the culture. Jackie provides the introductions and hands out the drink menus lying on the table. I order a Cuba libre, Jackie a gin martini, and Jocelyn a hot wine.

"What brings you to Peru?" Jocelyn asks.

"I've always dreamt of visiting Peru, the mountains, the history, the culture."

I hate the way I sound.

"So you're just passing through."

"Well, I've already been to Lima, Arequipa, Puno. But I am spending some time here volunteering in an orphanage."

"And how do you find that?"

"It's fine. Well, I mean, it's depressing of course. But, yes, overall, it's fine."

The drinks arrive, and I suck the cola from a straw.

"Jocelyn here is working on her doctorate from the University of Chicago. How long have you lived in Cuzco now? Five years, is it?"

"Too long," Jocelyn retorts.

"Well, anthropology doctorates aren't exactly known for their quickness," I offer. "What are you studying?"

"The effects of modernization among Quechua and Aymara women, specifically tourism."

"And what are the effects?" I ask, only half interested in my words.

"Objectification. How tourism turns Indigenous people into things without history. Love the Inca, loathe the Indian. Tourists are only really interested in learning about dead Indians anyways and buying pillowcases from alive ones."

"Jocelyn's super smart," Jackie says, grinning.

"Quiet now, Jackie."

"And where's this new Peruvian beau of yours? What's his name again?

"José" Jocelyn says, checking her phone.

"Yes, dashing José. Where's he at?"

"Running late, I guess."

"Jocelyn, here, has fallen for a local," Jackie says, turning to me. "She's so very taken with him."

"It's only been a few dates."

"Isn't it unethical to fuck the subject? Or is that what ethnographers mean by deep immersion and thick description?"

Jocelyn looks up from her phone, and her stiffened face slowly relaxes.

"Jackie, you're incorrigible," she says, sipping her wine.

"I'm just teasing."

"I know, I know. If you would excuse me, though, I must use the bathroom."

Once Jocelyn has vanished into the growing crowds, Jackie stares at me studiously, about to share something sacred or sacrilegious.

"He's cheating on her," she says.

"Who, José?"

"Yes of course José."

"How do you know?"

"A girlfriend. José has quite the reputation among expats."

"Does he?"

"He tries to seduce do-gooding women for a green card or any western residence permit or entry visa."

I am not sure where my allegiance should lie.

"That's too bad," I say.

"It's beautifully ironic," Jackie says, laughing.

"How so?"

"The anthropologist suspending her critical faculties in the name of romance? It's wonderful."

"Well, I suppose if each is getting something out of it, then what's the harm?"

"Oh, you're so cute, Jesse."

I order another drink and then another. Jocelyn and Jackie talk and laugh while I relax and fade further into the couch and deeper into the rum. The bar fills with locals and tourists, and the music becomes louder and louder until I cannot hear the words Jackie says to me, her face beautiful and dreamlike in the low light. We are leaving, she tells me, and after saying goodbye to Jocelyn, we stroll up and down the sidewinding streets, and Jackie screams she will find us a respectable club, and she will get me dancing. "You must learn to dance," she says to me, and I follow her blond hair through the white streets, past the leering faces of tourist men in jeans and jackets, who bark out trite, drunken slogans of frivolity, some obscene language only white people speak when abroad and drunk on experience, the unfamiliar scenes, the unstudied history, but I pay them no attention, my focus only on her, Jackie, my star on a summer's night, leading me safely through undulating darkened terrain. "Come on, Jesse," she is saying somewhere up ahead while I step through the cobblestones of a pedestrian street, Hatun Rumiyoc maybe, an old preserved Inca road, past the great stone walls of a dismembered Inca palace; past the distant Indigenous women in magnificent shawls, who wander these alleys daily, haggling a fair price for their culture; past the art museums displaying their opening hours and advertising their beautiful objects; past the many bars blaring music onto the streets, filling Cuzco with a fusion of sound. Cuzco, surrounded by terraced mountains, Cuzco, once a capital.

Inside the club, Jackie meets her people, she the proverbial monarch butterfly fluttering from group to group on the half-full dance floor moving to a hybrid of local and foreign sounds, swaying to the rhythms of a Cuzco Saturday night, dark with possibility, intrigue, and indiscretion, and sheltered from the rains falling day after day; these people immune from the daily chores suffered by us, the volunteers, who dig, conserve, love thanklessly. At the bar, a woman in a red dress catches my eye, and maybe she smiles at me, but no, she signals to the gentleman behind me, tall and appetizing with a curved chest and sculpted shoulders, and she disappears with him, and I think nothing about it, only trying to survive the night at the pool table until I ask a player where the bathroom is, and he points up the stairs to a secluded second floor with unused tables and chairs. On one table the woman in the red dress has bent over and is pushing herself against the handsome man, rotating her hips, simulating sex, the man holding her hips tight and secure, and she is smiling, beautifully happy here, upstairs and intimate, overlooking the lights and dancers. She sees me and only stares back, still smiling, sighing, unwilling to sacrifice her pleasure because of my presence and, as I walk by, she is still grinning, her teeth so white, her lips as red as her dress. And the image haunts me because it asks me how to exist in this world, how to find pleasure among the suffering, how to stay humble amid orgasm.

Back at home, Jackie's eyes have a glare to them. Her hair falls in braids, and she wears tattered jeans. One leg crosses over the other; her hands rest on the table. She looks at me. My eyes fall to her neck, lovely, long, delectable. Despite my best efforts, I see my lips there. I see my teeth leaving little marks. It is three in the morning. I want to taste her. I want to wake up next to her.

"Neil Young was a heroin addict, you know," Jackie says.

I know I am drunk because I am about to argue about a trivial thing. "He was not; marijuana, sure, but he eschewed the harder stuff."

Jackie laughs, and my left leg shakes in anxiety.

"Look at his eyes, man, drooping, bloodshot. In the early days, he looked as if he would keel over most of the time."

I sigh. "He lost some of his best friends to drugs; he wrote the fucking song 'The Needle and the Damage Done.' How could he write that if he were shooting himself?"

Jackie has an edge in her voice. "Are you serious? The redemption narrative, of course. He is all sage now, carrying his bucket full of wisdom and judgment."

She smiles her victorious smile, so beautiful that I almost hate it.

"Do as I say, not as I did."

The kitchen light has a brightness I do not like. In it, she lies on a bed among red pillows and presents herself to me. She commands me to pleasure her, to unbutton her jeans and pull them from her legs. She orders me to rip off her panties and to curl my tongue into her. I kneel before her and push my tongue in, and then again, in and out, surgically, expertly. I am patient. I am skilled. I am hers. My hands explore her torso, breasts, mouth while I glaze my tongue over her sensitive spots, over her nerve-filled organ awaiting the saliva of a studied sycophant. She tastes of iron. I lather her until my mouth goes dry, and massage her clitoris, her labia, until her hands run through my hair and tiny pleasurable sighs fall from her mouth.

I work until she finishes, until she touches my back and summons me. She licks my fingertips and lays her lips on mine; her pupils are so wide and vulnerable. I shut my eyes and allow her to study each of my features, my nose, chin, cheeks, eye lashes. She analyzes each as if memorizing them, as if she were preparing for an exam. Finally satisfied, she turns her back and inches closer. She drapes my arms around her and soon she sleeps. As I have her in my arms, the anger I carry in my heart, the cynicism heavy on my shoulders, lapses and vanishes into her rhythmic breathing. Inhale. Exhale. For once, the vulnerability of my ignorance does not make me run. I want to stay with her in this bed forever. I want to nod when she talks, listen when she cries, satisfy when she feels amorous. Most of all, I want the emptiness to dissipate for an evening, to feel connected if only for a night, to sit on the edge of humiliation and not care if I fall.

Jackie has returned the water jug to the fridge.

"What will you do when you return to California?"

She answers without looking at me. "I have a job lined up at Disney through a family friend, some marketing position."

"Are you excited?"

"No. No I am not, but it's what you do."

She slices the table with her hand as if cutting bread.

"Life is a ladder. And I am finishing another step."

She pauses for a moment, a second for herself, and I wish I were there with her.

"I saw a picture of you on Facebook," she says. "I think you were horseback riding through the Argentinian foothills."

"And?"

"You're right. You're not very photogenic."

Jackie's smile comes swiftly, and I cannot help but laugh myself.

"I am an ugly motherfucker," I say.

"You are," Jackie says. "You really, really are."

January 24

A dozen boys watching television lie entangled across the unswept wooden floor. Two sit cross-legged, side-by-side, holding hands; a little rascal creeps from behind and slaps their shoulders, startling them. The boys laugh and shove the troublemaker, but he flees from their grasp, giggling, looking for and then finding another unsuspecting target.

A burly teenager marches into the room. The prankster drops to the floor and becomes reserved, a model of restraint and discipline. The teenager surveys the scene with satisfaction and lies on his back, propping himself up by his forearms. A tyke scurries towards him, drops to all fours, and rests his head on the bigger boy's rising and falling belly. Soon the little boy has fallen asleep, but the bigger one does not seem to mind.

I sit against the back wall and watch them. A familiar face appears in the doorway, looking sullen. He spots me, wags his finger, and a grin emerges. He runs towards me, and I absorb his tackle, corralling him in my hands. He buries his face in my neck, and I feel the coldness of his nose and then of his fingers searching my collarbone and then my biceps. He shifts and shuffles in my lap in an eruption of giggles and smiles before calming and dropping his head against my chest. He quiets in my arms, yet I don't know his name.

He wears the same clothing as he did yesterday: a tattered sweater and blue track pants. Today, though, he wears sandals, and someone has combed his black hair. He coughs and snorts. Snot gathers in his nostrils, which he wipes with his sleeve. Every now and then, the tips of his fingers trace symbols in the palms of my hands.

Outside our bare room, the wind barks. Thunder pounds over the distant Andes, whose pointy peaks I can barely see from our fogged window. Rain pummels the terra cotta roof, and streams of water fall from the gutters, flooding the playground and coating each monkey bar in a sharp gleam.

With every boom, the boy clings harder. A journalist on the television says the rain has destroyed entire farms, homes, and communities in the Sacred Valley, heartland of the old Inca Empire. Violent images flash across the screen. Entire roads have turned to lakes; bridges have disappeared into chaotic rivers. Stranded at Machu Picchu, tourists wave at the cameras while helicopters circle them in the sky. Rescue teams work through the wreckage. The worst rain in decades, the journalist says.

After carefully placing the little one on the floor, the teenager rises and reaches for the antique set. He switches the channels while holding the antennas to get the best reception. He lands on a cartoon about adventurous children and returns to his place. But, before he sits, he looks at me, a penetrating glance of revulsion. His eyes accuse me of something. He says not a word, but I hear each one. Next month, he turns eighteen, no longer a ward of the state, and will go. Next week, I, too, will leave.

The boy in my lap pulls a piece of chicken, dirtied and withered, from his pocket. He turns, his eyes pleased and generous, and offers the meat. "*Por usted*," he says. Before I say anything, he pushes the chicken into my mouth, and his fingers brush against my lips. I swallow it without thinking. He smiles and returns to watching the television. "*Gracias*," I say.

Soon he falls asleep in my arms. Most of the boys in the cold and damp room have fallen asleep. An occasional flash of lightning illuminates the encroaching darkness. He breathes gently, but I don't remember his name. I glance at my watch; it is 5:00 p.m. *Only one more hour to go*, I tell myself. Only one more hour before I can leave. I look down at his closed eyelids, his reddened cheeks, his small body. *¿Cómo te llamas?* I wonder. What is your name?

January 31

Jackie and I walk down Cuzco's sloping streets, from San Blas's bars to the plaza's central gardens and past the closed cafés and souvenir shops. Inca history books along with paintings of peasants are exhibited behind a sheet of glass. The rain has ceased for the moment but has left a trail of glowing puddles. Along the rocky, steep steps, the water has wiped the surface in a slippery shine.

"Watch your step," Jackie says.

And just as she says it, I lose my footing for a second, and my arms flay in search of something to hold. I do not feel embarrassed when one lands on Jackie's white coat.

"What did I just say?"

Jackie smiles under the halcyon light. Side streets ricochet from the main path like strands of curly hair. At each intersection, street lamps shoot orange incandescence in hazy streams. The puddles swallow and absorb the light. Between the water and light, a colourful coalescence hangs in the night, covering centuries-old buildings and churches in blurry phosphorescence. At the central plaza, McDonald's arches glow under the Andes' silhouettes. A Big Mac wrapper drowns in a gutter.

"Were we ever that young?" I ask Jackie.

"As young as who? Matt? He's only a few years younger than us."

"I know, but I find something distasteful about youthful enthusiasm paired with ignorance. It was like trying to talk to a kitten. He can't focus. He meows in clichés."

"Matt is harmless, yes, a cute little kitten with a good heart, wide-eyed, open minded, et cetera, et cetera. He's just dumb. Or maybe inexperienced is the better word."

"But a volunteer straight out of high school? He's only volunteering to appear worldly on his university applications. What can he possibly offer?"

"And how are we any different? What value did you bring the orphanage?"

"None. But at least I have some self-awareness."

"Yes, to the point of caricature."

Jackie's intelligence again disarms me, and I debate how much of her wisdom I should swallow.

Cuzco is quiet and distant. Its historical sights and statues stand in eerie silence. I feel as if I stroll through an art gallery filled with humanity's masterpieces. But a velvet robe cordons off each painting so I can approach only so far. A woman who looks nothing like me guards each artwork, her eyes clasped to me, but she never turns to enjoy what she protects, never gets to sigh at the interplay of colours, the realistic portrayal of a farmer tending his flock, of boats on seas, of faces constructed of cubes. She only watches me and those who look like me, who come with cameras to snap photos of her and her art.

"I can't believe we left Matt at the bar with those three young Dutch women. Poor them," I say.

Matt is the newest volunteer to our house.

"Poor? If they can't see through him, then they deserve his trite routine."

Jackie watches a car pass us.

"Besides, maybe they aren't interested in his conversation. Perhaps what they find most appealing about him is his chiselled abdomen and his lack of thought. People make choices for whatever reason. Allow them that right."

We pass our volunteer organization shrouded in darkness. On the window, an employee has listed the program options, the cost of Spanish lessons, and possible excursions around the area.

"Why did you come to Peru, Jackie?"

"Honestly, I don't remember. Because I could, I guess. It was something to do. You were looking for the brochure Peru, wasn't it?"

"Yes. I guess to have an experience as well."

I don't tell her that the other night after a bout of drinking, while sleeping, I threw up next to my bed just as Matt had an earlier night. I don't tell her that when I confronted Matt about his own release, to tease him about his adolescence, his inability to handle his liquor, he denied it. I don't tell her that when I woke to find my pile of vomit next to the bed, my real shame arose not from forgetting the episode, not from hurriedly wiping the floor in pungent humiliation, but from realizing that Matt and I may not be so different after all. Peru has become our playground, our discotheque, our toilet. A country in which we feel comfortable vomiting.

"It's horrible not knowing why you do the things you do," I say.

Jackie only shrugs her shoulders.

"You act like you are above it, Jesse, this business of helping others. Yet here you are in it. Actively supporting it. In a way, you are worse than Matt. At least Matt believes in the nonsense, believes that he may be doing some good. You know that it's bullshit and that it probably does more harm than good. You know it's more about us than it is about them. You know you shouldn't do it, but you do it anyway. That's the epitome of privilege."

"And you Jackie? What about you?"

"I have no illusions. I am only one person living in a history not of my making. You cannot ask a single person to shovel herself from under an avalanche. Nowadays, to live ethically means living off a piece of tundra somewhere near the Arctic Circle, and I prefer warm climates."

At the front door, she takes a moment longer to look at me.

"What time is your flight tomorrow?"

"Early."

"I hope you find experience," Jackie says, laughing.

"And you as well."

When we enter the hallway, we hug and then go to our separate rooms. Later, Matt stumbles into mine, into his bed, but I do not acknowledge him.

I never see Jackie again.

Three nights later, I sit outside Trujillo's bus station and wait for my overnight bus ride to Máncora, Peru's hedonistic beachside city in the north. I lounge on the curb, a bag on each side of me, and smoke a cigarette. A fence separates me from Trujillo's streets crammed at this late hour with taxis, pedlars, and teenagers looking for things to do. A man leans over the fence and greets me in a pleasant way. He asks me if I could hand him a coin he has dropped on my side of the partition, since he does not wish to walk all the way around and into the bus station to retrieve it. I look to my right and, sure enough, a bronze sol coin lies on the pavement. I hand it to him, and he thanks me with a bow. He tells me, however, that he has dropped a second coin a little further back, and he would be much appreciative if I would retrieve that one as well.

Then it hits me hard: I am being conned. I turn to my left, and one of my bags has disappeared. The coinless man has, too, vanished into the night as if some spirit called back to the ancestral world. The street proceeds normally, cars come and go, passengers enter and depart the station. Nothing seems out of the ordinary, except I now have only one bag.

I race into the station and demand the attention of a bus company employee talking on the phone. "¡Ellos me robaron!" I shout at her and point somewhere outside. She puts her hand over the receiver, shrugs her shoulders, and tells me to go to the police station. My bus leaves in ten minutes. Either I get on the bus and sacrifice my bag containing my laptop and camera or spend many hours dealing with paperwork and testimony for a bag never likely to materialize. Around me, families sit on the uncomfortable chairs surrounded by suitcases and cardboard boxes. They watch me pace across the station, swearing and mumbling to myself. Outside, I have another cigarette to try and calm down. A woman approaches the glass from inside the station and clamours for my attention. Maybe she wants to help me. Maybe she wants money from me. Maybe she wants to deceive me. I ignore her.

On the bus to Máncora, I shake and twitch with anger. I am the victim. I am the wronged party.

The night passes outside. Few cars are on the road. A few seats behind me, a woman listens to music from her phone without headphones. The music simply plays. She listens without anyone's permission. Has she just assumed everyone wants to hear her taste in music? Did she think we would sing along to it? Did she think we would thank her for providing some background noise to an otherwise dull bus ride? I want to turn around and tell her to shut that fucking thing off. I want to tell her she's being so fucking rude, so fucking inconsiderate, so fucking impolite, so fucking selfish, so fucking self-absorbed.

I am about to turn around when I catch my reflection in the window. My fists are primed, my face snarled. But when I look closer at that ugly, stupid face, it softens and slowly drips into a smile and then a chuckle and then a laugh. And laugh I do. I laugh and laugh and laugh.

3
Evolution

San Cristóbal (Chatham) Island
Galápagos, Ecuador

February and March 2010

Atop Frigatebird Hill, overlooking boulder-covered beaches and sterile patches of shrubbery, stands a bronze statue of Charles Darwin. He wears a thick, silhouetted overcoat, opened at the breast and adorned with a snug collar and generous pockets. His trousers are creased and rumpled. His shoes are practical, pragmatic. His left hand secures a notebook against his abdomen while his right curls, his knuckles protruding upward, his fingertips grasping downwards, as if he were holding an imaginary telescope. His hair is brushed back. His eyes squint in seriousness, small slivers of concentration. They are stern, studious, and scholarly. They stare ahead. They classify, group, distinguish, measure. They are the eyes of taxonomy. They are the irises of hierarchy.

The statue marks the spot where Darwin landed on Chatham Island—a flat volcanic island, punctuated briefly by a green mound or hillock—in September 1835, the first stop on his five-week tour of the Galápagos Islands. He was the consummate observer, a diligent chronicler of sights, sounds, and smells. The world presented itself as a mystery to his precocious mind, something to be solved, a codex to be deciphered. All the clues were there; they only required assembly.

And he immediately noted something peculiar about the islands—their uniqueness, their flora and fauna, their natural history. Indeed, he surmised that it would not surprise him if the inhabitants, both plant and animal, were found nowhere else on earth. He recorded everything. He counted the number of craters, roughly two thousand, of which there were two varieties: lava and sandstone. He measured the brown sand with his thermometer, and when the mercury reached its limit, 137 Fahrenheit, he could not gauge how much hotter the black sand was. He compared the acacia and cactus trees, noted the differences between terrestrial and aquatic lizards, and contrasted the male and female tortoises while describing their diets, mostly berries and succulent cactus leaves; their speed, thirteen kilometres over three days; and their reproduction habits: the male utters a long bellow during coitus, while the female drops her eggs in sandy deposits. He remarked, however, that few insects burrowed and crawled through the island's arid soils.

Yet he was still only a young man prone to bouts of enthusiasm, and the islands, at times, filled him with a childish whimsy or an inappropriate level of giddiness for a Cambridge man, a man of science, with a prodigious knowledge of botany, geology, and zoology. Between his dissecting of snakes and his collecting of plants, Darwin found himself scrambling up craters hidden in low-hanging clouds, ridiculing lizards for their ugliness and stupidity, and even riding lumbering tortoises. But it was the birds that intrigued him the most. Their tameness astounded him; they had no fear of man. Whether a mockingbird, sylvicola, tyrant flycatcher, mourning dove, hawk, or finch, Darwin could hunt each with ease; switches and guns were almost superfluous. He could knock a hawk off its branch or grab a mockingbird by its legs. Maybe it was the proximity that Darwin could achieve, maybe it was his unfettered access to them, the unlimited time he had to examine their plumage and beaks, but something about the birds, particularly the finches, stole his attention. He saw that despite their uniqueness, their particularity to the islands, they shared common features—habits, colour of feathers, tone of voice, tail, and claw shape—with their American brethren.

What law accounted for this paradox? What about the islands produced the subtle but important gradations?

Years later, under sober London clouds, Darwin formulated his theory of natural selection and outlined his understanding of adaptive radiation. Millions of years ago, a ground-dwelling, seed-eating finch absconded from the mainland, survived the rough Pacific currents, and landed at a wood-brush beach on Chatham Island. From this one hardy finch, at least thirteen varieties evolved on the islands depending on the niche, the set of resources, and habitats available. The finch adapted. Some grew to enjoy cacti; some began to live in trees; others started to eat insects. The environment determined their fate, pushed them to transform or to perish under the hot equatorial sun.

Unbeknownst to Darwin, his original notes, those first brief sketches, contained the spores and grains for understanding not only the finch's or the tortoise's journey but also humankind's. And although Darwin never concluded humans descended from a common ancestor, an original ape—that human life is simply a spool that keeps spinning and keeps accumulating dirt, debris, and dust— he did already espouse a corollary that humanity is a ladder and different beings occupy different rungs on it. And throughout his voyages, the young naturalist brutally derided those he considered uncivilized, those who wore fewer articles of clothing, those who came of age under different rules and understandings, which is why, perhaps, he paid so little mind to the people of Chatham when he arrived at Frigatebird Hill, that young colony of two to three hundred just emerging, just growing, surviving on the soft sands, the first wooden structures rising, fires of savoury tortoise meat glowing, the smoke gently wafting up to the sky and above the prison colony, and the ships frequenting the shores more and more, bringing more and more people who, like the finches before them, were escaping something, moving for some reason, hoping that the Galápagos were the answer, praying to adapt and to evolve.

I've been drinking. And when I've been drinking, especially rum, I like to think about disorder, chaos—wildness. So I like to think it was not far from here, this stretch of three-storey red-bricked buildings, that Darwin watched a young boy, no older than eight, kill several finches, pluck their plumage, and roast their wings. And walking now, past the half-built homes, the laundry hanging across stiff lines, I hope, under encroaching drunkenness, that along this road, which leads to the highlands just twelve kilometres away, there lies a crater lake clothed in wood, and maybe, just maybe, that is where Darwin, in a picturesque scene of mist and cloud and plant, found the skull of a sealing-vessel captain, murdered by his crew at the height of their mutiny. I stop for a moment, while the others skip ahead, and savour the silence.

The four of us are walking in the back streets of Puerto Baquerizo Moreno, only city of the Isla San Cristóbal, formerly Chatham Island, southeastern corner of the Galápagos archipelago, one thousand kilometres from the Ecuadorian mainland. It is night and it is hot. I am in a black, buttoned dress shirt, cargo shorts, my hair tied in a ponytail. Most nights, I don't leave my room, but it is our last one on the island, and the others have been harassing me. We have been here for a month volunteering at a summer camp for a local NGO, babysitting the island's local children. My head is fresh with convenience-store-quality rum. It was five dollars at the shop near the pier, just down from Melville Street, along Darwin Street, and across from Shipwreck Bay, where the tour boats sway in the waves. I watch them sometimes from my bench while smoking a cigarette, the American tourists waddling from the hull, cameras around their necks, big sun caps, skin crisp and burned. They slink around in the heat and barge into the shop, buy their underwater cameras and T-shirts, memory cards and chargers. Sometimes they stop for a beer next door and watch the sun sink over the green forests, the lava-spewed beaches, and watch it fall right smack into the Pacific. And I always wonder if she's there with him, languishing on his every word, she a Brooklynite full of precocity, he an outcast from the Ecuadorian mainland, who ferries around other Americans, pointing out sea lions and octopuses, that same herd of tourists, demanding in its size, who now stalk the confines of the animals' last refuge.

We arrive at a fenced-in concrete football pitch that also moonlights as a basketball court. Everything on the island is versatile.

Adaptable. Local teenagers, four of them too, spot us and point to the gate. They kick a ball menacingly and watch, hands on hips, as the ball spirals towards us over the pebbles and tiny pieces of glass. They carry a boredom that must exist universally among the young, those minors who fall unconvincingly between child and adult, too old for silliness, the lightheartedness of childhood, and still too young for seriousness, the implied freedoms and responsibilities of adulthood. The feeling of limbo must sting even more for island youth, who have known the same streets for years, the same bends and knolls, the same neighbourhoods and neighbours, the same routines, the same teenaged insurrectionist flair that, after fifteen or sixteen years on this tiny volcanic island with one main road that leads nowhere, must become so diluted, so watered down, that the thought of stealing something or drinking something or smoking something becomes as mundane as doing homework. They must think that life exists out there beyond the archipelago, on the mainland, in the hustle and bustle of Quito or Guayaquil—oh god, the people who live there, their stories, their exploits. They must despise their parents for migrating from the mainland and colonizing this basaltic volcano, trading in the dangers of violence and drugs for the dangers of ennui and the occasional tsunami.

It is Friday night, and all they have is a ball.

We negotiate the terms in broken Spanish. Football is almost a universal language. Philip and Dylan hail from southern England, Londoners, who were raised on the pitch amid Chelsea glories. Marco comes from Amsterdam, fed, too, on the celebrity of Robben and Van Persie, the Flying Dutchmen, all draped in orange. We shake our opponents' hands, and then Philip points to Dylan, who sulks towards the net, while Marco fills the left forward position and I, the right. In the distance, waves break over the rocky beach, but the breeze barely reaches us. Deserted are the streets. Heat desecrates the night. A few children lean against the fence and watch, their fingers wrapped around the wire. Philip rests his foot on the ball and nods at his fellow centre man, who confirms the request. Marco shouts for the ball, and Philip obliges.

I last played soccer fifteen years ago on a southern Ontario field covered in snow. My best friend and I have broken the opposing team's defence, and we are racing down the field with only a lone defender and the keeper to beat. I have the ball in front of me, a rock of ice and snow, and as the defender unwisely goes for a block tackle, I chip it to my teammate, who fires the rock in one motion. I watch the ball sail into the air among the incessant grey and white of a winter's afternoon deep in rural Canadiana. I remember the goalkeeper, a girl of twelve in a pink jacket, reaching for the ball as it flies above her ponytailed head. I remember it ricocheting off her gloved hand, bending her forearm back as if it were a twig, the ball rolling over the goal line. My teammate breaks her hand, and she wears a pink cast.

Philip moves the ball artfully down the left wing, bypassing Marco, who runs to position himself in front of the goal. The Londoner taps the ball ahead with his left foot, teasingly, and twirls his right around it, tiptoeing and tap dancing, waiting for the defender to attack, to succumb to the temptation, to bite the juicy fruit. And when he does, Philip in one motion floats the ball over the defender's jab, the ball landing on his left foot and then is volleyed towards the net, sailing wide. He claps his hand in frustration and jogs back to centre, acknowledging neither Marco nor me.

Philip wears the illusion of fitness. He is slim and possesses a sexy anorexia, often mistaken for form. When he poses on Playa de Oro, hands on hips, with his remarkably even tan, delicious deltoids, and umber latissimus dorsi, and when he stares out at the youngsters frolicking in the waves, fleeing an errant stingray or crab, an anarchic scene of screams and splashes, he fools those around him, particularly the young women, other volunteers in green bikinis, tricks them into believing he possesses a strength or fortitude, as if he could charge into the waves and scoop up every child in the event of a shark sighting or an earthquake.

He does not. His abdomen buckles and crackles not so much from training but from debauchery and self-abuse. He drinks. He fucks. He sweats. He is an undernourished hunk. A gaunt god. A diseased perfectionist. He is an emaciated piece of pork. His strength as well as his charm are ephemeral. Nothing particularly remarkable emanates from him, except his lack of self-awareness. That void of self-consciousness. The world comes to him. His accent intones with the assuredness of future management, a moneyed position in the upper echelons of society. His forebears must have ushered in the Industrial Revolution, men in top hats investing in Manchester mills and poor houses, must have slurped the wealth from their workers, getting fat from their sweat. Philip is owed everything. Especially women.

He has a sociopathic smile of big white teeth. His boyish good looks disguise the vacuity within. He seduces in the way that narcotics do. An irresponsible *carpe diem*. A parochial mindfulness. A drunk Bodhisattva. At the bars and restaurants along the waterfront, I watch Philip entertain his girlfriend, Sara, some woman he met at some bar in some country. They try to make it work, travelling and intimacy, travelling and relationships, but she must know, sitting there reading *Persepolis* and drinking a fruity cocktail, that inevitability will swiftly arrive. I tell her I enjoyed the film version, and she smiles and says the book's better. Philip pays no attention, his consideration absorbed in the jovial, juvenile conversations around us, the young and altruistic, the garrulous gringo volunteers of the Galápagos. And, after she leaves the following day, Philip's eyes linger on the smoother skin of the near and available, the smell of life, of hot, moist experience.

The ball lands in their goaltender's hands. He rolls it to the winger, who delicately pushes it up the court. I block his angle and widen my purview to anticipate a pass across to his fellow winger angling on the other side, awaiting a break forward. He understands my intention and circles back while I close in. Philip screams something behind me; Marco stands indifferent; Dylan analyzes the scene in boredom. The winger must have momentarily lapsed in concentration, a rare blunder in form, as he obtusely kicks the ball towards the goalkeeper, but it caroms off his sneaker and flies to the right, towards me, and without moving a muscle, without surrendering a bead of sweat, I watch the ball hit my thigh and dribble into the net. I shrug my shoulders and nonchalantly receive the high-fives from my teammates, as though scoring a goal in a pickup football game on the Galápagos Islands were a regular occurrence. I beam within. I am secretly elated. I have convinced them that I belong. I am worthy. It does not last.

The locals push back and hem us in our own end. The five minutes of activity under this woolly afghan night has already exhausted me. Heat slows everything to a slither, making every movement somehow both pronounced and paltry, magnifying every mistake, the fat and flab; each and every unattractive and defective part falls under the heat's scrutiny, under its collective analysis and communal ridicule. The ball bounces on my trainers, lawlessly, refusing to still and submit to my control, and one of the local teenagers spots my weakness, my unsuitability, and descends on me, entraps me in his speed, his smothering attacks, his relentless ambush, his barrage of kicks and pokes, his feet ensnaring mine, his hands on me. And in desperation, a final plea for help, I boot the ball towards Dylan, but the ball rolls with a lethargic spiral, and I watch in shame as it stops perfectly on the toe of another local Galapagoan, who fires it into the net past Dylan, who sees the white blur glide past him and raises his hands in frustration, as if to say, *At least give me a chance, at least allow me the opportunity to contribute, to make the save, to do my job.* Philip turns away in disgust while Marco doesn't register a reaction, and as I apologize to Dylan, he nods at me in a stoic manner, and takes pity on my pathetic display.

Dylan and Philip have travelled together for several months now. Friends from university, they have embarked on a year-long, round-the-world trip to mark the gap between childhood and adulthood, the last hurrah before being gobbled by the rules of responsibility, the rigours of everyday living. They want the opportunity, as did Darwin 180 years ago, to explore the world and themselves before making those final, dire decisions, before choosing which soul-crushing, spirit-ravishing path best suits them. Darwin was set to enter the church, to become a man of God, before being asked to join the crew of the *Beagle* because of his natural curiosity, his love for rocks and organisms, his logical mind, which, as a result of his South American trip, eventually set the rules for humanity's journey from slug to soul, from microscopic mulch to sentient being, capable of art, poetry, music, love. Dylan and Phillip too, I sense, wish to uncover something drastic about themselves, find something beautiful in the world, some point in the future to strive towards, some great goal, some purpose. Following their countryman—Darwin too was only twenty-three when he left England—they have been swept to the Galápagos to be inspired, to gain knowledge and, like the finch, to adapt and grow.

The other day Dylan cried. Unlike Philip, Dylan has layers, pieces of himself that he reveals only after trust has established itself. And despite the muscular and masculine bravado he sometimes exhibits to match Philip's incessant one, despite the crass and crude jokes he makes during another drunken episode under oceanic stars, his is a romantic spirit, a dour, gloomy, almost maudlin soul, who would sacrifice his entire edifice, crack his own carapace with a hammer, just to wake up next to a beloved, to lie naked in her arms with the rising sun peeking through the blinds, creeping over the bed, and wrapping their bodies in early morning warmth. So when I saw him hunched over on a table in one of Moreno's tourist hotspots, his tense back heaving, his body collapsed and broken, embarrassed tears pooling on the table amid the fecund mangroves and unfeeling pelicans of the young Galápagos, where migration is endemic, where mutation is customary, where movement is the law, I felt nothing much at all other than a little remorse and a lot of smugness.

During the summer camp, Dylan, for the most part, organizes the sporting activities—obstacle courses, basketball, dodgeball—anything to tire the little rogues and their nonstop spontaneity. They are exuberant with life, deranged with its fever. During the first week of camp, for example, Carnival smacks the town from its doleful slumber and transforms it into a savage battleground. Children and teenagers hunt the streets with water guns and water balloons, lurking from behind doors, stalking from rooftops. They ride on bicycles and search for anyone foolish enough to wander the streets on these few days preceding Lent. The chaos infiltrates the school as well, with the rascals decorating the yard in liquid, dousing and soaking the volunteers with unconscionable abandon. Pieces of balloon litter the grounds. Cotton clothing drips and becomes heavier. The water fountain works as an ammunition reloading station. But their energy does not get quelled with the holiday's conclusion, does not lessen with the director's loud admonishments; it flows over into the next weeks, building in intensity and rigour, their hunger for joy and fun insatiable, and I reluctant to accommodate it.

Dylan, though, has a laudable empathy, a remarkable patience that he displays daily. Unlike Philip, who tries to corral the children into submission, bully them into acquiescence, Dylan tries to channel the calories, the sugar highs, into a manageable form, direct it into exercise, activities, and sporting events, and today, he has planned dodgeball. While half of the children paint and practise their English prose in the classroom, the other half assemble outside on the basketball court with us and are halved again, with a dozen or so standing on each side of the court awaiting instructions, looking attentively at the half-inflated basketballs sitting seductively at mid court. Dylan and Philip try to explain the rules in Spanglish, revealing that the basketball acts as a bullet, and if you are hit by the bullet, you are *muerto*, dead, but if you catch the ball, pluck the bullet in mid-air, the shooter dies. Each team also has a queen who must be protected at all costs because the queen can resurrect her charges, can reanimate her loyal subjects by touch; but if the queen is assassinated, she stays dead forever, and her subjects will slowly starve and inevitably surrender without her revitalizing brush.

The courtyard buzzes with the anticipation of permissible violence, and then a hush falls as they ready on the line, toes touching the paint, knees bent in an athletic pose, ready to sprint towards the ball, satiate old grievances, get vengeance and restitution, restore balance, unleash hell. Dylan surveys the line to ensure fair play, and Philip asks one last time if everyone is ready; Marco steadies the balls on the line. And on the command of "Go," the two armies rush at each other, and the previous moment's silence devolves into disorder, the rule of the mob, survival of the fittest. Madness invades the quiet. Shrieks stab the scenery. Frenzy comes in sharp slashes. At the mid court, two boys in T-shirts tussle over a ball before the smaller one makes a deft pull, stripping it free, and in a flash it rises high over his head and comes crashing down on the bigger boy's leg, who wears a mask of incredulity, unbelieving that he was bested by the little tyke but falls nonetheless, crumbles in a heap of shame, under cries of "*¡MUERTO!*" And here comes the queen, rushing to the rescue in pigtails and jeans. Guarded by a retinue of three, she drifts over the battlefield, ducking and dodging the bombardment of basketballs that fall and bounce nearby, and with the nimbleness of childhood, a cool flexibility, she stretches and reaches to her fallen comrades, goading them back to life, soothing their worries, demanding that they fight for her, ordering them to storm one more time into battle, assuring them that victory is imminent, that the sun soon rises. But amid the hullabaloo—enraged cries of competition and accusations of cheating and foul play—one girl, with the face of a dove, hangs back under the basketball net, demure and diffident, deferring to the stronger students around her until she sees a ball roll lackadaisically past the line, beyond the sight of the others, and bound to her. She collects her courage and wades into the fray, creeping forth from under the cloak of unpopularity, and I watch her sneak her way over shot schoolmates towards the ball that has fallen still just beyond her reach, sitting there in indifference, waiting for her, she who now stands above it, when a boy spots her, a brash, lecherous boy, too big for his age, and he winds his arm, five metres from her, and launches his orb. As I study the ball flying through the air, twirling in the mid-morning humidity, I understand the playground as a site of microscopic calamity, a microcosm of the world, a testing ground for tragedy, and when it hits her cheek and her budding, confident eyes turn to shock and humiliation, her face crumpling to confusion, her tears welling fervently, I sense the cold hand of nature at work.

Dylan rushes to her, takes her hand, and leads her from the court to a nearby bench. Philip and Marco wander over as well while I continue to supervise the game. From the gate to the school emerges Amy, a volunteer from Brooklyn, who upon seeing the little girl in tears hurries over to her aid. The girl sits between Dylan and Amy and slowly regains her composure, calming herself among the cooing and consoling of the volunteers. Amy is wrapped in kindness. She has a pleasing, welcoming smile that warms without intent. There is no hidden agenda, no maliciousness, no ulterior motive, only pure altruism. She is friendliness personified. She is bright. She is bubbly. Children sense this and gravitate towards her, and when they wrap themselves around her waist and glance into her dreamy eyes, they become ensconced in her compassion and believe that she cares for them, believe it so furiously that they refuse to shift when she gently shakes them loose. She does care. But Dylan is not a child, not in the physical sense and, unfortunately for him, he too is warmed by her spirit, but he desires something far more than friendship and nurturance, something far deeper than pleasantries, something beyond the daily greetings of civilized and mannered living. And as they sit together pacifying the child, assuaging her rumpled skin, allaying her caustic shame, I catch Dylan's eye hold on Amy a second longer than necessary, an indulgent glance, a tender gaze, signifying a turn from himself and an embracing of what nature has long mocked in humankind: affection.

We are behind. The locals have just scored, a beautiful give-and-go sequence that shredded our meagre defence and eviscerated our dwindling pride. 5 to 2. Marco looks to Philip for an explanation, and he just hollers some unintelligible roar to the sky, casting his burning look in my direction, while I keel over in exhaustion, panting under the court lights. I am sobering up. The inanity of the situation has begun to dawn on me. My rational mind has fought through the pall of drunkenness. I want to sit down. I want to throw up. I should be asleep in my vile room, lying shirtless on my mattress, the water-stained walls looming above me, the sweat glistening on my rash-covered, unsunned skin, the ancient fan rattling in exhaustion, the spiders spinning their webs, the pests multiplying, the heat unmovable and pervasive. I should not be among these men. I cough. I spit. I breathe.

A million insects float and dance in the luminance. The surrounding houses sit in silence. Not a sound comes from the town, except for Dylan bouncing the ball in mounting rage. Dylan motions to Philip to vacate the net, which he does, and he mopes to centre court to join Marco and me. Philip places the ball on the edge of his goal and points to the opposite one, indicating that he's going to give it a go and take matters into his own hands. I couldn't care less. The opposing team laughs and steps aside to allow Philip an unencumbered view of the net. He takes two steps backward and directs his eyes to the ball and then to the net, calculating velocity, height, curve, imagining the angle the ball will travel, its arch and dip, latitude and longitude. He smiles. And fires. The ball sails under the lights; well struck, it cuts across the night, shooting towards the goal and over us, who watch with a mild amusement as if it were a meteor, watch the sphere rotate towards the keeper; but it does not dip, does not drop, does not descend, and instead it rises further over the net, the fence, and onto the streets outside, where it bounces a dozen times and rolls away down a hill and out of sight. Philip shouts something obscene and reluctantly departs to retrieve it, muttering curses to himself as he traipses down the street following his errant shot. The rest of us stay quiet in our cell; an unspoken resolution descends: the game is over. Marco motions to his watch; Dylan nods. I watch him march out of the court and scream at Philip that it's time to press on to the club, the island's ramshackle discotheque, which I sense, nay hope, will become full of delightful horrors, what with the state Dylan's in, all heartbroken and vulnerable and ready to stab a stranger in the eye.

The previous weeks, I have watched Dylan bloom and then wilt. A remarkable cycle. With Amy, he has risen from being Philip's unctuous buddy, his sycophantic sidekick; he has stepped out from Philip's shadow. In the island's bars, he sits next to her and tastes her every word, careful to slowly digest each one, testing for subtle meanings, layered nuances, coated hints. In the classroom, he organizes the children's school bags and boots while spying Amy float from red table to red table, from student to student, praising each drawing, family pictures of beaming faces and disproportionate arms and legs; and when she calls him over to show one particularly nicely crayoned image, Dylan can only nod and smile, smile and nod. On the beach, they sit, chins resting on knees, waves breaking over their toes dug in the sand, amid a rookery of sea lions and their barking pups. Dylan makes fatuous comments about travel and life in general, trying to seem suave and debonair, a philosopher king, while Amy simply smiles in her intoxicating way, face turning to perfection, an oblong canvas of incandescence, there for the viewer to soak in, to drown in, to live in. Soon Dylan learns the value of shutting up and lets the scene, the Galapagoan tranquility, speak for him—the evening's caress, its gentle cloying, the wind pushing the clouds towards Ecuador, revealing the sun dripping into the ocean. I know Dylan has forfeited his resolve, suspended his critical faculties, sitting there stealing fugitive glances at her; he has fallen for the postcard of foreign bliss, succumbed to the potency of the expectation. He has become infused with infatuation, deceived by how easy everything appears under the spell of no tomorrow.

I see a man across the beach dive into the still water from a natural pier of rock. He swims towards us in an uninterrupted sequence of strokes. His crawl is effortless. His movement is hypnotic. His pace is languid. Each arm cuts the water in the same rhythmic fashion. He navigates through a maze of motorboats with sleeping sea lions resting on their bows. His lithe body moves streamlined, his feet fluttering in perfect harmony, his mouth sucking air in wonderful synchronicity. He emerges from the sea dripping, beads of water scattering over his browned, lacquered skin. Dylan waves to him; Amy shields her eyes from the sun and greets him as well. Carlos, the tour guide, another refugee from the mainland, extends his hand to Dylan and grins at Amy. He barely acknowledges me in the background. He is loquacious and charming, skilled in the art of marketing, of making gringos feel tall and big. He wants to take the group of volunteers on a snorkelling trip, only twenty American dollars a person, to Punta Pitt, on the opposite end of the island, inaccessible by land, to a secluded reef with great marine life. Dylan and Amy express their interest before Carlos asks them to join him for a beer later, which they agree to do. As Carlos saunters away, sans towel and barefoot, in the direction of town and its derelict houses, I catch Amy turn her head towards his fleeing image, her brown eyes wondrous.

One night at the beachside bar, a dozen empty beer bottles and several filled ashtrays litter the table at which we sit. I sit with Carlos and Amy; Dylan has gone to fetch Philip for another night of debauchery. Carlos remains shirtless and orders the barkeep to bring us another round. Amy is fluent in Spanish, and every now and then she will switch from English to converse with Carlos in his native tongue. I understand some. They laugh. She feathers her fingers over his bicep. They giggle in dalliance.

Carlos turns to me and says, "She's a real flirt, isn't she?"

"Maybe, she's just friendly," I reply.

"Thank you, Jesse," she says.

I feel satisfied yet saturnine. Carlos lights a cigarette and shakes his head.

"A girl can get into a lot of trouble being so friendly," he says. Amy sips her beer while I watch a crowd of tourists gather on the street.

"A girl shouldn't be punished too harshly for saying hello," she says. A sea lion pup has slithered through a hole in the clumsy barricade separating the beach from the promenade. Carlos unleashes a billow of smoke from his nostrils.

"Amy," he says, "a smile can both infuriate and infatuate a man; it is never innocent." The visitors take photographs of the transgressing pup, who struggles along the pavement; its fat is robust, yet its fins are young and inexperienced. Amy's face curls into mock outrage, playful with a tint of severity.

"Jesse," she asks, "what do you think?" Camera flashes burst in the twilight; a gaggle of children follow the pup down the path.

"I think a person shouldn't be judged based on another's expectations," I say. From the beach, the pup's mother barks an awful, disorienting cry, a desperate call causing the young children in baseball caps and blue shorts to cover their ears. Carlos snuffs his cigarette in the ashtray, his fingers sprinkled with ash.

"Just don't waste a man's time," he says; "don't tell and then not show." The mother wails from the hole in the fence as the pup bounces and turns around, supporting its barrelled body on its fins, its wrinkled fat glistening in the late sun, and struggles to return to its mother and the rookery.

"Don't expect the moon from basic human decency," Amy says, taking one of Carlos's cigarettes. He opens a flame and covers it, while Amy brings her end to the fire, gently touching his hand. Children throw fistfuls of sand at the pup; one tries to touch its glassy coat before his father pulls him back and scolds him. Amy blows a ring of smoke to the ceiling and only smiles. At the sight of her pup, the mother calms, and they turn from the onlookers, waddle down to the shoreline, and flop and then shoot out to the waves. Carlos stares at Amy in drowsy anticipation. Up ahead, Philip and Dylan walk towards us.

"What's the best thing about being a tour operator on the Galápagos?" I ask Carlos.

I don't care about Carlos or his job. He is a venomous and superficial tick, a man-child who frolics in the sea by day and fucks in the shadows by night. I do not care about him, nor do I care with whom Amy spends her time. She is twenty-three. She makes her choices and dies with them. She, the inscrutable butterfly with syrupy lips, floating from flower to flower, sucking herself satisfied, fattening and feasting on a tulip's nectar, devouring its pink, orange, and purple petals. She, the iridescent firefly lighting paths through long, voracious grass and muddied, rain-fed pools of stinking mulch, leading lost, lustful men to shelter. She is rapacious. She is ravenous. She is resplendent. I do not care about her. Let her be. But Dylan does care. Dylan, walking just ahead amid the vegetable patches and wired fences of back-alley Moreno, the concrete block homes and chicken coops, cares very much. Dylan, the impotent Casanova, has fallen prey to a common misconception, particularly for men, of mistaking neighbourliness for flirtation, friendliness for amour. Dylan, crestfallen and contrite, limping towards the discotheque, heart full of glass, was taken for a ride by her pouty and mopey face, a pretty mouth full of enchanting, spellbinding words, her whimsical flavour and sullen eyes, making him believe in the promise of beaches, of youth, of those mild indiscretions.

Towards the club we march, and I want to ask you, Dylan, *Where is she now? Where is she now? What is she up to?* I bite my lip and swallow the giggle, the laughter swelling deep within me, percolating in my belly, rising in my esophagus, knocking on my throat, demanding release through my mouth and out into the barren night. Oh Dylan, I do feel for you. All those hours Dylan, all that work you put in, for what? All those clever remarks, the unrivalled charisma, bathing her with attention, listening to her every anxiety and aim, soothing her with half-meant compliments, watering her with those splendid words. And now you, Dylan, slouch towards the club, on some seedy pilgrimage, forever Amy's consummate platonic friend, her buddy, her brother, her bestie. When she pulled you from your cave, Dylan, your self-imposed exile, when she tickled you with her comity, when she softened your shell, and beckoned you to come forward to the light, you, the terrified toddler, when she burned your bulwark, offered you her hand, and you took it, did you ever see yourself here, stepping into this putrid menagerie of flesh? You should have.

Stay home, Dylan. As I do. Or at least as I tried to tonight before you, Philip, and Marco knocked on my door and persuaded me to go out, last night on the island and all. Usually, though, I simply lounge around my room, sweating, thinking of her, not Amy but her, whom Amy masks; of her, whom I obsess over; of her, who no longer returns my Facebook messages with a regularity I think appropriate. Or I play video games, some FIFA football game, the computer always thrashing me even on the easiest level. Or I am lying on my bed thinking up stories to write, of western men getting drugged in colonial Quito bars by smooth-talking local women, awaking to find themselves tethered to tables, at the mercy of thorned goddesses breathing fire at their most delicate, precious spots. Or I am sitting outside the house, on a white plastic chair, smoking a cigarette, watching the family next door playing volleyball on the gravelled lawn. The father is a taxi driver who parades around the island in one of those ubiquitous white pickups, charging a fortune for a two-kilometre drive. The mother stays at home most days. Their two young daughters spend their time cavorting around the property, spinning Hula Hoops, riding tricycles. Then the ball rolls towards me, and I gently toss it back to the girl, who has always been a little panicky of the strange man living next door. The father waves to me and asks if I would like to play, as I have before. I shake my head, and he nods in understanding, before a sketch of genuine delight chisels itself over his cuddly face, and asks, "*Otra vez, ¿cómo se dice 'barrio' en inglés?*" "Neighbourhood," I say. "*Ah sí,*" he says, "*bienvenido al* neighbourhood." His girls laugh at the funny word fumbling out of their father's mouth. The littlest one tosses the ball to her father, but it hits the pole and trickles towards the garden; she giggles before her father scoots after it, his fingers just above the rolling sphere of leather, grabbing it before landing in the muddy soil. His family claps, and I sit there smoking, watching the family at play, dreaming of all the things I will do upon my return to Toronto—the volunteering, the schooling, the playing, all the wonderful stuff awaiting me as I disembark at Pearson airport and jump on the subway and head downtown to the teaming and buzzing streets, the Friday night frivolity, the jammed bars of excitable young intellects debating the finer points of Marcusian Marxism, because I am still young, only twenty-five, still more time ahead of me than behind; time, though, the quintessential straightjacket, full of bad faith and the tyranny of choice, because when you have everything, time appears as the elixir, a long field in which you may plant your crop and harvest at your leisure, but you end up just standing there over your fallow dreams, becoming the man you always despised, the man who was handed the world and forgot all about it, standing in a dusty corner, gently bumping his head against the wall to see how long before it starts to hurt, before the pain and frustration make him return to the world, make him sense the ineffable terror of living for another, that responsibility wrapped in a sweater of endless despair but delight too, delight in watching her grow, mature, evolve into something special, amazing, unique, both for herself and for others. But he never does move from his wall; it is never hurting enough to move, and that's the greatest fear, immobility, to be a beautiful statue conquered by choice, derided by time.

At school, a metal gate separates the classrooms from the playground. And when no gym classes are happening, the volunteers must ensure that the gate remains closed lest the little ones escape and flee into Galapagoan freedom. One morning, about a week ago, in the bedlam that falls between classes, the children screaming and scurrying from one class to another, a volunteer forgets to lock the gate. After the children find their respective rooms, and calm returns, I am cleaning up the courtyard when I see a lone girl standing in front of the doorway, which stands wide open. She is maybe seven years old, has long black hair, and wears a blazing pink dress. She sways in the early-morning breeze, on the cusp of action, as she places her hand on the handle and peeks outside. Her face is full of intrigue, the curious gaze that defines the kingdom of childhood, before rules and respectability replace the recess, the afternoons replete with sandcastles and reverie. She creeps further afield, her flip-flops stepping past the threshold, her eyes alight with possibility. At the instant she releases her grasp from the blackened door and is about to march forward into the unsupervised terrain—out from the school, away from the peculiar and imperious gringos, her parents, her church and town, their rules and regulations, and into an eyeless landscape, to roam and run with the wild things—just before her plunge into that wonderful world, I scream for her to stop. It startles her. She steps back into the school. Her eyes fall to her feet. She says not a word. No breezes stir. No voices mutter. No children abound. It is only us and the silence. I point to the ground and bark for her to come. "*Ven acá,*" I say. She registers the words and lifts her eyes to meet mine. They glow with indecision, burning on the brink of insubordination, dancing with disobedience.

She glances back to the breach, the window to her new world, as her body relaxes and readies for revolution. "*¡Ven acá!*" I yell again. She shakes her head. And her stony, submissive visage melts into a defiant insouciance. Her lips curl and cohere into a mischievous grin. "*¡¡Ven acá!!*" I scream, my voice quaking in anger and self-reproach. She shakes her head again and laughs, laughs at the strange guard full of animus and hissing threats, laughs at his laws and statues, the heavy crown of authority and judgment that he brandishes every morning, laughs at his sweaty and unformed face, glistening with insecurity and doubt, laughs one more time and then bolts. She is out the door and out of sight. Gone. I race to the gate and see a flash of pink tearing across the basketball court, past the pavilion, towards the local restaurants and hair salons, on a road that leads up to the highlands. I sprint from the door and scream for her to stop. She does not. I hear the amused hoots and hollers from a construction team working on a nearby home. I hear her voice too, a primitive howl emanating from her tiny frame, bouncing and bopping over the ground, arms flaying, knees bending, lungs heaving, her body personified joy. Her bark is the sound of the uncoiled, of desire and purpose unfurled. Her untamed shrieks blast the sluggish morning and kill the addled heat. She is breeze. She is wind. She is hurricane. And as she senses that I am approaching and can feel my boorish, uncouth paws entrap her, she lets loose one final cry, a deafening, piercing roar. She struggles in raw rage against my clasp before submitting to my strength and calming in my arms. On the way back to school, across the court, I carry her while the construction team claps. She fights no more. She only smiles.

The discotheque hides in the first floor of a decrepit old building in Moreno's dishevelled back streets, on its edge, a step from the wilderness. Climbing a knoll, we hear music break the lull and sense the long strands of sound plow over the pavement and die further afield among the thickets and cacti, the iguanas and lizards. Philip and Marco quicken their step; I hang back with Dylan, drifting towards the site. Dylan wears the long necklace of heartbreak with unabashed pride. He has mastered the mime and has claimed the cliché. He walks it well: heavy and cumbersome steps, tightened and inflexible body, wicked and wild eyes. He is on the edge. He holds that abeyant violence of a man wronged, of an ego pricked, a walking id desperate for retribution and reprisal, a wounded animal clinging to the fading sense that his claws still lacerate and his fangs still devour. I sense it. I want to see it: the fall. I want to see the tragic unravelling of a boy full of dead romance. I want to see the unveiling of his hamartia, his masculine unswallowing of her word, no. I want to see him fall apart.

The club is full of snakes. It is a claustrophobic room full of long-tongued, shedding bodies, who skin themselves and then slither along the dance floor, afresh, anew, unsaddled beings born again under the neon ball and hot strobe lights. The music pounds in uneven currents of machine-gun-fire beats. The percussion bounces and ricochets off the peeling walls, creating an orchestra of explosions, an enclosed artillery range. The space is warm blooded. The dance floor heaves with caroming bodies, gyrating, shaking carcasses that eventually blend to a single undifferentiated mass of sweating and throbbing flesh.

The people are a mixture of locals and tourists. I see familiar faces. A female photographer who has just returned from tree planting in the highlands. A young woman from California whose hair is braided and who walks around town barefoot and swims every morning at Playa de Oro. A Dutch woman conducting ethnographic research among Moreno's women for her doctorate. An older woman from Australia who has relocated to San Cristóbal and has fallen for another tour guide, a bronzed surfer god, who now sits shirtless on one of the club's couches and lets his abdomen be searched by her white hands. I remember seeing him and his brethren, a fraternity of surfers, rolling and rocking, sitting on their boards, just offshore from Playa Lobería, a few kilometres west of Moreno and the airport. There, the beach bends into a welcoming smile of soft coral sand and shrubbery, guarded on each flank by palisades of jagged, night-black, basalt rock that coils around the cove like an unkempt goatee. In the rock's crevices and nooks, lashed by foaming waves, crawl hermit crabs, and one suddenly gets sucked into the pummelling swells and must dodge a sea turtle, which darts magnificently through the cloudy waters towards that ten-legged, hibiscus-red crustacean. Snorkelling among them, I lose sight of the eternal battle. My goggles become fogged, the waters murky from the previous night's storm. I stand on the muddy seabed, my head just above water, the salt stinging my eyes, its bitterness falling across my tongue, and I gaze out towards the surfers waiting just beyond the reef for their beloved wave, bobbing beneath the afternoon sun, which burns the earth and sea in waves of shimmering, bending light. Then, a plane descends across the blue backdrop, scaring and scattering dozens of finches and warblers, boobies and frigates from nearby colonies, a plane delivering hundreds of tourists to the protected and endangered islands, filling the multiplying hotels and restaurants, souvenir and diving shops, ballooning Moreno's gut further inland, pulling its streets further into the dense, thicketed interior. Just as the plane lands, a wave rises from the sea, amping metres high, and the surfers paddle towards its cap, jump to their feet, balancing on their pieces of polyurethane, and descend its lip, gliding through the crest, under the curling waters, through the wet tunnel, until the wave breaks, and a few are sucked underneath, their boards flying through the bright sky until the tethered rope pulls them back to the sea. Before long, they all emerge from the waves laughing and celebrating, slapping the water in fits of reverie, screaming one-worded exclamations, and quickly they paddle back to their spot and wait. The birds return to their nesting places; a sea turtle swims by sullenly. And in the distance, tour boats congregate in the afternoon heat.

The club dances. Philip and Marco flock to the pool table and greet everyone. I stand at the bar and down a tequila shot with Dylan before handing him a cigarette, which he takes. I smoke and watch the crowd. They talk folderal. They talk pabulum. They talk experience, of things done, of things still to do. Their faces become indistinguishable to me, again metamorphosing into one blurred chimera, a gargantuan gargoyle, getting fatter on each word, on each tidbit of want and desire, feasting on their dreams and needs. They are the rootless grandchildren of Kerouac, the restless bastard offspring of Burroughs and Ginsberg, the affluent wanderers, searching for *it*, digging the scenery, scouring the earth for the beat, the word, an undiluted, unpretentious string of pure, unsullied, unsoiled images, desperate to feel something, enduring hunger, desperation, longing, melancholy, lust, experiencing every notch on the great spectrum of human emotion, desiring to become whole and complete under the fog, the druggy debauchery of unfucked bohemia. They bore me.

The club steams. The alcohol has touched me, as it has Dylan, who leans on the bar beside me. He barely supports himself, clinging to the rail, his eyes blurry, unfocused globs of wrath. He stares out to the madness, disposed to violence, determined to seek vengeance for some imagined slight, some affront to his mettle. Why Dylan? I order a beer. Everything flows. Everything drifts in a series of images, an unfocused mélange of portraits, photocopies from my past, photographs from my present. They blur in a dizzying soup of meaning. A young woman in an orange dress glides across the room, in between humping bodies and clouds of smoke, before landing on the dance floor. Men stop to stare. I recognize her from the ceremony. She has just won the island's beauty pageant. She is beautiful, undoubtedly, but I put that thought away deep inside, locked and bolted. She moves on the dance floor. She is pliant. She adapts to the music, each tempo shift, each rhythm change. She is agile and supple and nimble. Her hips undulate. Her body is magnetic and pulls men towards her. And she does not spurn their advances. She welcomes every one, bouncing from each grasp, jouncing from hand to hand, pivoting to a new set of lustful eyes, until she chooses her suitor and sashays into him, hands draped across his shoulders, his fingers exploring her lower back, and then he twirls her and pulls her close, his hand over her midsection, his lips above her neck, her body rippling, bending into him.

An urge seizes me. I wish to approach her there on the dance floor and kindly inform her that she need not perform for these men. She is not their plaything. I would lead her by the hand to a secluded beach, away from Philip, Marco, and Dylan, where she would tell me why she does the things she does, and I would listen and nod and say kind, sympathetic words, and she would cry and thank me, thank me for caring, for understanding, for treating her as a person with thoughts, fancies, dreams, and wishes. It would be like when I was a child on the school bus watching the girl with the pink cast walk towards her bungalow under snow-dusted pines, through the slush, over her icy porch, and finally to her wooden door. And as the bus pulled away, I would always think that it was I, and I alone, who could see her for who she truly was, special and lovely, pretty and unique. And as she fell from sight, I would dream of taking her away, rescuing her from the tyrannical eyes of fellow boys, who only want one thing, to own, to possess, to dominate, and I would never see her like that, never ever treat her like that. I would hold her in the palm of my hand and protect her from the night.

Miss Moreno kisses him on the dance floor. Dylan grabs another beer and lurches towards the mayhem. Philip has his hands around Rebecca, another volunteer; Marco whispers something in the ear of a local girl. I watch Dylan drunkenly stumble from group to group, widely swinging his arms around strangers, interrupting conversations, stalking uninterested girls. I smile and feel the agitation stir within me. Dylan is a bedraggled spectre, a mere mirage of a human being, yet he plays the card of exception, of enlightened man. Philip is a pig, a lascivious lout, but he has the decency to drink his slop and munch on his mire. He does not sweeten his shit. Dylan is the pig who thought he could fly, which makes his fall, his caving to gravity, his capitulation to the natural order that much more riveting and spectacular. I watch him leech onto other groups and receive indulging salutations. I watch him slouch across the room, amid the rotating lights and dancing bodies, a crippled and defective lad, licking his wounds. I see him hobble towards Philip, who wraps his arm around Dylan and pats his chest. Images of Amy splash across my mind. Amy meeting me the day I arrived in San Cristóbal. Amy introducing me to my host. Amy informing me about the school and our role in it. Amy assuaging all my worries. Amy full of infinite smiles and boundless energy inviting me to meet the other volunteers. Then later the whispers come, rumours about Amy, swirling innuendos about her and Carlos, daring us to believe that she could— could she be there in his apartment, lounging on his bed, Dylan? I'm asking you, Dylan. I'm asking you, Dylan, whether you can see her with him, she on his bed, undressed and willing. She wanting to, Dylan. That's what hurts the most, isn't it? That she chooses him. That he does something for her that you could never do.

Dylan's voice rises among the noise. He is getting excited. He is getting closer. And as I study him that much more closely, under my hazed and intoxicated trance, which has somehow sharpened and strengthened my senses, slowing every movement to a crawl, stifling every flicker until it stretches out for seconds and minutes, he appears so insignificant and infantile, so unworthy of comment, so pedestrian, so fucking banal, that I almost feel sorry for him, as you would for an insect mindlessly scurrying about in infinite circles, round and round without intelligence or sense of purpose or any inner knowledge. But I do not. Because I ally with Amy, Dylan, with my girl in her pink cast, because your alleged heartbreak, Dylan, licenses atrocity, sanctions violence. For hundreds of thousands of years, from Australopithecus to *Homo sapiens*, expectation has eviscerated Amy and her ilk, punished, often brutally, just for saying hello. Can you imagine that, Dylan? The weight of the fucking world dropped on you for saying hello, for smiling, for asking, "How are you?" Fuck you, Dylan. I have nothing but contempt for you, nothing but scorn for your limp heartache, your wilted despair. Fuck you, Dylan. You don't get to burden Amy with your assumptions, your hidden desires of South American flings, exotic romances; you don't get to include her in your own *Bildungsroman* as some static character who was just a great fuck you had on your trip, a scrumptious story you'll tell all your mates back in London; you don't get to call her a coquette, some trollop who tempted you with silky words, a harlot from whom you expected heaven, cool conjugal rights, unlimited affection, someone who would smother you in attention and adoration. Fuck you, Dylan.

And then the inevitable happens. Dylan pisses on the wrong hydrant. He is face to face with a local as they bark at each other, saliva spraying, more forming, foaming at the corner of their lips, eyes inebriated and bellicose, two mammals manoeuvring, sparring for territory, for supremacy, for mating rights, for their futures. Oh, Dylan. I sip from my beer and light another cigarette. They growl inexact threats in a dozen words or less, mostly articulating themselves through body language, puffed-up chests, flexed muscles, or readied poses. Dylan points his finger at the other's gnarled face, and he bats it away as if it were a moth, some innocent, innocuous pest, drab and dull, irrelevant and impotent. Oh, Dylan, you silly boy. Soon the rest of the revellers notice the rising tension, and begin to mingle and loiter around the two, shouting their own encouragements, negotiating bets, discussing odds. Philip turns from his girl and sees his comrade in peril and rushes over, interjecting himself between the bucking animals, which only enrages Dylan further. With Philip's arms wrapped around him, Dylan lunges for the local, fingers bent, nails unfiled and raw, teeth snarled, and is held by Philip, who laughs and cautions his mate not to do anything stupid. Philip pulls Dylan away, pulls him by his chest, drags Dylan out, who still shouts and screams and yelps at his antagonist, the local who just stands where he was and waves, waves goodbye at Dylan, the tadpole, the puppy, the suckling, the boy who is now hauled out of the club like junk, litter, rubbish, out through the pack of spectators, the rollicking bodies and filthy couches, past the pool table and bar, past the young people in the midst of an experience, all the frivolity and fun of a Saturday night on the Galápagos, and finally past me, while I grin and silently thank Dylan for the entertainment.

Behind the bar stretches a mirror, and in it I see myself surrounded by bodies in motion, and a strange sensation descends of being swallowed. I feel trapped in the belly of a humpback whale with its innards a great ceiling of eyes peering down on me, a myriad of colours, iridescent irises that stare in unflinching rigidity, just gawking and glaring at me in unending silence, no words, no whispers, just eyes forever. The terror envelops me. I run but am met by white orbs everywhere. The girl with the pink cast appears and approaches in swift steps. In the stomach full of eyes, I drop to my knees, and she stands over me, her brown hair covering her face, and with her unbroken arm, digs her thumb into my eye socket, thrusts it deeper and deeper until my eye loosens and pops, until she has hollowed it out. I kneel still. And after she excavates the second one, she takes both and adds them to the wall, and there they stay stuck, watching me walk in circles, blood dripping down my cheek, walking in circles with a smile on my face, until I straighten my course, feeling along the eyes, and walk out of the stomach, out of the mouth, into bright sunlight, azure skies, which I can no longer see.

In my blackness, everything calms and freezes. In each careful step from the discotheque, my mind softens and slows; each image recedes further from view, the voices stop, and a wonderful quiet takes hold. While I walk, my mind and body become one, with each supporting the other towards the simple goal of movement. And I remember the afternoon I arrive in El Progreso, a farming community in San Cristóbal's highlands. The town, nothing more than a few shacks and beaten buildings selling life's basics, was founded in the mid-nineteenth century by Manuel Cobos and José Monroy, two entrepreneurs who harvested moss for dye, made leather from wild cattle, and produced fish and tortoise oils. In 1880, San Cristóbal was chosen as the site of a penal colony that would host convicts from the mainland, and local workmen built it not far from El Progreso, among the verdant forests that have lain dominant over the old sugar plantations, restoring natural law, the ancient estates that Cobos had built to exploit the free labour at his disposal. And exploit it he did. He beat the inmates down, whipped and degraded them beneath the equatorial sun, the severe sky, but one afternoon the prisoners decided that they had endured enough and murdered Cobos in his own prison, among his own sugarcane, struck him down beneath his own palm trees. They fled among the *Scalesia* thickets, the humid and lush woodlands, and scattered like an invasive species, their seeds digging into the soft soil, hiding there in craggy caves, the rock roofs blackened from the smoke of their lonely fires. They disappeared into the scenery.

I wanted to walk further into the island's interior, to El Junco lagoon, and forgo the thirty-dollar taxi ride, but the heat has proven too stifling, too insufferable. Clouds trot in and form cumulus bunches over the tropical greenery. Rain seems imminent. Humidity hangs heavy. I buy a Gatorade and consume its electrolytes beneath a melancholy street lamp and hanging telephone wires. The street is vacant. Herman Melville visited the islands in 1841 and wrote of their forsaken quality: the impenetrable interiors, the dehydrated land, the haggard mist. He saw them as specks of forgotten rock, the ideal environs for outsiders, men foreign to civilized code, the whalers, the buccaneers, the adventurers, men who relished the solitude, who could endure and survive. He envisioned a race of hermits, men who had either been abandoned or forgotten on these rocky outcrops, forced to survive in a shanty, feeding on birds and reptiles, waiting for a passing ship, praying for rescue. Of course, some men developed a taste for the vanquished life, the exquisite loneliness, the ideal isolation, and dreamt not of saving but of endless abandonment, evolving into a sort of turtle, a tortoise man with an unbreakable shell, unimaginable longevity, and unthinkable resiliency.

Just a dozen kilometres or so away, past El Junco lagoon, one of the island's few fresh water sources, which sits in a bed of clouds atop a dead volcano, just past a lonesome stretch of straight asphalt that runs beneath a line of green hills, stands the island's giant tortoise sanctuary. *Galápago* is the old Spanish word for "saddle," for when Tomás de Berlanga arrived in 1535 with his Spanish retinue, the carapaces of the giant reptiles appeared to them as such. The giant tortoise is the archetypal survivor, an emblem of endurance, a solitary roamer. It has adapted remarkably to this inhospitable terrain, evolving in such an ingenious manner that it can subsist without food or water for up to a year. Yet, despite their adaptability, despite eons of trial and error, a millennium of malleability, which made them ideal for their environment, a paradigm of perfection, a miracle of suitability, it was their very uniqueness, a cruel paradox, that guaranteed their slow decline. Once the whalers and fur sealers discovered that they could stock live tortoises in their ship's hull for months, feasting on fresh, succulent tortoise meat at their leisure without having to support the creatures, the exploitation of the giants began in earnest. They were hunted in their homes and massacred in huge numbers, their oils processed and shipped to the mainland to light Quito street lamps. Rats and pigs, introduced by early colonialists, devoured tortoise eggs or their little hatchlings; other mammals competed with them for scarce resources. Over the second half of the nineteenth century and into the twentieth, close to 200,000 tortoises were slaughtered, and several varieties went extinct.

I find a deserted bench and sit. A solitary palm tree sways in the light breeze, its branches stiff and resolute. The breeze is a lovely reprieve, as sweat has broken over my rumpled and tired face. A Doritos bag flutters down the road. The deep jungle behind me teems with unseen wildlife. But I do not hear it; in fact, I hear nothing save the leaves. Silence is endemic here. Except at times, perhaps inspired by a heat-induced daze or the unmarked graves of old tortoises dotting the landscape, I think I see a magnificent tortoise bumbling down the lane, sun glistening from its shell, crawling with its neck stretched, its eyes vigilant, its beak clamping for nourishment. Melville speaks of a superstition pervasive among the seafarers of his time that wicked captains and unruly officers were punished upon their deaths with a grotesque transformation, their skeletons and skin mutating into scales and scutes, their backs becoming hardened shells, their jaws protruding into beaks, and their nails curving into claws. Resurrected as tortoises, they are cursed to dwell forever on these hot and arid rocks, unable to swim, to flee across the currents, to join their brothers on the mainland.

I begin my return to Moreno. The road bends through the rolling hills and farms, whose tilled land beats back the encroaching vines and weeds in the everlasting battle. The fences are flimsy, worn things, better suited to rustic photographs than as protection against the island's crawlers. With each step, as I ascend and descend gentle knolls, I feel electricity within, a subtle joy building and building, pumping from my heart, permeating through my veins and arteries. Green has kissed the landscape, painting the vegetation, the rebellious brush, in shades of emerald, strokes of olive pigments, splashes of lime dye. A virility accentuates the scene, a fertility writ large. The clouds gently drop through and along deciduous branches and cover the saplings and their jade leaves in cool mist. The vista exhales. Every few minutes, the sun breaks through the cloud, and its slicing rays illuminate a section of wetted grass in sparkling effulgence.

I press play on my MP3 player, and the shimmering and organic beats swell in my ears, enlivening my step, animating my movement, melting my iced consciousness. Everything is alive. Everything is vital. The road runs straight into a moss-coloured mound, an uppity hill dreaming of becoming a mountain, before shooting left and spiralling down to a plateau. The sprigs clutch at me as I pass. They reach out over the road from the impassable morass beyond the roadside, the tangled knots of wiry ferns and shrubs, a carcinogenic vegetation. But the feeling is not deterministic of all life eventually, inevitably fading to black. Nor is it one of pure cruelty, of nature devouring all anemic life, watching it atrophy in a chorus of screams and cries. Melville was wrong. What is remarkable about the island is neither its desolation nor its loneliness; it is its vigour, its dynamism, its life. The island vibrates with creativity and quivers with transcendence; it speaks of an unquenchable desire to survive, to reproduce, to prolong each breath in the face of overwhelming malice. It is an island for the tortoise, for a soul who needs no validation from others, no claps or words of approval, no verification, no little nudges of encouragement, no rain-swept kisses, no Saturday night forays, no clever remarks, no corroboration, no co-optation, no acceptance, no conformity, no Dylan, no Philip, no Marco, no Amy. To be a beast today is to exist in solitude. Everything is permitted except loneliness.

The road begins to flatten, and I see the glimmering Pacific waters in the distance. A battered pickup slows down and offers me a lift. I politely decline. I pass a farmhouse with two children playing in the yard. They wave and scream for my attention, but I keep my eyes focused ahead, under the lonely spell, the reclusive vibe, and walk on towards Moreno, the new noise, the baby homes, the struggle against the void, and the world again shivers for me as voices cluck and crack under crumbling corrugated roofs and creaking banisters, and the world begins to darken, the clouds and sun dissipate, and stars pierce the dark fabric above, which keeps the awful nothingness beyond at bay.

I am sitting on a bench on the pier under a halcyon street lamp between Dylan and Philip with a crate of twenty-four beers at my feet. Philip has procured the *cerveza* from one of his contacts in the town, and when, not an hour ago, at three-something in the morning, we arrive along the empty street at a dark building and knock, the gentleman who answers, with the crate of beer in his hands, does not seem upset to be disturbed at such an inconvenient hour. No. The entire episode seems rather ordinary for him. And now we sip warm beer and watch the few boats see-saw in the calm waters. The late night is still black, but in the distance, towards the horizon, a glow softly emanates. The birds chirp in optimism. Dawn has begun.

Dylan and Philip have retrieved their bags, and two hardy backpacks sit obediently next to the bench. They will take a boat to Puerto Ayora, on Isla Santa Cruz, meet Philip's girlfriend before returning to the mainland, Quito, and then fly to Santiago, then to Easter Island, New Zealand, Australia, Indonesia, Thailand, and so on. Dylan's mood has improved, and he slouches in a somnolent stupor, arms crossed, and coolly gazes at nothing in particular. Philip's exuberance has not lessened, and he continues to clamour about this and that as curls of his auburn hair fall over his hazel eyes, which scan the scene in a slapdash manner.

This stretch between late night and when morning breaks, an hour before the sun rises, before the consequences of the night become apparent, before the headaches, the nausea, the regrets, is my favourite. It is the dissolution of drunkenness, when the fluidity of intoxication, the river of feelings, images, and thoughts abates. Everything slows. It is a time of reflection. The fog slowly lifts. But the cruel clarity of sobriety has not yet come. It is the in-between zone. There is still time.

Philip turns to me and says, "Rebecca told me she couldn't do that to Sara, couldn't betray her trust. What trust? They knew each other for five minutes." Philip slaps my shoulder and says, "Well, it's all part of the experience." He tilts his head suddenly as if struck by an idea, a question, that has just occurred to him. "And you," he says, "you must have done alright throughout your travels, must have had your fair share of girls." I sip my beer; it tastes of swill. I do not answer and feel his hand leave my shoulder.

I remember two weeks ago after conducting an English class for adults with Amy, after working through the difference between *going to* and *will*, after writing sentences of future plans, tomorrow or in five years, debating the certainty of action, the degree of probability, I am sitting outside on the street with Marco, sharing a cigarette in the insufferable heat. The evening is busy, people hurrying about, and Marco asks me if I am in a relationship. "Not anymore," I say. He smiles, as if predicting the answer, and in his tactless, charming way, wants to know why. He wants to know what happened. "It didn't work out," I manage. "It never does," he replies. "No, I suppose not," I say, turning to see Amy exiting the building. She smiles and says, "Everyone has left, could you lock up, Jesse?" I nod as she bounds past us. "Good night, gentlemen," she says. We wave and watch her fade into the crowd, confidently moving through the maze of people, knowing which route she wants to take, knowing exactly where she wants to go.

The sun has crept over the darkness. The dawn glows with a soft phosphorescence. Every inch of light has sewn itself into a gleaming mosaic of transparency. The morning has been revealed. My eyes are heavy with sleep denied. A few people now mingle at the pier, readying the boats, cleaning the docks. Philip nudges Dylan, who has fallen asleep, and motions to the sea. Philip finishes his beer and places the empty bottle back in the crate. Dylan draws his shades over his bleary eyes and rises to his feet. We walk towards the dock, where Philip asks the attendant a few questions. The figure nods and points to a small boat sitting gingerly in the water. The boys toss their bags in and climb down a mossy set of stairs and onto the boat. They balance on the bow, adjusting to the wobbly structure, and move to the stern. Beyond the last bench, in an open, oval space in the boat's back, Dylan descends and curls into a ball. Philip relaxes on the bench, hovering over Dylan, and places a hand on his shoulder. It rests there a moment, maybe two, before Philip takes it away and waves to me. I salute in return and watch the boat push out of port, pick up speed, and pound over the open sea, water spraying and spitting from the punishing motor, before disappearing into the sky.

I turn back towards Moreno and its haphazard buildings, a metallic stain on the greenery, and saunter over to Darwin Street. The restaurants are closed; the patio chairs are neatly stacked. Everything is tidy. The shops, too, are locked. Hanging from the windows are T-shirts adorned with Darwin's older face and his greying beard and images of the evolutionary journey from ape to man. A tourist agency advertises diving excursions. Snorkelling trips are half price. Along the rocks, somewhere close to here, I know without seeing it and without hearing it, a crab is being devoured.

I remember a few years ago sitting with a friend in a university dormitory drinking rum and listening to music. I try not to like anything, I say to him; it's a horrible dependency, it makes you vulnerable, open to attack, you have to defend things, fight for things, and everything can be so easily taken, destroyed, ripped, ravaged. And it's true, I still believe, opening the door to my room, the heat as omnipresent as ever, gathering up my few belongings and stuffing them in my bag. Yet it is also true, I think, mentally plotting the last few stops on my trip, Cuenca, Quito, Popayán, Bogotá, Cartagena, that somewhere in this young town, right now, Amy wakes in a warm bed full of sunlight, smiles at Carlos, and together they plan their day.

4
Aftermath

2010

During my time in Peru, Ecuador, and Colombia, Lovely and I speak less and less. I try to maintain frequent contact, a phone call from Cuzco, a Facebook message from the Galápagos, but the distance has become concrete, beyond argument. But as she drifts further from me, I dream more about our reunification. I picture surprising her at her convocation, like some hero returning from war, and I imagine her face curling into happiness, a joyful realization that we may continue from where we left off. I imagine her resuming her life with me. I imagine our conversations, the wonderful silences, the long walks through Toronto's various personalities, our moods subtly lifting with each kilometre ambled. I see her there waiting for me. I see her, the poem, the picture. I see her.

Two weeks before my return, in April 2010, I am walking across Plaza Mayor in the beautiful Colombian town of Villa de Leyva. Sleeping deep inside the Andes, this colonial jewel of adobe and cobblestone splendour seduces visitors with its timelessness. The big stones comprising many of the town's streets mean that vehicles are a rarity, and that residents and visitors alike must watch their step, taking the requisite time to get from point A to point B. Waiters are busy setting tables at the chic restaurants lining the plaza's perimeter; they add a plate, a napkin, cutlery, followed by a candle, the final touch. Many of the old white colonial homes have been transformed into boutique hotels, which appear this April Friday afternoon to be bursting with guests from Bogotá, who have escaped the traffic fumes of the capital for a few tranquil days in the mountains. A line of schoolgirls in blue dresses passes in front me, led by a teacher taking them to their school hidden down some side street. The children remind me that this town is still a home for some, still functions, still breathes.

I find an internet café along the plaza and log in to my Facebook account. I ignore the news of my feed and the postings of my friends and look to see if Lovely is online. I click on her name, the conversation box opens, and I type "hey." Travellers sit at the computers around me, undoubtedly updating friends and relatives on their travels and adventures, and I wonder whether they have more grand tales to tell than I do. Lovely responds with a "hey" of her own. I ask her what she has been up to, and she tells me about how busy she is with school and her work placement as well as the headaches concerning her loan repayments. Her rent has increased, and she is worried about making it this month. I tell her I will be home in two weeks, and she says, "Whoa, that's neat." She is silent. She does not say anything else. I can hear the typing of the travellers around me. The room is suddenly thick and heavy. There is pressure. There is tension. I ask her what I always knew I would: "Say, would you like to go out for dinner when I get back?" Her response is swift: "No, thank you." And then she is gone.

Outside, clouds have gathered over the plaza. Night approaches and with it will come rain. A few people eat at the restaurants but do not seem concerned about the weather. A waiter lights the candle at each table. I sit on the steps of a church and light a cigarette. As the last light becomes erased by the fat clouds and the Andes in the distance, a few lanterns come to life casting the white buildings in a sultry orange. A feeling of emptiness suddenly replaces the once vibrant plaza. Few people are about. Everything is quiet except for the voices of the restaurant patrons, whose words arrive to me only as sound.

A woman nestles up to me and lights a cigarette of her own. She speaks, but her Spanish is incomprehensible to me. All I know is that she, too, is a visitor here, maybe from Colombia, maybe from another Spanish-speaking country. She is a fellow traveller. I have no desire to speak to her. I smile. I try to answer her questions. She wants to impart some advice, some nugget of wisdom she feels I could profit from. Something that travellers tell themselves. Something vital and important about how we see the world. But I am in no mood to humour her. She senses that. She senses I am not in social space and have no interest in her musings, in her philosophy. And when she leaves me, I watch her disappear down a side street, and the last trace of her existence I encounter is her cigarette smoke floating up towards the church's steeple illuminated by lantern light.

I light another cigarette and the nicotine calms me. The first drops of rain fall. I will go eat at one of those restaurants and return to my hostel bed. Tomorrow, I will travel to San Gil and make my way north to the coastal cities of Santa Marta and Cartagena. For once in my life, the journey does not hold much appeal. For once in my life, I want to be home.

Toronto is full of puddles the May day I see Lovely. It is cold; it is rainy. Before I visit her, before I make that mythical trek back to the Junction, I stroll the downtown core, see a movie, sip a pint of Stella, and wonder at how, even after eleven months, things haven't really changed. I stroll the travel section at Chapters, eat a Subway sandwich, and smoke a cigarette, all of which I did before. The familiar restlessness returns. On the bus towards her place, though, I pass all the familiar landmarks, all the sidewalks and parks infused with such memory and significance that I have trouble settling my stomach, the excitement building to intolerable levels, for I had envisioned this moment even before I left: the triumphant return. And standing on her stairs, I press the doorbell and peer into the hallway, waiting to see her, and that sly grin, come bouncing down the stairs, unlocking the door, and letting me in.

We go out for drinks at a local pub, with Samantha, and talk about my trip, the highs and lows. We talk about Lovely finishing her master's degree, her search for employment, her fight to make rent. Genevieve has gone to South Korea to teach English and has left Lovely with her chubby cat, whom Lovely despises but must clean and feed, an irony that I can't help but find delicious. The conversations are safe and pleasant affairs, very surface and skin, and I don't fail to notice Lovely skirt certain issues, avoiding segues I wish to troll, dodging topics she knows will come. When Samantha leaves and we are left alone in the bar's music and merriment, we discuss trite themes and drift in and out of silence. And I know that an unmistakable gulf has arisen between us, a great lack, and that underneath her passive front, there beats a past, a hurt, longing to speak, to scream, to deafen the surroundings with cries of recrimination. But I refuse to see it.

Back in her kitchen, we sit at the flimsy table and drink rum and diet Pepsi; the sink is full of dishes; the washer, empty; the fridge, full of perogies and pasta. The walls are familiar with its calendar and mementos. I am full of memories. And when I ask her if we could talk about us for a moment, my desire for her past again muffles her hesitation, masks her reluctance because I know this is inevitable, this is history coming to its end, this is prophecy. I wax eloquently about her. I gush that there hasn't been a day, nay an hour, since I left when I haven't thought about or dreamed about our reunification or desired the opportunity to restart what was killed too early. She stays quiet, looking at her nails, and seems uninterested, only a faint glint in her eyes. But when I say that all night, I have wished to kiss her, Lovely's eyes flash with rage, and she no longer aims to be polite, to be a good host, no, that force she had buried chooses to stay dormant no longer. She glares at me, on the cusp of tears, and tells me that it is amazing that I can come back after all these months, after leaving, and assume we'll just make out, we'll just go to bed. She wonders at my sense of entitlement, my assumptions, my arrogance. She is shaking, her voice cracking. She says she does not want this, does not want us, does not want to rekindle what is long dead. She says I left and don't get to come back. She doesn't want me. And then silence. She regains her form and dumps the contents of her glass in the sink. After she goes to bed, I have a cigarette on her balcony, the maple as beautiful as it always was, and think about going away. In the distance, condominiums are raised, and little convenience shops are boarded up. I drain the remaining rum, shut the lights, and fall asleep on the couch, just by the staircase, just below her room.

Over the summer, we stay in a nebulous fog, a barbed-wire border zone between two countries. My nights are full of rum, cigarettes, and writing. We talk. We talk. We talk too much. But not about us. About breakfast and globalization, about jobs and the weather. Yet an intimacy still persists despite the history, the sorrow, the betrayal. And I throw away everything else, all others, all other outlets, all possible alternatives, and rest my eyes on her, on my computer screen, on that seed that was planted almost two years earlier. But nothing ever grows. In the darker recesses of me, full of faint screams of harder truths, I ignore the whispers that say I prefer the seed, the beginning, first dates, and new countries. I can love only the dawn.

In the fall, she starts a new job and goes away. Email messages go answered, as do my Skype calls. I spy on her through Facebook and uncover the germs of a new relationship, a fresh someone in her life. I dissect and analyze the flirtatious lines, the clever comebacks, the status and photo likes, the planned events, the fusion of two online entities. And from within comes a jealousy unbeknownst to me, and it floods my arteries and veins, fills my cells and organs, covers my skin and hair. I phone Lovely, and after we talk about her job, and present other pleasantries, she confirms her new romance, and I control the tempo and texture of my voice and stay calm. When the phone clicks silent, the levee breaks. And I watch her life unfold through the bright lights of social media.

I become obsessed with her, the past, our story, and wish to put my thoughts to paper. I write her a letter to lay bare the truth. I wish to apologize. I wish to set the record straight, to have a firm account of the events for future historians. I apologize for leaving in the midst of her troubles. I apologize for assuming we would reunite upon my return. I apologize for not recognizing that life reveals itself in the minutiae of the everyday. I apologize for not understanding that epiphany knows no borders, that people can travel great distances within their own home, city, and country. And I apologize for refusing to see that somewhere along the line, she stood on her balcony in the snow and decided to shut the door. She has excitement, purpose in her life, and I do not. It's how it was for me then. Only now, it's reversed. Only now, it's my turn.

I give the letter to Samantha, and she says she will pass it on. Over the next months, I see Lovely everywhere, at shows, on the streets, and in my dreams. I want to approach her and say, *Don't be afraid, I don't want to talk about the past, I just want to say hello, I just want to know how you've been.* But it is never her. And then I am furious with her for moving on. Every spat of anger is followed by a wave of guilt. I oscillate between bouts of redemption and regression. I swing between narratives of reunification and rupture. I try to live in the moment, but the past always sneaks in, intrudes uninvited, and blankets me with warm memories.

And over time, Lovely has become less a person and more a picture that I hang among the others, my photos of Bruges, of Berlin, of Barcelona. She too is a place I once visited. I no longer know her. I see only what she was, only those things she said before, those things she believed, those things she did. I don't see what she does every day; I don't see the work; I don't see the effort; I don't see the growth. And it is fine because just as people collect experiences, little moments of learning, I collect countries. On my deathbed, I will have my photo albums out and say to the walls, *Look, this is me at Uyuni, look at me on the Galápagos, look at me under the granite spirals of Torres del Paine.* I have submitted a life. I did this. I did this. Some people stay; I decide to go. I leave. I exit. I escape. After Lovely, I travel to stay innocent. I am unaccountable. I am not guilty anymore. I haven't been guilty of anything in years. I stay safe in other people's histories, other people's countries, other people's stories, other people's lives. Every morning I wake up in the nothingness of the everyday, and I dream of Africa, America, Australia, and Asia. I dream of Tanzania and California, of Fiji and Kuala Lumpur ... I dream of Cairo and Calcutta, Rio de Janeiro and Rabat, San Francisco and Seoul ... of Tehran and Tunis ... far away ... Mozambique, Madagascar, Mauritania ... in my dreams, I am so far away.

Part II

The Balkans
2016

Introduction

On the night of Friday, November 15, 2015, I am sitting in a Korean restaurant in Barrie, Ontario, enjoying kimchee and bibimbap. Around me are Genevieve and her husband as well as his brother and wife. Genevieve asks me about my new job working for my mother's publishing house as its copy editor.

"It's good," I tell her. "I like working with language and sentences. I like having words as my tools."

I grab a piece of kimchee with my chopsticks.

"Plus, I can work from wherever I want."

She takes a sip of her ginger tea.

"Anywhere else than Bradford," she says smiling, referring to the fact that I have been living with my parents for the last year and a half. It's a source of shame for me. Thirty-one and still living in my childhood home. But that will change soon. It must.

"Indeed. I am saving up some money and then hitting the road early next year."

"Another trip? How unlike you."

I laugh.

"I know. So out of character."

The kimchee has some kick to it, and I take a sip of water.

I ask Genevieve about Lovely.

"She's good. Working lots."

"Seeing anyone?"

"I don't think so."

I excuse myself and go to the washroom. The kimchee has elevated my body temperature, and I sense the first drops of sweat amassing on my forehead. I sweat easily. A shortcoming. A flaw. I turn on the tap and let my hands receive the cold water. I cup a little in my hands and splash it across my face. The effect is instantaneous, as the water enlivens me. In the mirror, I see myself. On the cusp. On the edge. I am going, going, going.

"Where are you off to this time?" Genevieve's husband asks me upon my return to the table.

"The Balkans."

Silence.

"You know, the countries of the former Yugoslavia. Eastern Europe, generally."

"Isn't it dangerous?" The brother wants to know.

"Not particularly," I say. "No more dangerous than anywhere else."

"Why the Balkans?" Genevieve asks.

Yes, why the Balkans? I want to say, *Why not the Balkans?* and fall into my standard monologue that each and every country deserves exploration. Every single country deserves to have its history known, its culture appreciated, and its sights seen. And although I subscribe to such a sentiment, the Balkan region has always captured my interest. In high school, I wrote a report about the rise and fall of Yugoslavia, and the sources I consulted were full of names and places I had never known existed in Europe. Names like Tito. Places like Zagreb. I had trouble making sense out of the events. I could draw no neat line from point A to point B. The history confused me, and when I delivered my findings to the class, I even had difficulty understanding the words and sequences falling from my mouth. It wasn't as if this history was so different from the history of other places; it was just that I had no familiarity with it. These events had been hidden from me, locked away in some closet. It was as if I had discovered a trunk full of books in the attic about countries I had never heard of and was just told to summarize its history in a ten-minute presentation. The task overwhelmed me. But it also sowed the seed of curiosity, which blossomed over the years, especially as more and more news stories portrayed the region as a place of never-ending violence.

My audience is satisfied with my answer, and we go back to chatting about this and that. Work. Plans. Dreams and ambitions. The last great film we saw. They talk, too, of responsibilities. Mortgage payments. Taxes. Car insurance. Debt repayments. Baby things. Genevieve is asked whether they have decided on their child's name yet. "No," she says. "But there's still time." The baby is not due until the spring. The other couple is expecting too. Around the same time. They talk about how great it is that the cousins will be the same age, how they will grow up together. Instant friends and companions. Instant joy. Both sets of parents are excited but cautious. They fear the sleepless nights, the higher cost of living, all the things they will need to learn to look after a baby, a little human being. They exchange ideas and information. Where to find the best deals on strollers and clothing and car seats. Ideas about childcare and future schooling. Potential hiccups. Potential remedies. Together. They are entering this new chapter of their lives together.

I am uncomfortable. I have nothing to contribute. Theirs is a language I do not know. In my blue pants and black merino T-shirt, I again feel the first pricks of perspiration. Sweat prepares itself to march across my skin. The restaurant's lights seem brighter, like spotlights in fact, the kind of lights that flash across the night sky and across the ground whenever a prisoner escapes from prison. I feel cumbersome, awkward. I feel fat. My body seems to be growing right before my eyes. My pants can no longer contain my bulging legs; my belly pushes out against my shirt. Have I gained weight? I must have. Too much sitting. Too much editing. Not enough exercise. There's the door. Outside, it looks as if it could snow. Here comes a family—a young couple with a toddler in a stroller. We all watch them. The waiter shows them to a table and sets menus on it. The woman requests a high chair for their toddler, who looks at the surroundings with great wonder and curiosity. Everything must seem so new and fascinating. So great. How lucky the child must feel, deep down inside at least, just to be able to sit and stare. That's what I need too. New sceneries. New city streets. New languages. New histories. Free me from the world's weight, its expectations, its narratives. Let me run. Let me go.

"There's been an attack in Paris," Genevieve's husband suddenly says, looking at his phone.

I watch the toddler smack his tray and delight in the sound it makes. His mother playfully admonishes him to be quiet with an index finger to her lips. But he smacks it again and again. Always smiling. Big giggles.

"What happened?" Genevieve asks.

"Gunmen opened fire at a music concert. Dozens killed."

"How awful," Genevieve says.

The mother tells the toddler, "Shhh," but he's not having it. *Look where I am!* the toddler's actions scream. *Look how great this restaurant is. How can I be quiet in a place like this?* I am envious of that wonderment—that freedom to be.

"There's more shooting in the streets," her husband reads from his phone. "The whole city seems to be under attack."

The baby laughs.

"They are speculating on a possible Islamic terrorist link."

I feel his words pulling me back to the world. But I wish to resist a moment or two longer. I wish to avoid the inevitable conversations that will come. I wish to dodge the myopia that will afflict those who refuse to believe in history or context, who are too scared to trace the roots of violence. I am afraid people will wrap themselves in flags and beg their leaders to make the bad men go away by any means necessary.

The toddler has made a mess of the food. The tray is a puddle of liquids and solids. Food decorates the little cherub's face and fingers. And he could not be happier. The mother takes a napkin a gently wipes the toddler's mouth, who buzzes with joy.

I want nothing to do with Paris. I want nothing to do with the fallout. I don't want to go searching for snakes under logs or in long grass. I don't want the trouble. The inconvenience. The work. The soul searching. Put headphones over my ears and let the music come. Pack my bag and put me on a plane. Put me in front of a brilliant cityscape and hand me a camera. Let me appreciate the world behind the safety of my hotel's walls. Let my credit card and passport speak for me. Just let me go. Please, just let me go.

I set everything aside.

I focus only on the place.

The destination.

And what it evokes.

5
Doppelgängers

Sarajevo and Srebrenica
Bosnia and Herzegovina

May 2016

In the southern Bosnian city of Mostar, Stari Most, the arched stone bridge, has linked the opposing sides of the Neretva River for centuries. During Ottoman times, Bosnia was a frontier zone and a busy intersection for many worlds: Christian and Muslim, Austro-Hungarian and Turkish, West and East. And in its southern parts, between the dramatic mountains rising towards Sarajevo and the raspberry fields winding down to the Dalmatian coast, a spot where western Europe's steppes are within reach, where the Neretva flows a little wilder, its waters a rough turquoise hue, the Ottomans built a town and then completed a bridge in 1566. They called the town Mostar, after the *mostari*, the bridge keepers, and the settlement grew. It became a cosmopolitan cauldron: its mosques, churches, and synagogues sprung up on both sides of the river, spreading the messages of various prophets; its merchants filled the narrow laneways, bartering goods from distant lands; and its citizens were polyglots, speaking an array of languages as diverse as those of Babel's Tower. At the centre rose the bridge, an architectural wonder, a pearl. Standing twenty-four metres high and stretching thirty metres wide, Stari Most reached across the steep riverbanks as if extending a hand, connecting the city's various shards, linking each piece of a delicate, fragile mosaic. In the sixteenth century, the Ottoman traveller Evliya Çelebi said it was the tallest bridge he had ever seen, rising to the sky like a rainbow.

The keepers of the bridge developed a peculiar tradition. Every now and then, they would struggle atop the bridge's railing, stand on the limestone, stare across the city, and step off. Before long, the citizens cultivated a reputation for recklessness, and visiting dignitaries would sit in the bridge's castle and wait for the next mad Mostarian to jump, putting his fate in God's grace, purring little prayers as he fell through the air, landing in swirling, shallow pools of water, surrounded by jagged rocks, emerging with yelps of thanks, biceps flexed, fist raised, amid the claps of thanks of the spectators, who might have donated a few coins for his trouble. In the air for only three seconds, the man defined dexterity and finesse. After leaping, he flipped, locking his hands behind his knees, pressing his thighs against his chest, his toes pointing skywards, his arms taut, keeping his body tight and controlled. He rotated once, twice, three times, body tucked, eyes towards his toes, each millisecond the river inching closer and closer, he spinning, losing his sense of self, hurling to the earth, merely an object falling faster and faster, the landscape around him a dizzying blur. But before the final splash, he released his legs, unsnapped his body, and faced the water, stretching and straightening arms, his torso and thighs becoming a line, a knife that pierced the water, stabbing its surface, disappearing into the depths, producing the lightest of splashes. After he rose from the water, another diver dove, and then another, each one coming from a different corner of the city, each corridor represented. And the divers soon joined forces and formed an organization, a group dedicated to punishing fear, embracing passion, no matter the concomitant risks and dangers.

They named themselves Icari, after Icarus, son of Daedalus, the master craftsman who built a labyrinth under the court of tyrannical King Minos of Crete to hold his Minotaur, which needed the daily sustenance of a dozen Cretan boys and girls. To keep the layer secret,

Minos imprisoned both Daedalus and Icarus in his palace tower. In the dark room, Daedalus crafted two sets of feathered wings for himself and his son. Before they flew to freedom, Daedalus cautioned his precocious tyke not to ascend too high, as the sun would melt the wax that held the flimsy wings together. Icarus ignored his father's advice, feeling the wind on his body and through his hair, marvelling at the ground below, the patchwork of farms and forests, canyons and gorges, Crete a world onto its own, and he climbed and climbed until he could no longer hear his father's cries, until the earth was mere splotches of blue and green, until he felt the sun hot against his skin and saw with alarm the wax melting, saw himself falling and falling to the sea below.

The gods punished Icarus, so it goes, for hubris, for flying too high, for trying to touch the realm of the celestial. In a sense, then, the Icari jumpers defied God with every dive, with each leap towards his sky, before ultimately tumbling back to earth, surrendering to his laws, his order, but surviving. Unlike Icarus, they survived. They survived God's wrath. And an unlikely camaraderie grew there, under the bridge, along the Neretva, with each hairy head popping from the water, alive and rejuvenated. A brotherhood of survival emerged in the city at a crossroads, on a bridge that soon connected a predominantly Catholic side with a predominantly Muslim one.

On November 9, 1993, Bosnian Croat forces obliterated the bridge. Its centuries-old pieces sank to the bottom of the Neretva, severing the links between the city's Bosniak (Bosnian Muslim) eastern side and the Catholic Croat western one. The siege of Mostar was just one piece of the larger dissolution of Yugoslavia, the decade-long bloodbath that destroyed Josip Tito's vision of a unified and united federation. Before, Serbs lived among Croats; Croats mingled with Bosniaks; Bosniaks existed beside Serbs. But from the 1980s onwards, nationalism renewed or simply invented old hatreds. Parochialism replaced unity; harmony splintered. Since the early 1990s, Yugoslavia has birthed seven nations: Bosnia and Herzegovina, Croatia, Kosovo, Macedonia, Montenegro, Serbia, and Slovenia. Borders have reappeared, and some people find they no longer belong. Animosity remains; violence lurks beneath the self-serving discourse of corrupt and overpaid politicians. Peace is fragile and tentative.

Between 2001 and 2004, a team of European engineers and architects rebuilt the bridge as close as possible to its original shape. Hungarian divers combed the bottom of the Neretva searching for the original limestone pieces. Walking in the light May rain towards the refurbished bridge, I imagine those stones rising from the river's depths. I imagine the ropes and pulleys, the blueprints and sketches, the scaffolding and tools needed to restore Stari Most to a pearl. I see people from the western side, with its pointy minarets and buildings with old bullet holes, reach the apex and meet people from the eastern side, with its Croatian flags and churches and the crucifix that stands atop the nearby Huma Hill. I approach from the west, past the bookstore that shows footage of the bridge's bombing on repeat, past stone markers that advise one not to forget 1993. Turning right onto the bridge, dodging women carrying umbrellas, I sense commotion. Voices rise from the zenith; excitement is palpable. With dozens of tourists, I ascend steep Stari Most, stepping delicately over the slick wooden grooves towards the top. A man dressed in a parka and flip-flops parts the crowd from the east and strolls to the ledge. Camera flashes blink in the hanging cloud. All eyes follow him. From his parka pocket, he removes a cap and goggles, and adjusts each. He disrobes to his trunks, steps on the ledge, and sits. Cross-legged above the river, gazing at the distant hills hidden in gloom, he appears as chiselled and defiant as a gargoyle. Below, on the shoreline, onlookers have their cameras and cellphones aimed; atop, we all wait, quiet, hoping. He raises his hand and rubs his thumb and index finger together as a gust of wind ruffles the short hairs down his legs. But then he decides to step down. He grabs his clothing and vanishes into the crowd.

Disappointed onlookers disperse. Patrons return to their meals, shoppers to their browsing. I look at the river, its waters emerald, its currents mellow. Only he knows why he did not jump. Maybe he will return tomorrow when the winds blow less, when the sun shines a bit more. And if he does, people will watch, ready to celebrate Icarus resurrected from the waves, his wings intact and flapping, propelling himself up, rising above Stari Most, the spectators and city, above the minarets and steeples, above Sarajevo and the distant graves of Srebrenica, flying towards the sun in defiance.

1. Sarajevo

When I was growing up in the 1990s, Sarajevo was on the tip of everyone's tongue. I remember I liked the way it sounded: a wonderful blend of the familiar and different. Some letters followed English phonetics, whereas others formed unpredictable notes. Sarajevo. It rolled from the tongue in a pleasing way. Sarajevo. I enjoyed saying it. Sarajevo. In my twenties, I considered naming my daughter Sarajevo, if I were to have one. I imagined cradling her in my arms, running my fingers across her cheeks, and whispering, *My little Sarajevo, my rebellious little daughter.* I would welcome her home from school and listen as she recounted her stories of triumph, of besting some boy, outsmarting him or outrunning him. I would hear her defy some expectation, defeat some assumption, dismantle some discourse. She the proverbial underdog would prove everyone wrong. Whatever obstacle she faced, she would rise from the ash and transcend it. She would struggle and suffer, yes, but she would persevere like her namesake, the city with a thousand lives, a thousand accents, a thousand faces. Her name would guide her through anything. For me, Sarajevo was the epitome of endurance.

In my high school history class, my teacher said the First World War started on Sarajevo's streets when Archduke Franz Ferdinand, the heir to the Austro-Hungarian Empire, was assassinated by the Bosnian Serb Gavrilo Princip on June 28, 1914. The Austrians annexed Bosnia and Herzegovina in 1908, a provocation that enraged Serbia, which saw the territory as its ancient appendage, its antique arm that had been unjustly severed. For six hundred years, the Serbs sought to reassemble its imagined heartland, which had been torn and split when the Ottomans advanced through the Balkans in the fourteenth century and defeated the Serbs in the Battle of Kosovo in 1389, which, coincidentally, also fell on June 28. The significance of the day was not lost on the Black Hand, a Serbian nationalist organization of young radicals determined to restore Serb sovereignty. Franz Ferdinand was the prize, a rare and delicious varmint, and they longed to see him roasting on a spit.

The archduke had come to the Bosnian capital to inspect the imperial army and was touring the city in an open car with his Czech wife, Sophie. And as the automobile swerved through the streets, bypassing the hordes of pedestrians enjoying an afternoon out and about, a young man, Nedjelko Čabrinović emerged from the shadows and tossed a bomb at the archduke and his wife. The bomb hit the car and rolled to its rear before detonating innocently at a distance from the royalty, injuring only an officer. Later, on the way to visit the injured man in the hospital, the motorcade stopped briefly on Appel Quay, an attractive street following Miljacka River and its many bridges. In one Quay café sat Gavrilo Princip drinking a coffee, undoubtedly agonizing over the earlier missed opportunity, when he looked up and saw Ferdinand sitting idly in the street. He raced outside in the afternoon sun, unbelieving of his luck, fate's inexplicable humour, drew his pistol and fired into Franz and Sophie. Within a few months, the world was at war.

Sitting in my public school in Bradford, Ontario, I remember thinking how odd it was that the world should descend into bloodshed, millions of men should die in muddy trenches, countless more poisoned by mustard gas, all because some strangely dressed archduke was killed in some European backwater. This was not London, Paris, Berlin, or Vienna; it was not even Istanbul. This was Sarajevo, a city I could not locate on a map. That would change, however, as the early 1990s unwound, as murmurs of Balkan madness crept into newspapers, over the evening newscast, and into my life as a Grade 4 student with an unhealthy passion for the Toronto Maple Leafs. During the siege of Sarajevo from 1992 to 1995, when Bosnian Serbs encircled the city and starved it to death, journalists reported the carnage and blood that the citizens suffered through. Death and atrocity were commonplace. Sarajevo became a synonym for suffering, for hell itself. Everyone knew the name *Sarajevo*, but no one could explain it or understand it. Sarajevo was just a place where bad things happened, where violence was as ancient as it was predictable. I did not try to understand the details, or to put the event in its proper historical context, to study the cause and effect of historical movement, or to grapple with how something as legendary as Yugoslavia could collapse so irrevocably in a dozen or so years, cease to exist, vanish from all maps. I was nine. And in love.

In spring 1993, with the siege in full swing, the Toronto Maple Leafs were making their deepest playoff run in decades. They had beaten the powerful Detroit Red Wings in seven games. Doug Gilmour owned the ice; Dave Andreychuk's orangutan arms reached every puck. They had survived another seven-game series against the St. Louis Blues. Félix Potvin goaltended like Johnny Bower of old; Wendel Clark played with the tenacity of a man half his age. And they had taken Wayne Gretzky's Los Angeles Kings to a seventh game in the conference finals, only one game away from a berth in the Stanley Cup Finals. I breathed the Leafs. I adopted pregame rituals that would have put the most religious of zealots to shame. After school and in the hours leading to the game, I played street hockey outside in my Leafs jersey, imagining that it was I scoring the winning goal. My excitement would build as the games got closer, the seconds ticking down. I sang songs of thanks whenever the team scored on my rickety television; I spoke to mysterious men in the sky making sketchy promises in exchange for victories. I would have conversed and negotiated with men below as well if I had thought they were better plugged into the hockey world. I would have traded my soul for the Stanley Cup.

I did not know it at the time, but children across the Atlantic in the southeastern crevices of Europe were also speaking to mysterious men in the sky, yet for different reasons. Deep in dark cellars, huddled around candlelight, the upstairs apartment covered in glass and sandbags, they sat listening to the gunfire ringing out from the nearby mountains. They prayed that they would not get shot by sniper fire in the playground, that their parents would not die from shelling while selecting potatoes in the marketplace, that their schools would not stay closed long, and that they would not celebrate another birthday in wartime.

My prayers went unanswered. The Kings prevailed in game seven and broke Toronto's collective heart. I was devastated, inconsolable. I hid in the laundry room with my tears and sobs. I moped around the playground, played less hockey, ate less food. In my childish way, I vowed never to love anything again, to quit from the cruel game of caring, to become a shell, immune to the yo-yoing of emotional investment. But after a few months of self-pitying, I returned to the world, watched my favourite television shows, took pleasure again in my pastimes.

The children of Sarajevo did not return to their old world so swiftly. As I watched *Fresh Prince of Bel-Air*, their television sets were dark. As I listened to my favourite compact discs, their stereos remained quiet. As I studied long division and practised my French, their schools stayed shuttered. And as I played basketball in the playground, the summer sun warm on my freckled face, they mourned the deaths of friends pierced by shrapnel while running under the same sun. The vagaries of fate, luck, and circumstance separated me from them. Growing up, I had Sarajevo in the back of my mind; it was a name that would turn my head whenever I heard it, a word I recognized but did not understand. The city was a subtle reminder of my luck, a gentle nudge not to be too critical of the boredom and dullness of southern Ontario. In many ways, the children of Sarajevo, indeed of Bosnia, were my contemporaries and became my doppelgängers. And today, I will meet one, a child of Sarajevo, a boy of the siege.

It is early morning when I cross the Miljacka River into Baščaršija, the old Ottoman heart of Sarajevo, which hawkers, mongers, and barterers of all stripes have filled since the fourteenth century when Isa-Beg Ishaković, an Ottoman general of Bosnian origin, founded the city. Despite the earliness and cool and cloudy conditions, the old market stretches into action. Merchants lay out their goods—copperware, ceramics, embroideries, jewelry, wood carvings, pirated DVDs, CDs—and proprietors assemble their patio tables under minarets in the hopes that patrons may brave the weather (and religious foreboding) to enjoy a Lovac, a local Bosnian beer. An uneasy truce between the holy and hedonistic, between devoutness and debauchery, exists in Sarajevo, as if the long war had taught both the sacred and the secular that life is too short to be continually at each other's throats.

Standing by Sebilj Fountain in the heart of old Ottoman Sarajevo, I see a giant of a man with a little red knapsack lumber towards Pigeon Square. I have arranged a day tour of the city over email with a local outfit, and when I asked my guide how I would recognize him, he wrote that he would be the "fat" one. Instead of his husky frame, I focus on his gait, watching while he trudges past honking cars and the growing crowds, parts a sea of aloof pigeons, and plods through the first drops of rain.

"Samid?" I ask, extending my hand. "Yes," he says, taking it. "I told you that you would recognize me." His boyish looks—stubble beard, shiny skin, sly smile—belies his attire: a worn winter coat falling lazily over faded jeans. He opens his umbrella and looks at the sky with a pronounced nonchalance, as if the stratus clouds, cold rain, and rapacious grey were everyday attributes of a Sarajevan spring day. "We are still waiting for two others," he says, peering at his cellphone. "I need to buy a few things for the tour. I'll be back in five minutes. If you see two Koreans walking around, get their attention. They are usually so punctual." Slightly unnerved by his casual stereotyping, I study his moving—a curious mixture of confidence and inhibition— to a stall hidden in one of Baščaršija's many lanes, deep in his Sarajevo, a city still rebuilding from a war that serrated it, and from an ethnic violence that has forever scarred it, Sarajevo, the cosmopolitan city.

At the fountain, with the group assembled, Samid says, "You may ask me anything about my past, about Sarajevo, about the war." He has sympathy for the visitor who comes to Bosnia with only a cursory knowledge of the country, who knows it as a place of violence, a city full of ghosts, with an incomprehensible history, its story a layered labyrinth. Samid has grown up in that history and knows it intimately. A Bosniak, or Bosnian Muslim, he came of age during the longest siege in modern warfare, the siege of Sarajevo, in which for almost four years, Bosnian Serbs encircled and ensnarled the city and tried to strangle its Bosniak residents into submission amid a decaying Yugoslavia. Samid grew up then, among the bombings, landmines, and shattered glass. Among the frost and the need. So when Samid speaks, we listen. When he regales us with exhaustive knowledge of the land and the city, an amount befitting his size, we absorb it. And when he sometimes jokes with politically incorrect grit, I, at least, take it as a sign of his candidness: a desire, perhaps misguided, to joke at our supposed differences. He has no use for tactfulness, no time for delicacy. After growing up in hell, perhaps he thinks life too short for such seriousness, as he himself has witnessed the logical conclusion of all ethnic chauvinism: death. Perhaps it is his way of welcoming a Bosnia respectful of difference but not defined by it.

"Have you done your homework?" Samid asks. We all look at one another sheepishly, pupils at our desks, each terrified to speak first. He has provided a printout, a four-page Word document outlining the fall of Yugoslavia, beginning with the 1976 constitution granting more self-determination to each region, through the death in 1980 of socialist strongman Josip Tito, through the rising nationalisms, through the emergence of a man named Milošević, and culminating in the early 1990s with Slovenian and Croatian referendums, the first wars of independence, and the implosion of Bosnia, its three ethnic groups—Bosniak, Croat, and Serb—turning the gun on each other. We nod. "Good," Samid says. "In my experience, guests get more from the tour when they know a little before. This country has a complicated history." He checks his phone and peers across the street in his studious manner. "Our driver has arrived."

We zip through the dense, tightly packed Turkish area and past the more ornate and ostentatious buildings and boulevards, relics of the former Austro-Hungarian Empire, another of Sarajevo's many faces; past the Eternal Flame, a burning torch that memorializes Tito and his Partisans' efforts against the Nazis; past the refurbished apartments and glitzy shopping malls, which, as Samid sardonically notes, "no one has money to spend in"; past the gargantuan American Embassy, a city unto itself; past the bullet-holed History Museum full of personal artifacts from the war and solemn stories; and past the derelict and damaged airport, once the home of the UN peacekeeping mission to Sarajevo, and now receiver of a handful of daily international flights.

Throughout the drive, Samid rails against the crises plaguing his city and country: the 40 per cent unemployment, government corruption, ethnic politics, the bewildering political system, and Kafkaesque bureaucracies. "They make it impossible for me to work," he says, turning in the passenger seat to face us in the back. "The government now requires me to get all these new certifications to work as a tour guide." He looks out the window as the driver switches on the wipers. The raindrops are persistent but light. "Sixty per cent of the country's budget goes towards paying government salaries." He does not elaborate. The words are more for him than for us. They are meant to remind him of something but fall flat. They have lost their fervour and passion; they sound hollow, beaten and bare. Beneath his monotone remark, though, I hear a subtext of frustration, a sense of this resurrection being squandered, of hope dissipating.

On the city's outskirts, near the airport, we stop at an unassuming assemblage of houses, decaying dwellings that have not changed much since the war's end. Under grey skies, they stand stark and stoic, worn brown eyes into the past. Bullet craters bedeck the facade. I ask Samid why the city does not pay to have the bullet holes plastered or painted over: "Is it to remember?" "Partly it is to remember," he says. "But mostly the government cannot afford to do the work." The concrete has cracked, creating sharp pieces that protrude from the weakening foundation like the fangs of a cornered beast. Trees have gone unpruned, and their branches reach towards the second storey and its walls of scratched paint. Vines crawl across the brick. The interior is hollow. On a rusted door, someone has written "*tunel*." Samid points to it and says the door was one of the entrances to the

Sarajevo tunnel, an eight-hundred-metre underground corridor connecting the besieged citizens of Sarajevo to freed Bosnian territory on the other side of the advancing Bosnian Serb forces. This was freedom's gate. Food, petrol, weaponry, cigarettes, and people all passed through the tunnel, one of the only linkages that Sarajevans had with the outside world. "It was not easy to leave," Samid says. "Only the wealthy and connected could buy their way out."

The siege of Sarajevo was the longest in modern warfare, lasting from April 5, 1992, to February 29, 1996, and claiming the lives of fourteen thousand people. When Bosnia declared independence from Yugoslavia on March 3, 1992, Bosnian Serbs, fearing Bosniak and Croat domination in the new republic, carved pieces of land for themselves and ethnically cleansed the areas. They formed their own republic, Republika Srpska, led by Radovan Karadžić and, to guarantee it, they had to defeat the Bosnian government and beat Sarajevo.

The tunnel complex has been transformed into a museum, where visitors can look through displays documenting the difficulties living under the siege and the perils of smuggling goods under enemy-crowded hills. Mannequins clothed in army attire push wheelbarrows full of sandbags. Heavy leather boots and shovels lean against display cases. Helmets rest below an array of flags. Mortar shells hang from the wooden ceiling like icicles. Boxes of artillery sit on trolleys. Old pistols lie under sheets of glass. Framed photos of visiting dignitaries cover the walls. The space is compact. Heroism is the underlying motif.

A model of an under-siege apartment, full of books and cartons of cigarettes, stands outside the museum. "People used to burn books to keep warm in the Sarajevan winter," Samid says. "Former academics usually stayed the warmest." I smile and think of my parents, academics themselves, and the dozens of bookcases stuffed with monographs and essays on feminist and Marxist theory. I imagine them ripping pages from Gramsci or Wollstonecraft and dropping them onto a weak fire of paper and twigs. Samid tells about how his own family survived the collapsing streets of Sarajevo, about dodging the bullets of Sniper Alley, surviving the market blasts and mortar shelling, and just keeping a sense of hope. "It was difficult," he says, his voice heavy with remembrance. "Food was scarce, as Serb forces prevented most food relief from entering the city." He pauses for a second longer and points to the cigarettes. "No matter how bad it got," he says, "there was always tobacco." We laugh, but Samid has already moved onto the next stop on the tour.

We arrive at a plot of wet grass, cordoned off by barbed wire and a handful of poles. Pieces of metal and plastic sprout from the ground, so close that I could touch them. On the gnarled wire hangs a red sign adorned with a skull and crossbones. Above the beaming skull reads "mine." An estimated 120,000 undetonated landmines still lie in the Bosnian countryside, and six hundred people have died from stepping on them since the war ended. The late-April clouds cling tight to the mountains surrounding the city. Across the fence, past a muddied field of tilled earth and dandelions, the airport looks desolate and abandoned, some postapocalyptic shrine to what was. Samid, too, studies the scene. I wonder if it loses its visceral power the more you stare at it, the way a horror film becomes that much more absurd the more you watch it. Does familiarity numb this image's effect? Samid checks his cellphone and begins his monologue. "After Tito died in 1980, it took only ten years for Yugoslavia to die. First Slovenia declared independence, then Macedonia and Croatia, and finally Bosnia." He examines us the way a teacher would after explaining a tricky math equation. "The process here did not go well."

Independence in Bosnia required the approval of the three different ethnic groups, and consensus simply did not exist in the early 1990s. The fear was that Bosnian Croats would follow Croatia, the Bosnian Serbs would follow Serbia, and the Bosniaks would be left to fend for themselves in a disintegrating Bosnia. And when Bosnia did declare independence in 1992, this breakdown is exactly what transpired. Bosnian Serbs, backed by Belgrade, launched a secessionist bid, and newly independent Croatia also joined the fray, backing the Bosnian Croats against the Bosnian Serbs and, at times, against the Bosniaks. The three-year, three-sided war left over 100,000 dead.

In another room, decorated by maps and army paraphernalia, a television screen shows grainy, unfocused footage of Sarajevo burning. Smoke billows from apartment blocks. Men perched on mountaintops fire onto the streets. The occasional shell explodes, shaking the camera. A woman carrying bags walks through the wreckage, her city a heap of burning memories. Everything is grey and impoverished. Even the interviewed generals and commanders, with microphones shoved below their mouths, look coarse and disfigured when they bark their rhetoric, eyes inflamed with historic grievance. But Samid, sitting on the wooden bench to my left, attracts my attention. He scrolls over his phone, checking his work email no doubt, seeing whether he has tours for the afternoon or tomorrow or whether he has any journalists to guide, fixing contacts for them, arranging meetings, telling his story again and again, for their documentaries, their news programs, to show the world Sarajevo reborn, emerging from the rubble revitalized, a phoenix, a city of Lazarus. I hope he can make a living from what he has endured. I hope a semblance of peace, a trace of tranquility, comes from daily reliving the madness. I wonder, though, whether such memories will ever dull, will ever end up confined to history books and the objective accounts of journalists. Every now and then, Samid looks up from his phone, intrigued by something the narrator has said, perhaps bothered by his interpretation, ready to interject his own opinion. But each time, he decides not to speak and instead returns to the comfort of his phone.

A large group of Turkish adolescents enters the museum. They walk with the imperviousness of the young, seemingly unaffected by the museum and its meaning. The Turkish government has invested heavily in Bosnia since the war's end, much to the Bosnian Serbs' outrage. It has helped to rebuild mosques and has financed infrastructure projects. Along the river in Sarajevo, rusted trams from Konya chug. Turkish flags flutter throughout the city. The Turkish language is easily overheard in cafés and restaurants, in guesthouses and tourist agencies. During the Ottoman times, many of Bosnia's inhabitants converted to Islam, and Muslims became the majority group. Over the course of the nineteenth century, general disillusionment with Ottoman taxation grew along with Christian antipathy towards both the Sultan in Istanbul and the increasingly oppressive local rulers in Bosnia. In 1875, Christian peasants in Herzegovina rebelled, followed soon by those in Montenegro and Serbia. Russia then declared war on the Ottomans and, by 1877, Bosnia was under the nominal control of the Austro-Hungarian Empire. The Muslims of Bosnia were now under Christian rule.

Before leaving, we descend to the tunnel. Pieces of frail and bent metal criss-cross the floorboards. The tracks disappear around a bend. No carts carry supplies now. No voices whisper orders. The only sound is our breathing. Blinding light bulbs hang from the wooden beams that support the ceiling and sides, holding the structural integrity, stopping the rubble of rock from crushing us. Stepping forward, I crouch and bend my head slightly to keep from banging it. The glow shrinks the space further. I cannot see a step ahead. I feel my breathing intensify, my pulse quicken. The walls move in; I suspect the bulbs could blow at any moment. I imagine mortar shells detonating above, the ceiling shaking, pebbles falling, then bigger ones and bigger and bigger. I sense the beams fracturing under the weight, splintering into kindling. The wood breaks and the rocks tumble. I am concussed and crumble. Everything blurs and bounces in a haze. The weight crushes, and the light fades under raining rock. Piece by piece, the darkness envelops me. My mouth is too full to scream.

Exiting the museum, we pass a sign honouring the victims of the siege. From this distance, I cannot read their names.

We drive towards the mountains and pass a blue sign welcoming us to the Republic of Srpska, written in English and Cyrillic Serbian. A semiautonomous Bosnian Serb entity, the Republika Srpska, along with the Federation of Bosnia and Herzegovina, comprise the contemporary country of Bosnia and Herzegovina. The 1995 Dayton Accords secured peace in the nation but not integration or reconciliation. In many facets of postwar life, ethnic chauvinism has hardened, as the three major ethnic groups still live apart. "Every year, the government promises a new census to see who exactly lives in this country," Samid says. "But we are still waiting." The accords, in fact, normalized ethnic division, cemented ethnic loyalty, and made ethnic politics a reality in contemporary Bosnia. "Our country has three presidents," Samid explains. "Each must come from one of the three groups: one Bosniak, one Serb, one Croat. There is no such thing as a Bosnian." Below the presidency, each region has its own political framework, its own system of representation, a network of cantons and legislatures, producing a bewildering array of professional politicians who promise to serve the interests of their own groups. Ethnic loyalty becomes enshrined in the political language, a perpetual cog in the wheel. "We have elections here every other week," Samid laughs. "Becoming a politician is the only lucrative career path in Bosnia."

In the mountains, snow melts at the foot of cedar groves, the last traces of the weekend's spring snowstorm. Fog covers the forests in an impenetrable grey and leaks across the thin strip of asphalt. Our driver turns on the headlights. "This is Mount Igman," Samid says, the road getting progressively steeper and disorderly. "The hub of the 1984 Winter Olympics." Through the fog, we see cables cut through pine clusters and climb higher. No chairlifts rumble through the forests, however. Bobsled tracks and ski ramps lie in ruin. Only corroding monuments remain, eerier reminders of how things can suddenly change. We take pictures of ourselves standing on the vacant, abandoned medals podium, shadowed by the Olympic rings. *I was born in 1984*, I think, looking at myself in the camera. The podium consists of two right-angled concrete triangles and three uneven platforms, corresponding to bronze, silver, and gold. A space opens between the triangles, whose hypotenuse sides slide away from the podium, showcasing the gold-medal platform, on which I stand and smile. On the higher triangle to my right are written the words "Sarajevo 84." The structure is a cloud of water droplets. Only I and the podium are visible. "Is it okay?" Samid asks. "Yes," I say. "It is perfect."

Around another bend, we arrive at the skeleton of Hotel Igman. The six-storey hotel stands in a heap of its own bones. Its innards—

windows, carpets, wallpaper, furniture, lights—have been hollowed and scooped out. Only its ribcage stands now, licked clean, a concrete shell protecting nothing; it reminds me of a fossil from some prehistoric beast that once roamed the forests here, some mythical chimera that ruled the mountains before going extinct and left to rot in the snow. It is ghostly. It is spectacular. Built for the Olympics, the hotel was once ritzy and swanky, the place of choice for the moneyed and lavish. In 1993, the hotel was bombed and blasted. "The government cannot afford to tear it down," Samid informs us. "So unemployed youth now come here to play paintball among the bullet holes and ripped tiles." It is an ideal setting for paintball, for any kind of urban warfare simulation really.

Walking among the debris, past the demolished walls and mountains of cinder blocks and stone slabs, I cannot comprehend how this hotel was built less than ten years before the war's beginning. What a sense of optimism the Olympics must have represented at the time, a coming-out party for Sarajevo, a showcase for the rest of the world. Now, water leaks from the ceiling among old wires that drop like snakes. Stalactites have formed from the leached lime and hang from the cement roof as if in a cave. Plumbing pipes obtrude from the floor. Nails and screws lie among the glass and garbage. Mud and mortar coalesce into sludge. Graffiti decorates the discoloured brick. The blasted-out walls, broken as if by a sledgehammer, offer clear views over the pine trees dotting the sloping earth. The fog slowly enters the space, stretching into the cool and empty hallways. Our footsteps crunch the wreckage, breaking the silence.

Samid hands me a piece of broken tile with the word "Tito" carved on it. The material feels cool in my hand, light and fragile. "You want it as a souvenir?" he asks. I imagine carrying it around with me on the rest of my trip, a symbol of another people's struggle buried deep in my nylon backpack. "I don't have enough room in my bag," I say, handing the piece back to him. Samid examines its texture, its coarse and grainy surface. "I'll keep it then," he says, putting it in his pocket. He seems satisfied, a genuine moment that transcends the superficialities of tour leading. "Is Tito still admired?" I ask. "Among the older generation he is. He reminds them of a time of greater opportunity, greater hope I suppose. Nowadays, people find hope difficult." Samid says nothing more and disappears down the stairs.

About the time local teenagers discovered the hotel's warlike atmosphere and replaced lead bullets with paint pellets, my friends and I discovered the James Bond GoldenEye 007 video game for Nintendo 64. Every few weekends, we would assemble at someone's basement, huddle around the television, slip the cartridge into the machines, pass out the controllers, and go to war. We would play in teams and travel to a variety of countries and cities—Arkhangelsk, Severnaya, Kyrgyzstan, Monte Carlo, St. Petersburg, Cuba, Mexico, Egypt— armed with AK 47s and magnums. We would hunt each other in bunkers, parks, laboratories, airport hangers, cityscapes, underground layers, frigates, and dams. We knew each level by heart, had memorized where the ammunition was hidden, learned where the best sniping and ambush areas were. We were experts in the art of killing, and art it was. The kill was not nearly as satisfying as watching a beautifully laid plan come to fruition, eyeing with quiet relish as your prey fell into your trap, stalking him as he fumbled and stumbled across the terrain, closing in on his backside and deciding whether to gut him with a hunting knife or shoot him with a pistol. It was thrilling. And we could be brazen, experiment with different weaponry, test different techniques. Because if we erred and got killed—watching with embarrassment and disappointment as the screen went red, the music climaxing in dramatic fashion, our avatar dropping to his knees before finally keeling over—we knew it was only temporary. Death was short. A few seconds. Before long, we would reanimate, standing there strong and ready, prepared to have our revenge after learning from our past mistakes. We were amazed, as well, at how realistic the game was, the weapon details, the blood, the shrieks of pain, the tension and suspense. Even more remarkable was that when someone shot a wall, the bullet would leave a small hole, a tiny later crater. Sometimes we would try to spell our names in bullet holes on some wall in Siberia. How many glorious hours we spent killing each other, amid laughter and goofiness, it is impossible to say. We loved the slaughtering.

Our last stop is a park overlooking the city. We see the minarets and mosques, the cemeteries and churches, the red-tiled roofs and distant skyscrapers. From this vantage point, Sarajevo looks contained, hemmed in by Bjelašnica and Jahorina mountains. Constricted. The city runs in a horizontal line, following the river, orderly and predictable. But we know none of this is true. Sarajevo is neither contained nor predictable. It exists in constant motion, forever shifting. A city that withstood hell, rebounded from rapture, and survived serration. It could do nothing else but get up and get on with it. Samid waits in the car while we snap our final photos.

At Pigeon Square, the car slows along the sidewalk, bustling with afternoon shoppers. A decrepit bus rumbles down the narrow street. A child scares a group of bobbing pigeons, which rise and dart over a group of elderly men drinking Turkish coffee beneath a canvas cover. I wonder what fortunes their coffee grounds tell. Samid turns from the front seat and asks whether we enjoyed the trip. We nod like schoolchildren. I shake Samid's hand and thank him for an illuminating morning, for his sharing his experiences, his knowledge. And when he takes my hand and tells me to enjoy the rest of my time in his city, I sense his veneer of professionalism momentarily soften, and a flash of mischievousness erupts in his eyes while a playful grin forms over his lips. Holding his hand, I imagine for a second a different story, one in which Samid and I have been lifelong friends, for I have noticed similarities between us—the cynicism, the sarcasm, the flouting of custom—and a different history unravels in my mind. We have grown up together. We have shared secrets. We have stayed loyal. We have defended each other against every foe. But dropping his hand and exiting the car, I know it to be a childish lie, a product of my at times romantic, naive thinking. Samid comes from a different world and knows that world better than I ever could. Samid is my shadow. He reminds me not of some universal brotherhood, in which all souls belong to the roots of the same tree, but of an unbridgeable gulf that exists between those who have come of age during war and those who have not. I am neither his friend nor his brother. I am a tourist in his city, in his Sarajevo.

I sit on a patio sipping a pint under the glare of a minaret. A Muslim family walks by, the women covered in colourful hijabs. There is talk of banning the headscarf in courthouses. In the countryside, more and more Bosniaks depart to join Daesh in Syria and Iraq. Bosnia as usual bubbles with tension. I ask the waiter if I could buy a cigarette from him, but he tells me he is all out. At the next table sit three young men, and the one closest to me hands me his opened pack of Marlboro, and I eagerly take one. I nod in thanks as I light it and feel the nicotine calm me. "Where are you from?" he asks. "Toronto, Canada." He takes a drag from his cigarette. "And you?" I ask, completing the well-worn routine. "Here, but I live in Berlin. I am showing my German friends the city of my birth." He points to the two sober-looking gentlemen sitting across from me who greet me in a detached way. They are in their mid-to-late twenties. The proprietor returns with a tray full of glasses and hands one to each man. They raise them and gently bring them together, before shouting "*Živjeli!*" and tossing the contents down their throats. "What is the drink?" I ask, intrigued by the ritual and salubrious effect the clear liquid has had on its drinkers. "Rakija," he answers, beaming. "Have you tried it?" "Only the Turkish variety," I say, recalling its awful licorice taste during my younger Istanbul nights. "And I did not like it." "Well, of course not," the young Bosnian says. "It wasn't true rakija. Bosnia makes the best." He laughs, undoubtedly aware that every country in this part of the world claims to make *this* the best or to have invented *that* first. "You must try it," he continues. "It's made from …" And he cannot think of the word in English. A serious conversation in German follows before one of the Berliners looks to me, his face serious and eyeglasses balancing on his nose, and says, "Plums." "Lovely," I say.

Soon, they return to their conversation, and I sip my beer. I think of Rebecca West's 1937 voyage through the Balkan Peninsula. She, too, was drawn by the region's turbulent history, intrigued by its propensity for violence, its remarkable ability to shift the world. She spent five years travelling through the landscape, talking to people, taking notes, and wrote a classic of travel literature: *Black Lamb and Grey Falcon*. Part ethnography, part journalism, part memoir, part encyclopedia, her half-a-million-word magnum opus tries to pinpoint the cause of the region's seemingly endless strife. Yet when she travelled through Sarajevo, war was the furthest thing from her mind. The people, she says, are the city's greatest resource. Its luxury has less to do with material goods than with its citizens. They are a garrulous group, she exudes, who delight in life's pleasures, take such delight, in fact, that they hoard the bliss and buzz. Beauty is kept tucked away in cellars, hidden deep in basements and closets. They are prudent and judicious in its use, careful not to spend it all on a summer afternoon, perhaps because they know to save some joy for a cold January night or for something far worse. I feel it, too, sitting there along Ćurčiluk mali Street, the careful frivolity among the restaurants with packed patios, families and friends gossiping and chatting and laughing over dishes of ćevapi, burek, and baklava, among the shisha joints, with its young patrons blowing fruit-flavoured smoke from elaborate pipes in my direction. I sense the cautious optimism despite the country's continuing corruption, ethnic tension, unemployment, and slow reconciliation.

Around me, the faces are still bright, lively. I cannot help but wonder what they hide, what lurks underneath the giggles, the white teeth, the lapping tongues. What have I missed? I ask the man next to me if I can steal another cigarette and he yells, "Of course!" as if asking him were an insult to the scene's communal vibe. I take one from the clearly marked Marlboro package and light it. I think about my own Sarajevan narrative, constructed as a convenient journey from death to resurrection, from tragedy to cautious hope, and I wonder how much of this I actually understand. All conventional stories beg resolution; it is the arrogance of the present, however, to assume anything has been resolved. Things go on. Memories in tow. And my words inevitably distort reality, fictionalize it to a degree. My punctuation corrals life's flow. Every moment is an olio that defies syntax. Every edit is an unfolding lie. Every period is a silence, a selection.

I think of Samid, my doppelgänger, doing his afternoon tour, reliving again and again his memories for the enrichment of strangers, trying to reveal his hidden logo, his sealed pack of cigarettes. But I cannot hold him in my thoughts, and already he has moved into the fuzz of recollection, a blurry image moving through the forests of my memories. And writing is pointless if its purpose is causality, if its sole goal is to sequence the world into understandable and manageable chunks. I embrace bricolage. All I can do is cast my net and pull in everything I see and hear. All I can do is stitch together a series of representations fitted to an indescribable reality. Yet I feel rejuvenated and excited in thinking about the work involved to say anything intelligent about a place. To enter a discussion takes much effort. And most of the time, one should simply listen.

I thank the gentlemen for the cigarettes, pay the bill, and rise from the table. Around me a thousand narratives go on, following not the dictates of story but the rhythm of wind. I swerve through the afternoon crowds. The spring's sun squeezes through the clouds, the warmth a reminder of summer's closeness, yet all the metaphors of rebirth and resurrection stay closeted within me. And I make a promise here, vanishing into the people whose language I do not speak but whose history I want to know, that if I ever have a daughter, I will never call her Sarajevo.

2. Srebrenica

In 1995, I was eleven, in Grade 4, and different. I had long, curly brown hair that cascaded down to my shoulders. My face had no real outline, no distinguishable features—a chubby canvas in which passersby could paint whatever they wished. And most of the time, they saw a girl, an ugly girl. For most people, I was an androgynous abyss, a genderless gap. I was confusion personified. Terror came whenever I set foot outside familiar places, wherever people had not been told that the thing before their eyes was, in fact, a boy. In restaurant washrooms, standing at a urinal, I would watch men burst through the door, spot me, spout a torrent of apology, exit post-haste, and then re-emerge seconds later perplexed, chin scratching, no longer trusting their eyes. Little children appalled me the most. Unfamiliar with rules of decorum and polite etiquette, they would stare at me, mouth hanging open, dumbfounded and uncouth, a large-mouthed bass. I would feel the beasts' eyes watching me, addicted, summoning the courage to ask their parents, "Mommy, what is it?"

Sunday nights, my father and I would venture to the hockey rink to watch the local team play. Chewing toffee and sipping hot chocolate, I enjoyed the intimacy of the action, being so close to the body checks, the shooting, the scoring. My father would playfully rib the opposing goaltender while I tried to disappear into my seat, secretly pleading for him to stop drawing attention to us. Because even if the goaltender was mediocre, even if he had surrendered an easy goal, some lazy wrist shot from the blue line, I knew when he removed his helmet, sprayed a line of water into his mouth from his bottle, and glared in our direction, that he was recognized as a boy and that was a power I would never have. At intermission one day, I was walking towards the foyer when I heard a familiar shout from a row of seats. "Hey you," the voice repeated. I stopped and looked. Four big-shouldered male teenagers stood on the second level, staring down at me. "Are you a boy or a girl?" the largest one demanded. I felt the familiar humiliation mixed with fear smoulder within. The hot, probing lights of judgment were on me, pinning me down while I watched the scissors, scalpels, and forceps slice and incise me.

"Are you a boy or a girl?" he barked again. Although I was used to this erosion of dignity, I stumbled on this particular occasion, tripped over my tongue, too eager to show these boys that I knew what I was. "I am a gir—," I stammered. "I mean, a guy." Laughter spewed from their excited bellies as I struggled into the foyer. "It doesn't even know!" I heard him shout. "It doesn't even know."

It is the English pronoun reserved for those things that lack sentience, that ineffable quality that marks a human being human. An *it* is subhuman, an inanimate object, or unthinking animal. It has neither sex nor personality. It exists to be used and degraded. And on several occasions during my early adolescence, I was an *it*.

Since I was an adequate long-range shooter, I had joined my school's basketball team. Before the start of one home game, I stood at half court with my teammates—the opposing players from a different school talked strategy on their half—as both sides waited for the referee's instruction. I saw one boy whisper something into the ear of his crew, point to me, and laugh. The referee blew his whistle, and I approached the line. The whispering boy lined up across from me. His teammate stayed in the backcourt and said, "So, a boy or a girl?" The whispering boy looked at me and replied, "Neither. An it."

Despite the frequent bouts of embarrassment, however, those moments of shame that internally released torrents of angst and self-loathing, the pain of being different and expendable, I still knew at some instinctive level that I could not be killed for it. I knew that even though I suffered, I could not be stripped naked, thrown into a dirty room, and gassed. I knew that I could not be taken into some desolate field, forced to kneel, and be shot in the back of the head, slowly slumping into an unmarked, mass grave filled with people like me, people that for whatever reason were marked as other and killable. I knew that despite being labelled an it and mocked for my appearance, I was still part of the universal family, and its humanity protected me from the shadowy members, brothers and sisters who felt the pang of rage or disgust whenever their eyes shone at me. They would not reduce me to mere bare life, the Roman *homo sacer*, man outside of law and rule, with no protection, a thing as disposable as garbage, to be tortured at will. And I need to restate it: they could not kill me for it.

That year, at school, I heard about people who were killed for resembling an it, who fell outside humankind's warm grasp. In a little grey portable, slumped at my wooden desk full of crumpled papers, pens, and pencils, surrounded by light walls covered with artwork, familial scenes of humour and hand holding, I learned that not too long ago, millions of people were murdered for being different. The Nazis believed that everything wrong with their country, Germany, was the result of outsiders, distasteful elements of society who polluted the purity of the authentic fatherland: Caucasian, of Nordic stock, blue eyes, blond hair, white skin. To eradicate this diseased portion of the body politic, the Nazis quarantined the impure stock first in ghettoes, and then shipped them—Jewish families, Roma wanderers, homosexual men and women, dissidents of all shades—to concentration camps, where they were executed. I learned about the words *Holocaust* and *genocide*, about how women and men could be targeted and exterminated based solely on their ethnic or cultural makeup. What scared me the most was how quickly and easily the Nazis had convinced an entire citizenry that whole populations were less than human, some vermin in need of eradication, a pestilence in need of erasure, how seamlessly a banal bureaucracy of death had appeared, how efficiently the entire machine worked, how rapidly its operators stopped thinking. When the lunch bell rang, my teacher encouraged us never to forget the lesson of the Second World War.

And on one summer afternoon in 1995, around the second week of July, on the eve of my twelfth birthday, playing on a local baseball team, I was forced to have my picture taken by a professional photographer while I held my bat in a swinging stance. Before he pressed the button, and to get me to smile, he told me to imagine that a group of cute boys sat in the stands and were winking at me. The anxiety forced my lips to slide sideways into a half-hearted smirk. I rejoined my friends as we fielded ground balls and caught pop-ups. But I couldn't stop thinking about those boys in the crowd winking at me. What if they approached me and realized that I was not what they had assumed? What if my reality made them feel something they did not want? Then, I saw them phantomlike creeping along the ball diamond, stopping at each base to gossip with my friends and teammates. Each would whisper something into their ears, and my friends would nod, and their eyes would harden and glare at me. We would still play, but something had changed, and I knew it. We joked less. We talked less. We smiled less. They refused to see me. I wondered there alone on the field, beneath the swaying willow trees and emptying bleachers, the floodlights illuminating the solitary bases, the quiet dugouts, whether my friends would bear witness to my death if it came to that, whether they would defend me against the unruly mobs, or would I see them among the ugly, twisted faces, mouths foaming with hatred. Or would I forgive them, knowing full well that if not for the force of history, it could easily be me with my rifle aimed and knife ready.

A ground ball to my left side broke my daydream. I snagged the ball in my glove and fired it to first base. No, I could not believe it. It would not happen to me here in Bradford, Ontario, innocent land of marshes and farms. Little did I know then that in the mountainous eastern corner of Bosnia, at the same time that I positioned myself underneath a lazy fly ball, other young men were waking to the fact that it could. And when they were told to kneel blindfolded by men in commando uniforms in the soccer field in which they used to play, did it seem so farfetched for them to conclude, maybe, that the events of the Second World War were not so extraordinary? When they were castigated as "Turks" and had their limp and muddied bodies sprayed with bullets, did it seem so outlandish for them to think they had become the other? I was not killed for having long hair. But in Srebrenica, thousands were killed simply for having the wrong last name and, maybe, for believing in the wrong God.

Srebrenica has been famous as a spa town since Roman times. Above the community, streams trickle down the mountains; their mineral-rich waters purport to cure any skin ailment. Ottomans afflicted with leprosy once soaked in the pools under a canopy of maple and oak leaves. Nowadays, Bosnian doctors have legitimized these historic claims, lauding the medicinal properties of the iron-laden creeks and recommending them to treat anemia and multiple sclerosis.

"It can also help with sinus problems," Zoran says as he saunters from the van, down a path, and to the water's edge. "Watch," he instructs. He crouches, cups his hands, scoops some water, and quickly sniffs at it. He suddenly stands, takes a big whiff of air, and exhales, head tilted towards the sky. "Great," he says, smiling. He motions for us to join him, and I, two American women, and a German couple dutifully oblige. "The trick," he says, "is not to completely submerge your nose in the water; you only want to smell the surface." I squat over the brook. From deep within the deciduous forests, the waters flow, rising and falling over a series of tiny knolls, undulating over smooth rocks, drowned pebbles, and dead branches, rippling between muddy banks the colour of copper. I take a handful of water and quickly inhale.

A slight burning sensation expands inside my nostrils, and my eyes water. But then relief arrives in the form of freshness. My nasal cavities become unblocked, the snot and mucus buildups destroyed, my nose breathes unimpeded, naturally, absorbing the vigour of the mountains, of spring on the verge of bloom. The others look at me, awaiting the verdict. "It works," I say. Zoran grins before bending to fill a few bottles, which he will bring home for his daughters. He never forgets the legendary, magical waters of Srebrenica.

We follow the narrow *Crni Guber*, or Black Spa Road, up the mountain until it dead ends at a corrugated metal fence. Past the fence, trees have been felled, an open space built where forest once was. The frame of some structure reaches towards the clouds. Across the barricade, I expect to hear bulldozers, hammers, drills and to see scaffolding, pulleys and hardhats. Yet only silence emanates from there. "The town of Srebrenica has long planned to build a posh hotel and spa here," Zoran says. "They wanted to put the town back on the tourist map, like before, attract visitors, create jobs." On the fence, someone has fastened an artist's rendition of the complex. It looks grandiose, a veritable castle compound, a chain of high-rises with green roofs. It looks like no other building I have seen in this eastern corridor of Republika Srpska. It appears futuristic, not of this time, belonging to a different chronology, with a dissimilar history. Zoran spins the van around. "But the money has run out," he says, steering the van down the mountain road. "Now, there is only a half-built hotel deep in the mountains."

As we descend the curving road, past the pools of medicinal waters, something large approaches. Zoran slows the van. Teenagers, and a lot of them. They reluctantly move to the shoulder as we squeeze through the web of boys and girls in jeans and light jackets, so close to our windows that I could reach out and high-five each one. Some walk and talk in groups; other solitary ones hang back. A few teachers yell orders, which only the more conscientious students adhere to. I turn around to watch them climb down the embankment to the streams that we just visited. There, they touch, taste, and smell the healing rivulets.

We stop at a scenic lookout over Srebrenica. Zoran has driven us from Sarajevo on a day tour to the genocide memorial honouring the eight thousand Muslim men and boys murdered by Bosnian Serb soldiers and paramilitaries on the order of General Mladić. On the three-hour drive, Zoran gave a lecture on what transpired here during the first few weeks of July 1995, the panic of the Muslim refugees, the failure or inability of the Dutch peacekeepers to protect them, and the incompetence of the international community to defend Srebrenica, a designated safe area since 1993. We gaze over the town.

The minarets of two mosques rocket to the hazy clouds; no one stands on the balconies. The speakers make no sound; it is not yet time for the *adhan*. Just beyond, on a bluff, stands an orthodox church. Its cupola, topped by an onion-shaped dome, shoots to the sky. The parking lot surrounding the nave, however, is carless. Not a soul enters its doors. White apartment blocks with rust-coloured balconies sit below the hills. No one peeks through the square windows. Below the apartment buildings are bricked townhouses with terra cotta roofs. No smoke gently wafts from the chimneys. All of Srebrenica, it seems, is silent. Peace has ruled Srebrenica since late 1995, for over twenty years weapons have stayed holstered, yet a gunless war still rages between the survivors. A war over history.

The town's name derives from the Serbo-Croatian *srebro*, meaning "silver," which was found in the nearby mountains centuries ago. Along with its healing powers, Srebrenica became known as a mining community. The people here mined not only silver but also zinc and lead, which remains an important industry today. "Though not as much as before," Zoran says. "Unemployment remains high." The land does not provide as much sustenance as it once did. Restaurants and shopping malls have sprung from the cemented ground; a service industry has replaced the extractive one.

The forests and mountains encroach on the community like an advancing army. Walking through Srebrenica's streets, one can become claustrophobic and feel as if surrounded. Though picturesque, nature has cornered Srebrenica, imprisoned it in woodland. In between the steep ridges and cliffs, roads wind perilously. A network of local trails dissects the bush. Movement remains hazardous around here. It is difficult to arrive and difficult to leave. The nearby peaks provide a perfect vantage point overlooking the valleys and rivers if one had the weapons to defend it. A hawk perched on a fir branch, for example, could see the highway curl out from Srebrenica through a corridor flanked by crags towards the village of Potočari and the old Dutch peacekeeper compound, past the town of Bratunac, over the River Drina, and into Serbia, less than ten kilometres away. Despite its isolation, this terrain of interlocking mountains and valleys has seen much migration over the years.

Before the dissolution of Yugoslavia, northeastern Bosnia had been one of its most integrated regions. Srebrenica was three-fourths Muslim, one-fourth Serb. Bosniaks and Serbs lived in the same apartment blocks, shared sugar, chatted over tea, spread gossip, and vented their frustration over whatever municipal controversy befell their mountain hamlet. With the secession of Slovenia and Croatia, rumours of possible Bosnian independence emanating from Sarajevo, and nationalist rhetoric ratcheting up from Belgrade, Bosnian Serbs worried about becoming a minority in a land that they considered, despite the rollicking waves of history, to be an integral piece of Greater Serbia. In 1991, they voted against seceding from Yugoslavia, and encouraged by such staunch support, Bosnian Serb politicians formed their own state within Bosnia—Republika Srpska—a horseshoe-shaped territory surrounding the Bosniak-dominated interior. And when Alija Izetbegović declared Bosnian independence in April 1992, those integrated areas, the country's most multicultural and ethnically diverse towns and villages, would become the most violent spots, in which every effort was made to purify those areas, to cleanse them of their discordant parts, and to replace a mosque's qibla wall with the orthodox church's patriarch flag, to substitute the Latin alphabet for the Cyrillic one, or vice versa.

As fighting erupted throughout Bosnia, Serb paramilitary groups purged many communities of their Bosniak citizens, including Srebrenica, where Muslim residents were forced to flee into the nearby forests. By January 1993, however, the Bosniaks, under the leadership of Naser Orić, retook Srebrenica and committed their own atrocities against Serb villages and prisoners of war. But by March 1993, Bosnian Serb forces had reversed all of Orić's gains, retaken many towns, and forced sixty thousand Muslim refugees into Srebrenica.

Looking at the town, I cannot fathom how sixty thousand people lived here. How could the town's meagre infrastructure support such a deluge of human beings? I try to picture the vacant streets packed with people. I try to imagine the panic and dread of watching supplies dwindle, hearing shells explode nearby, waiting for the Bosnian Serbs to arrive. I try to imagine what I would have done, a child here in a river of confused and frightened adults. I see myself holding my mother's hand while she pushes her way through the crowd begging for bread, a sip of water, meeting other mothers who are trying to save their children as well as their dignity. Dirt smears my face. My shoes fall apart. Long rips along my pant leg flap in the wind. Through legs and arms, I see an old man who does not look like me standing in a green jeep surrounded by people. He tells them that he will never abandon them. I try to imagine my reaction. Later, we hear that the United Nations has declared Srebrenica and thirty square miles around it a safe area under the protection of peacekeepers. I watch the UN flag rise in the town. I see foreigners collect the guns from our soldiers. Has the fighting stopped? I wonder. Overlooking Srebrenica, I try to include myself in its history but cannot.

Zoran ushers us back into the van, and we drive towards Potočari. He is a compact man in his forties, austere and responsible. He is extensive and exhaustive in his explanations, his voice even and steady. On the drive from Sarajevo, manoeuvring through the knotted landscape, Zoran did not once stop speaking, sensing it his duty to ensure his clients be as informed as possible before arriving at rows of white graves. He is disciplined and methodical. A former military man, he served in the Yugoslav People's Army, once one of the most powerful armies in Europe, and saw action when the federation splintered in the early 1990s. "The army became too nationalistic," he says. Whereas Serbs once trained and fought next to

Bosniaks and Croats, the army shrank in vision, becoming parochial and insular, helping the Serb cause alone. He left. And now he splits his time between Montenegro and Sarajevo, finding work where he can. Despite the self-assurance one would expect from a man who can kill in a myriad of ways, I sense a slit in his armour, a fragility and unease heightened by the intensity of Srebrenica.

"The people of Srebrenica fled this way on July 11, 1995, after the town fell," Zoran says, driving along the road to Potočari. "They wanted the Dutch peacekeepers to protect them from the Serb army advancing from the south." After suffering through Serb shelling for days and growing increasingly pessimistic about the UN's willingness to use NATO bombing to counter the Serbs, the Dutch abandoned their posts in Srebrenica, and the Muslim soldiers, partially disarmed as they were by the peacekeepers and dismayed by the inaction of the Sarajevo government, did not mount much of a defence either. NATO planes did drop two bombs on Serb targets that morning, but after the Serb generals threatened to kill the peacekeeping hostages they held and to shell the refugees into oblivion, the UN mission withdrew the planes. So on the morning of July 11, 1995, twenty-five thousand refugees departed Srebrenica. Twenty thousand tramped through the woods to march towards Tuzla in Bosnian-held territory. The other five thousand filled the road we now drive along, suffering through the summer heat to reach the Dutch compound in Potočari, five kilometres away. Behind them, through the abandoned homes and garbage-strewn streets, came General Mladić and his forces. The burly general, face glistening with sweat, spoke to the propagandists from a local Bosnian Serb news outlet. He told them that he presents Srebrenica as a gift to the Serbian people, and that the time has arrived to take revenge on the Turks in the region. In Mladić's mind, no difference existed between the Bosniaks and the Ottomans of yesteryear; the former would pay for the latter's crimes against the Serbs. "Onwards to Potočari," the general said.

The marble tombstones sweep across the field. They stand in neat and long rows, evenly spaced, spreading out for hundreds of metres in every direction. Each row has dozens of graves, and each line rises and falls along the uneven ground. Groundskeepers have kept the grass immaculate and finely cut. With the recent rains, the lawns are as verdant as the mountains standing sentinel over the memorial site. Among the rows stand a few trees, whose branches stay still in this windless morning; likewise, the gold and blue Bosnia and Herzegovina flags hang lifelessly. The tombstones are shaped like thick rectangles, which rise vertically from the earth. From the top of the knoll, they resemble the quills of a porcupine or the thorns of a lizard, a protective covering, a skin of palisades or spikes guarding the soil. Arabic and Serbo-Croatian script as well as the name of the dead and a fleur-de-lis adorn each marker. At the entrance, a curved wall displays all the names in alphabetical order: Tuzlić, Udovcić, Varnica, Zukanović. The Zukić family has almost two dozen entries; Ramo was only fifteen when he was killed. A stone marker notes the number killed or missing from that July day—8,372, followed by an ellipsis—of which over six thousand are buried here.

Zoran gathers us under the pavilion and tells us we are waiting for our guide, a survivor of Srebrenica. In between the graves, I notice families dropping flowers. A black cat saunters by. The forlorn atmosphere disintegrates as another group of teenagers, thirty or so, undoubtedly on a field trip, enter the memorial site. They possess that youthful energy, a universal vibrancy of those on the edge of adulthood. They wear their identities on their sleeves. I am sure they know each other's names. "Where are they from?" I ask Zoran. "They are from around here," he says, determining such from their accents. I wonder from which side they come. I have read that most Serbs do not acknowledge that anything untoward happened here. The dead Muslims are just like the casualties that any war produces, no different from the countless Serbs who were massacred by Bosniak and Croat forces, no more special than the hundreds of thousands of Serbs displaced from Croatia or Bosnia. In nearby schools, teachers make little mention of the events of July 11, make no mention of remains still found in the adjacent hills. Whatever the students' origins, their vitality contrasts with the melancholy of the site. Their movements are fluid and quick. Some are loud, some joke. Others simply wander through the rows. One of the Americans on the tour says their behaviour is inappropriate. "It reminds me of those teenagers taking selfies of themselves at Auschwitz." I concur that their actions seem ill-matched to the seriousness of the place, but I am reluctant to judge them too harshly. They are younger than Srebrenica. They know only life, not death. They possess the detachment of a generation that has eluded genocide. Still marked by it, no doubt, but not necessarily defined by it, or so I think.

Zoran motions to a solitary figure crossing the highway, a cigarette hanging from his mouth. "Our tour guide," he says. The man walks gingerly, appearing fragile and brittle, as if a passing car could blow him over. Behind him, on the opposite side of the street, looms the former Dutch compound, an old derelict factory building that also appears ready to decompose and disintegrate, to topple and crumble in a heap of metal, brick, and glass. Before he enters the memorial site, the man takes a final drag of his cigarette, flicks the butt, and crushes it with his heel, among the glowing ash.

Where we stand is where the refugees stood twenty years ago. From the tops of their armoured personnel carriers, the Dutch peacekeepers, in blue helmets and sleeveless green vests, watched the spectacle arrive. Along the asphalt road lumbered a desperate mass of humanity. Muslim women in brightly patterned pantaloons inched forwards pulling confused and startled children. Older men pushed wheelbarrows full of anything they could grab from their homes. The younger ones had frustrated eyes and muttered curses at the Dutch, who sat above them with megaphones barking out orders, the gatekeepers, the last line of defence against the coming marauders. Other adults waded through the crowds looking for family members they had lost in the chaos. Elderly women fainted from the heat; younger ones went into labour. The Dutch permitted the first few hundred refugees into the base itself but, once the main factory hall had filled, they reassembled the hole they had cut in the barbed wired fence. They allowed no more to enter. The rest of the refugees stood or sat outside the complex, exposed to the elements, or hid in nearby factories. They simply waited in the July sun.

Zoran introduces the guide underneath the pavilion as a survivor of Srebrenica and curator of the memorial centre. The man has short black hair that falls lazily over his forehead. The fine lines under his eyes seem etched, sanded, and burnished; they are experience's tell. His shoulders slump, his arms sag; he strikes me as fatigue personified. Yet his voice betrays his body's tiredness. It is defiant. Uncowed. In perfect English, he says "My name is Hasan. And I lost my father and twin brother at Srebrenica." Zoran stands behind him, arms folded across his chest, and watches him in respectful silence. The teenagers still parade through the tombstones, but Hasan pays them little attention. He tells us about the history of the site. He speaks in exact sentences, pithy and engaging, honed and sharpened from years of practice. We listen. Bill Clinton opened the site in 2003, when six hundred bodies were interred. In the subsequent years, as workers found more and more gravesites and exhumed their contents, identifying the missing and putting a name to a heap of bones, the number of tombstones rose. "When Srebrenica fell," Hasan says, "my father, brother, uncle, and I, along with many other boys and men, fled towards Tuzla, sixty miles away in Muslim-held territory." He recounts the journey through the mountains and minefields, ducking the Serb shots and shells thundering in the woodlands, ignoring the Serb voices over megaphones promising safety and shelter for every man who surrenders his arms, hiding in streams and caves waiting for Serb patrolmen—who had the area surrounded and were hunting the fleeing men as if for sport—to pass. Somewhere during the odyssey, exhausted and terrified, Hasan lost contact with his brother, father, and uncle, but he could only limp on, bolstered by the desire to survive. And when he did arrive in Tuzla and was eventually reunited with his mother and other family members, all he could do was wonder what had happened to the others. "I buried my father here in 2003," Hasan says. "And my brother in 2005." He moved back to Srebrenica in 2009, and now has a wife and daughter. He says it is hard to live in a place so thick with emotion, to have daily reminders of everything that was lost and all that he survived. He pauses, and a sudden rush of anger replaces the poignancy. "Many local Serbs still do not acknowledge anything happened here," Hasan says. "Many know who the perpetrators were; many know where other mass graves are. But yet they stay silent." He looks past us to the tombstones. "That's why it's important for more survivors to return to Srebrenica and to speak their stories so to fight this silence."

When Mladić and the Bosnian Serb forces arrived at the Dutch compound, they separated the men from the women. They told the Dutch peacekeepers that they needed to interview the men to ascertain whether any were war criminals. The deportations began in earnest. The Dutch acquiesced without too many questions, outnumbered as they were. But when some peacekeepers travelled around the enclave, they could not help but notice that the men they had seen huddled in a field or in a nearby factory suddenly disappeared. They could not help but hear single gunshots ringing out one night or the rumours of mass executions circulating the compound. They could not help but question the Serbs' motives when they robbed the Dutch of their weapons and equipment. Yet despite these warnings, the Dutch did not complain much when the Serbs entered the old factory and rounded up the three hundred or so Muslims who had taken sanctuary there.

The factory holds a chilling quiet. Most of the machinery has been removed. The floors have been swept. Small puddles of water, though, accumulate here and there. Between the walls is merely space. Circular tubes bisect the ceiling beneath the rafters, criss-crossed by silver beams. The factory is cavernous. Its thick white walls reverberate sound so that despite the size and distance between people, the atmosphere feels much more intimate and stifling. Sunlight bursts through rectangular windows. Metal columns stretch to the roof. The factory appears solid despite the cracks in the wall and corroding tiles.

On the walls hang enlarged pictures. Some are of objects found in the gravesites, pocket watches and toothpaste. Some are of the opened graves themselves, with workers plying through the remains, reassembling bodies of bone. Some are of Bosniak families having picnics before the war's start. But one photo grabs my attention. A young woman in a white tank top glares at me. Her stare is penetrating, trenchant. She has tied her hair back, and a few strands have fallen loose. Her lips are sealed. She only peers at whoever may be watching her. Across her torso, someone has written the following: "No teeth …? A mustache …? Smel like shit …? Bosnian girl!" Zoran stands next to me, and I point to the photo. "Is this typical Serb propaganda?" I ask. He looks at me quizzically. "No, the Serbs did not write that. The Dutch peacekeepers did." I find this difficult to understand. "You mean, the peacekeepers thought this about the people they were sworn to protect?" Zoran only raises his eyebrows as if to confirm.

Outside the factory, we listen to Hasan talk about reconciliation. "Reconciliation is impossible if there is no acknowledgment. If there is no acceptance of the past, then there is no possibility of moving forward." We thank Hasan for his time and for sharing his story. Zoran shakes his hand before Hasan retreats into the factory. Walking back to the van, across that lonely piece of highway, my mind is full of condemnation of the Serb perpetrators, of the Dutch enablers. I think of the Serb teenagers, sixteen or seventeen, still children under international law, standing over a kneeling, blindfolded prisoner of war. I try to see myself as one of them, a high school student, face of acne, possessing a personality not yet completely defined and opinions not yet fully formed. I see myself pointing the gun to the back of the prisoner's head with the hateful presence of my commander breathing down my shoulder, telling me that if I do not kill him, how am I different from him? I do not necessarily believe in Serb supremacy; I do not believe these young men should die. I only want to go home. Would I pull the trigger? I want to say that I would drop the pistol and walk away. I want to say I would refuse, refuse to participate in injustice, refuse to be another unthinking cog in a genocidal wheel. But I cannot say anything for sure.

Ahead of me, I hear the German gentleman, a retired journalist, explain the difference between Srebrenica and the Holocaust. "Here, you had a handful of Serb soldiers commit genocide; it was sporadic and of smaller scale. In Germany, there was a complete bureaucracy, an entire machine of death. It infiltrated every aspect of society. It was planned, calculated. It ran efficiently, so very smoothly." It took an entire citizenry to forget their moral responsibility towards the other, to abandon their humanity. "There are ongoing trials in Germany right now, aren't there?" I ask. "A ninety-five-year-old former Auschwitz bookkeeper who is on trial as an accessory to the murder of 300,000 people." "Yes," he says. "Oskar Gröning." I do not know why I say it. Maybe it is because I doubt my own resolve, my own strength to confront injustice, to sacrifice my own being in the name of humanity, to be the lone voice crying out in a chamber full of complicity. "He was only a child," I say. "He only did what he was told." The German's response is strong yet measured, cool yet oddly categorical. "No. There is no excuse. In times of great moral debasement, there can be no nuance. An individual must act, and an individual must choose. He must look beyond his everyday wants, his personal well-being, and inwards to his own humanity. He must see himself in others. Above all, he must think."

On the drive back to Sarajevo, I watch the farmlands twinkle in the afternoon sun. I do not know whether we are in Bosnia and Herzegovina or Republika Srpska. Zoran drives along the narrow roads; fields of remarkable green blanket the horizon. Farmers using antique tools go about their tasks, as their parents did. The other passengers stay silent in the back. From the comfort of our seats, the land looks picturesque, devoid of history and strife. I try to wear the shoes of both Bosniak and Serb, imagining myself in each respective role, killer and killed, perpetrator and victim. But as through a foggy window, I see only blurry figures in indecipherable uniforms, their faces smeared and runny, and I cannot tell which I am. If the Serb, I want to believe I would just walk away. If the Bosniak, I want to believe I could forgive my captor. But this is arrogance. Being outside those specific histories and cultural spaces, and inoculated against their muscle and power, I cannot say anything for sure.

I watch Zoran at the wheel as he navigates the unruly roads with great skill. His eyes look heavy, ready to submit to exhaustion.

Outsiders tend to understand the peoples of the former Yugoslavia as driven by antique hatreds, forever doomed to spin along a vicious spoke of tit-for-tat. Journalists always appear flummoxed by their irremovable opinions and are frustrated that they cannot put aside their differences and come together. Yet reconciliation remains a distant dream. I have no ideas on reunion or settlement; I would not presume to know any solutions. I choose, though, to hold onto an image of Zoran, standing behind Hasan, while he listens to the survivor speak his story. He has just driven another van full of tourists to Srebrenica and has told them the story of hate, betrayal, and death; he has presented the narrative to the best of his ability. And now he shakes hands with Hasan, introduces him, and stands aside to listen. He then takes the group to the town's healing waters in the mountains, takes a sniff, and fills several bottles for his family.

Mountains ring Sarajevo. Any road that leads out from the city centre invariably goes up. And the one I take is called Trebevićka, named for the mountain it reaches for, and winds up from Muslimana M5 towards Regional Road 446, which treads the line between Bosnia and Herzegovina and Republika Srpska. Trebevićka thins quickly, and I soon share the slice of asphalt with speeding pickup trucks, who must find it odd to see a stranger climbing this back road. The city soon dissolves into a string of block-shaped homes with triangle roofs covered in rust-coloured shingles. Makeshift gardens dot the lawns of some. The road rises under drooping spruce branches as the path becomes steeper and steeper, the city falling further below. At the intersection of Trebevićka and R446, Sarajevo seems a million miles away. Here, the green hills undulate in such a harmonious fashion that one could be forgiven for thinking it Switzerland. Islands of pine trees case the distant peaks. Low-lying homes lie scattered in the valley.

Not far along R446, Vraca Memorial Park comes into view. The park, which overlooks the city spreading across the valley below, was built in 1981 to honour the eleven thousand Sarajevo citizens who died during the Second World War. More recently, Bosnian Serb soldiers used its perches and panoramas to shoot and shell the descendants of those same citizens. Since 1995, city officials have given little money for the park's revitalization, and it stands in a forgotten state of disuse.

The park is overgrown: Blades of grass sway in the afternoon breeze uncut. Weeds puncture cement staircases. Shrubs and bushes proliferate unlandscaped. Branches hang across the pathways. Vines drape old buildings, whose foundations appear cracked. On a wall, someone has spray-painted "Kissing Spot" in deep red.

The park is empty except for two young men in hoodies drinking beer. I pass them following a pathway leading into the park's forested area and soon uncover an old Austro-Hungarian fortress drowning in brush. Past it a little further, up a staircase covered in dirt and wood chips, a clearing opens, and at its centre stands a grey monument, almost monolithic, painted with blue and white graffiti. At its base, the earth is blackened as if someone has just had a field fire. In the middle of the pillar, an artist has chiselled a face. The man wears a beret; his short hair is combed back. The bones running under his squinting eyes are sharp and well-defined, as are his cheeks. His neck muscles are tense, stretched. His face is muscular and strong; it exudes power and confidence. He gazes to the distance as if tracking the movements of an animal or army. Yet despite his glare, the artist has not defined the eyes. The corneas and pupils remain obscure, buried somewhere in the stone. The shape of the eyes has not been sculpted, and where those spheres of sight should sit, only uncut rock endures. The sockets are empty, eyeless. The man cannot see. Towards the base of the column, beneath the stone visage and string of sentences, is written a name: "Josip Broz Tito."

6

Drunk in Kosovo

Prizren, Kosovo

May 2016

On a cloudy afternoon in Prizren, I walk along the Lumbardhi River (Bistrica in Serbian), towards the cobbled Shadervan Square, filled with youths milling about like the pigeons congregating around the antique fountain, whose waters, when drunk, are said to guarantee a return to this immortal city sitting diffidently at the base of the chimera-shaped Sharr Mountains, which, I notice, have been surmounted by the sun. Restaurants and bars crowd Shadervan's edges, close to Sinan Pasha Mosque, whose imposing minaret does not scare the scores of waiters who wait on the patrons with trays full of meat and beer, fresh ashtrays, and new serviettes. The proprietors look skeptically at the amber sun, which is effacing the retreating grey, and wonder if they should give the order to roll back the patio covers. On the Ottoman-designed Old Stone Bridge, the criss-crossing citizens close their umbrellas on cue; children emerge from shops, footballs in hand, smiles on their faces. They scurry to the square before kicking the ball, scaring the pigeons to higher ground, up towards the old fortress, Kalaja, which stands guard over the city and has defended it over the centuries from various foes, whose descendants now live together in this young and fragile Republic of Kosovo.

I sense the rains have ended for the day and grab an empty table at one of Shadervan's many restaurants. I order a beer and watch people traverse the square and blend into one another. A group of high-school-aged children flows through the crowds. They lift their heads to the ripening sun, as a flower would, and bounce off and around people hurrying about their business. They are oblivious in a way that youngsters are, concerned merely for their friends, newfound lovers, or other minor catastrophes befalling young people on the cusp of adulthood. They pass one cellphone among them and laugh at whatever shines from the screen. They all wear dull blue jeans and black jackets. The young men have their hair cut short, the young women brandish ponytails. This army of young adults has a certain whiff, a curious confidence, which blunts my previous perception of Kosovo.

The tranquility almost unsettles me. Fed for years on the interminable news cycle of endless violence, rootless refugees, and merciless terrorist/rebel organizations, I am surprised by such an insouciant scene, doused in a carefree vibe. I have come to this corner of northern Albania and southern Serbia expecting gloom and grief.

When I stepped off the bus last night, after an eight-hour trip from Ulcinj in southern Montenegro and through northern Albania, Prizren appeared to confirm my expectations. The bus station was littered with potholes and muddied puddles and was encircled by a steel fence as if protecting its passengers from the menaces lurking outside. Under a light rain, the city looked impoverished. Sidewalks were nonexistent, only slabs of broken concrete. People in monochromatic clothing seemed to blend into the night, only popping out under a street light or when brightened by a fluorescent burst emanating from a closed retail store. I felt the night threatening, full of unseen dangers, and I walked with a sense of urgency, not fear per se, only an awareness of the city's unsavouriness, a feeling of risk, a premonition of dread. As my backpack jiggled and shifted on my waist, I couldn't help feeling exposed, a strip of steak used to lure a herd of coyotes or jackals, and I couldn't help reaching for my wallet whenever I passed a haggard and forlorn face. I often reached for my phone and checked the GPS map to note my whereabouts and the distance left until the hostel. A blue triangle marked my presence on the screen, my hostel, marked by a red circle, less than a kilometre away. I twirled, as did the triangle, pointing me in the right direction. *You're not lost*, I told myself, *only another fool checking his messages or sending a text.*

Across the stream, Prizren's streets devolved into erratic and narrow circles. Cars sat parked on the shoulder so close to the shops that passengers couldn't open their doors. Such little space existed that I couldn't navigate a parked car while dodging the one barreling towards me at a speed unwise for such a tight corridor. I had to wait until it passed, then scoot around the stationary one before the next pair of headlights landed on me. All the while people passed me unconcerned, completely at ease in their surroundings, completely attuned to the risks. I stepped fast and moved with purpose, and my pace did not soften until I saw the sign for City Hostel, dark and unlit, protruding from a sad-looking building painted in a fading grey.

But sitting on the square now, in the light of day, I sense an unmistakable optimism exhaling from the people moving back and forth. Each step seems purposeful and driven, each laugh seems sincere and enjoyed. After years of violence, every citizen seems to savour each moment free of gunfire. But maybe I am naive, maybe my eyes lie to me, maybe my narrative tricks me and blinds me from an actual truth, or the series of truths, or the thousands of opinions, that make Prizren tick and tock. Maybe they sense violence's return inevitable and only want to enjoy a spring afternoon. Maybe they have little hope in peace and believe more in its ephemeralness than its permanence. Maybe the sun, which has now broken through the clouds, is a mere prelude to another squall.

I finish my beer and walk the stream's length. Around a bend, past more mosques and churches, manicured trees, and a few beggar children, I watch Prizren fade into the green hills and then mountains. In my ruminations, I fail to notice the elderly man in front of me, draped in a shawl, with his hand extended, and a crooked smile smeared across his lips. I take his hand.

"Where are you from?" he asks, his shake firm and tight.

"Toronto," I reply, disappointed as I always am when I fail to blend into the ebb and flow of the local milieu.

"Are there many Serbians in Toronto?" he asks, his English flawless and direct.

I pause for a moment and gauge the situation. Is this a test? Is he trying to pinpoint my loyalties? Which side I cheer for? Which flag I fly?

"I believe there are," I manage. "I don't know any personally, but Toronto is a very diverse city with people from every corner of the world."

He nods, his expression jocular and cheery.

"Are there many Albanians?"

His frankness unnerves me. Is my strangeness licence to probe? Does my foreignness permit such delicate questioning? Or, in his age and in his experience, is he past the point of caring? Have such questions lost their political potency? Have they just peacefully moved into everyday parlance, into the simple platitudes of plain greetings?

I look around, expecting to see film crews or hidden cameras, expecting to be a future participant in some documentary or propaganda piece measuring the sympathies or hostilities of every visitor to Prizren.

"I believe there are," I stammer. "But, again, I don't personally know any."

He chuckles, somehow satisfied, and releases my hand.

"I am sorry to hear about the fires in the West," he says.

"Excuse me?" I reply.

"Yes, the forest fires in ... what is the name of the province? ... in Alberta, yes, Alberta."

His sunny visage has sombred; his eyes become heavy, downcast, while his lips fold and curve. I only recently learned about the fires and put them out of my mind, just like that. I try whenever possible to keep Canada in the closet. It historicizes me, reveals my nerves, and I prefer the history and stories of others.

"Yes, I was sorry to learn about the destruction, the pain."

"Thank you," I say, even though in those brief words, he has shown more compassion than I for my so-called compatriots. For as long as I can remember, I have been suspicious of nationalism, skeptical of flags and anthems. In public school, whenever the teacher forced us to stand for the anthem, I was always jealous of the Jehovah's Witness girl who got to leave the classroom and stand outside. Although I wanted nothing to do with her God, the idea that something else beyond a country could inspire such devotion and that could arouse such defiance in the face of tradition fascinated me. I began to ask why I should care more for the well-being of a Canadian than for an ethnic Albanian. I saw that nationalism was asking me to mourn the life of a Canadian soldier more than an Afghan one. Nationalism told me to love colonized rock, to imagine a community where I saw only strangers, to forget the past for the sake of the present. When I thought about Canada, I saw residential schools, slavery, and discrimination. I saw a people who adored wrapping themselves in a flag in order to forget such a history. Nationalism and amnesia go hand in hand. And as much as I wanted to believe that my ability to critique such a reality as well as my desire to leave and experience the world separated me from the others, I knew I remained forever tied to the language of nationalism because it was its silences and its power that provided me with the privilege to move in the first place.

The old man smiles one last time before disappearing into his city. I walk back to my hostel with the image of evergreens on fire dancing in my mind.

"So is Kosovo a country?" Etrit asks while he pours me a beer from one of the several jugs standing on the table behind him. A short and stout man of maybe twenty-five, he is the heart and soul of the hostel, the living embodiment of hospitality. He wears a loose grey sweater, and its hood wraps firmly around his head. A sardonic, playful smile forms on his lips, as he places my beer on the reception counter. He loves joking with his guests, and I'm sure he adores watching the anxiety grip them as they search for the politically correct answer to his question, or at least something intelligent to say about a place they've heard so much about but of which they know next to nothing. He never seems to sleep. Night and day he sits at the reception window and stares at his laptop, surrounded by empty Peja bottles, asking everyone if they would like a beer or a sip of his homemade rakia. He wants everyone to have a good time, to enjoy themselves. Life is a party, he must think. Every day without gunshot is cause for celebration.

I avoid his question. "I met an elderly man today who wanted to know about Toronto's Serbian and Albanian populations. I felt it was a trap."

"No, no," Etrit replies. "Everyone here is curious about visitors. Everyone here wants to know about the world outside."

I have a sip of the beer, and Etrit smiles as if he's won something.

"Just the one," I tell him.

"Of course. Of course."

A young woman in blue jeans and a black top enters the hostel and proceeds to take the seat next to me. Etrit pours her a beer.

"So Katerina, how was Pristina?"

"Boring."

"Oh Katerina, the truth teller. I told you it wasn't the best of cities."

"I did see Bill Clinton's smiling statue."

"Did you take a selfie with him?" Etrit asks.

Katerina laughs and shakes her head. "He's creepy looking."

"Hey, now," Etrit, says, boyishly smiling, "That's the adopted father of Kosovar Albanians."

"There's a Bill Clinton statue in Pristina?"

Etrit glances at me as if I'd just asked if the sky was blue.

"Of course. The Clintons fought for Kosovo independence. They led the 1999 NATO attacks in Serbia that stopped Milošević's advance."

Katerina takes a sip of her beer.

"In the early 2000s, every Kosovar Albanian family was naming their children Bill, Tony, or George," he continued.

Etrit pours himself a beer, then suddenly stops. "Where are my manners? Jesse from Canada meet Katerina from Bulgaria."

We shake hands.

"You're from Sofia?" I ask.

"No. I am not from Sofia. I hate the city. I am from Veliko Turnovo, city of kings."

I put my hands up in faux apology.

"No offence intended. My knowledge of Bulgarian geography is not as strong as it should be."

"Can you name another Bulgaria city?"

"Plovdiv. Varna."

"Oh. Very nice."

"Why do you hate Sofia?"

"Not Sophia. Sofia. Pronounce the *f*."

Her top row of teeth drops to her bottom lip as she hisses *fffffff*.

"It's too busy. Too many people."

"Is Veliko close to Sofia?

"Everything is close. Bulgaria is small. Not as big as it once was. Let me show you."

She points to the green map of the Balkans hanging on the wall, and we slowly approach it. The map is large but not detailed. It has only country names and principal cities. A child's map, maybe. Mountain ranges have been drawn in Bosnia, beaches coloured along the Black Sea. Lines neatly demarcate the countries. Borders are clear and beyond doubt. The country names are written in big black letters. Unmistakable. Every inch of space belongs to someone.

Maps have always impressed me, their power and language. How they order a chaotic world. How they tame geography. How they seamlessly group people and places into tidy little boxes. You need to accept a certain ordering of the world for maps to be legible. To say a country or culture ends at an artificial line is a remarkable way to think.

As a child, I would spend hours spinning my globe and gazing at my world map. I would run my fingers softly over the coloured countries—pink, red, orange, blue—as if sanding them, smoothing the crumpled material. There was something so comforting in seeing the world split like that. Its simplicity soothed my childish worries. Maybe the world wasn't so terrible if everyone could just stay in their little boxes. I would memorize country names and their capitals. I would remember where each belonged. And I would get frustrated, so annoyed, if one split or divided, if my new atlas had a black line where previously there'd been only space. I had to learn a new name, memorize another city.

Katerina points to Plovdiv and her finger moves just north to Veliko.

"It's about three hours from Plovdiv. You need to cross the mountain range."

The mountains on the map jaggedly move right to left and cross from Bulgaria into Serbia. The Balkan range.

"So Bulgaria is considered part of the Balkans?"

She looks at me, and her eyes flash in surprise.

"Of course. The Balkans is a region, not a political unit. Just because Bulgaria wasn't part of Tito's Yugoslavia, people think we aren't part of the Balkans."

She steps towards the map, rests her finger just above the word "Bulgaria," and traces out an imaginary circle enclosing all of Macedonia and parts of northern Greece.

"All of this was once ours," she says, a tinge of melancholy mixed with resentment in her voice.

"I hear that a lot in the Balkans," I say, but she does not respond.

Beside the map, someone has taped a piece of paper listing the top ten European cities for nightlife. In the number two spot, between Ibiza and Amsterdam, is written Prizren.

Etrit has topped up my beer when I return to the stool. His eyes shine with a mischievous light, a toddler caught with his hand in the cookie jar, and he grins.

"Don't fight it," he says.

"Etrit, I had no idea Prizren was such a popular party city. You've even beaten Belgrade," I say, pointing to the list. "When I arrived last night, the streets were dead."

"Did you check inside the mosques? That's where the pre-parties usually happen."

"What?"

"I'm joking, as is the list. Prizren is not the second-best city in Europe for partying. Did you think it was?"

"Of course not," I say, lying.

The beer has already affected me. It tastes of my youth. It recalls those long drinking nights in Toronto, those arguments I would engage in with both friends and foes, those sensations of excitement, of not knowing what the night would introduce. In my university dorm room, drunk on rum and diet Pepsi, we would argue about geopolitics and neocolonialism, about identity and systemic poverty. With my Turkish-Canadian girlfriend, and our other Armenian and Kurdish friends, we would discuss the history of Anatolia, the hushed Armenian genocide, the countryless Kurds, the Sykes-Picot Agreement that carved up the Middle East following the Ottoman collapse, Atatürk and the rise of Turkish nationalism. I would always side with the underdog—the Armenians and the Kurds—against the big, bad Turks. Each person represented their respective people in my mind and became a stand-in for the state and citizens. It's how my mind sorted things then, and sometimes I would confuse their names with their nationality. But in the morning, with a fresh hangover and a mouth flavoured with the aftertaste of rum and cigarette smoke, I would no longer find those discussions as pressing or necessary. As I vomited into a toilet, Kurdish nationalism was the furthest thing from my mind.

"Have you ever met a Bulgarian before?" Katerina asks.

"I have not. Have you ever met a Canadian?"

"I don't think so."

"So what do you think?"

"As dull as advertised," she says and laughs.

"Well, to be fair, I am exceptionally dull. Do not judge all Canadians based on me. Some are almost interesting."

They both laugh.

"Where did you both learn English?" I ask.

"America," they say together.

The hostel door opens and in steps a young man with a toned physique revealed by his tight-fitting black shirt. He has a solid frame, not overly muscled, but trim and defined. His face is smooth and hairless. He looks younger than his age and possesses a boyish charm. Pretty. He is pretty.

He shakes Etrit's hand and the two speak in Albanian. Big laughs separate each sentence, and the two friends slide back into their well-worn routine of camaraderie.

His name is Gëzim, Etrit says, and we all shake hands and make introductions. He works as a driver for a British-owned tour company and has requested Etrit give his clients, a troop of elderly English gentlemen, a walking tour of the city tomorrow.

"Are they staying here, too?" I ask.

"Oh no," Gëzim says. "They're staying in far nicer hotel."

He winks at Etrit while sipping the beer his friend has given him. He takes a seat and leans back into the chair, his legs spread wide.

"So Katerina. What do you do in Veliko?"

"I am student but lead walking tours of the city as well."

"Ah. Like Etrit, here."

"Yes, but I am much better," she says, laughing.

"And what do you study?"

"Law."

"Impressive." Gëzim savours his beer. "How old are you, Katerina?"

"I never say."

"No, no. I don't mean to be impolite." He smiles. "I'll tell you mine if you tell me yours. I'm twenty-seven."

"I never tell my age," she says, suddenly serious.

A silence falls on the room.

"Who wants rakia?" Etrit asks.

Gëzim shoots his hand high. Katerina begrudgingly nods.

"And you, Jesse?"

"I shouldn't."

"I understand," Etrit says, as he places a plastic cup in front of me and pours his silvery liquid. The odour has a fruity quality, and its scent offers a promise of intoxication. It opens a door to my past. Nostalgia fills the cup.

"It's here if you want it."

The cup sits in front of me. I know how it tastes. I know how this ends. But when the three others raise their cups in toast and bring them to their lips, I mimic the action. The alcohol promptly produces tears in my eyes and burns my throat. I cough, as I am out of practice, and the rakia takes immediate effect. The atmosphere suddenly loosens as if one were untangling a scarf in a fire-heated cabin. The lights glow a little more brightly. A stronger effulgence hangs in the air. Everything appears easier and simpler. All the words become effortless, all the answers obvious.

"You've been travelling for four months?" Katerina asks.

"Yes, two more to go."

"Alone?"

"Yes, I can become disagreeable rather quickly." I laugh.

On the train from Ljubljana to Zagreb, I shared a cabin with a young man who was writing math equations on a notepad. We rode past farmlands blending smoothly into the countryside as if the ground had always been shaped as such. Pine trees stood over wind-touched lakes next to villages that seemed untouched by time. Not even a railway station. I couldn't even see a road. I saw people, though, ambling about, doing their work, completing their tasks. The landscape was so verdant and fecund, so rich in potential. The man next to me looked up from his math occasionally and seemed contented by the blue skies.

At the Croatian border, serious-looking officials came and collected our passports. And when my neighbour passed his, I noticed the familiar Canadian coat of arms. A part of me wanted to ask this man from which part of the country he came, to discover what propelled him to this less-visited corner of Europe. But as I watched him return to his notepad and equations, I realized that beyond the opening exchange, determining where in Canada he lives, nothing connected us, nothing bonded us together, except for being members of a fictional space, except for the fluke of being born on the same soil.

As for the things that unite people, the shared ideals underwriting a sense of community and solidarity, I had as much chance of sharing them with the Croatian border guards as I did with this man who happened to reside in the same imagined nation as I. So I decided to let the moment pass in silence; instead, a sense of pride swirled within me. I had transcended nationalism's frivolities and its desire to understand human beings only as flag bearers, only as representatives of certain invented traditions. I left the man sitting there in serene reflection, as complex as other individuals whose passports I hadn't managed to see.

Another man has joined our party in the hostel's reception area. A big, burly, bearish man from Finland, whose English has a muffled, sputtering quality—the sound a car makes trying to start on a winter's morning. He's in his late forties and is a sweater and jeans wearer, the uniform of budget travellers. He knows the Balkans intimately, has stayed in every hostel from Skopje to Tirana, has tried every local dish, sampled each type of rakia. In fact, his name, which I've already forgotten, resembles the word for *soup* in Croatian. He tries to dominate the conversation with his stories, and I dislike him immediately.

"Cigarette?" Etrit asks, and we all rise and follow him outside. Huddled in the doorway and on the narrow sidewalk, we watch cars race down the narrow road. Otherwise, the street is quiet.

"Smoking is Kosovo's national pastime," Etrit declares. "For two euros a pack, how could it not be?"

"It's popular in Bulgaria, too, throughout the Balkans," Katerina says, and she takes a drag from her Camel cigarette. She sits on a step next to a green dumpster. Beside the hostel, there is an empty parking lot. The street lights illuminate the cracked and torn space topped with pebbles and debris.

"Nobody smokes in Finland anymore," Soup says.

"I was on a bus from Dubrovnik to Sarajevo," I say, "and as soon as we crossed the border into Bosnia, the driver lit a cigarette."

"Fucking EU never lets people enjoy life anymore," Soup says.

"Did you like Sarajevo?" Gëzim asks.

"Loved it."

"Everyone loves it; it has a good nightlife," Etrit says.

"I prefer Belgrade's," Soup interjects.

"Well, Prizren has a better nightlife than them all," I joke, and Etrit smiles.

Katerina and Soup snuff out their cigarettes and return to reception.

"Are there many Serbs in the city?" I ask.

"Not anymore," Gëzim says.

"So it's mostly Albanians."

"Yes," Gëzim says, smiling.

"I met a guy in Budva, Montenegro, who was convinced that the Albanians of southern Montenegro and Kosovo would eventually join Albania."

"It's nonsense," Etrit says, shaking his head. "The Kosovo constitution wouldn't allow it." Etrit raises his eyebrows and slaps me across the shoulder. "Kosovo has its own constitution, has a functioning parliamentary system, over one hundred countries recognize our existence. So it must be a country, right?"

"But the UN doesn't," I retort, too quickly. I am speaking too much. Too much.

"Fucking Russia and their veto vote. Putin will drag Serbia back into the nineteenth century," Gëzim says.

A man carrying two white plastic bags filled with canned goods walks past us and towards the closed supermarket at the end of the road.

"I remember the strong Albanian influence in Ulcinj in southern Montenegro." I say. "I loved the mosque overlooking the small beach. Such a wonderful contrast."

"Ulcinj is my hometown," Gëzim says. "But I live in Tirana now."

"Do you like Ulcinj?"

"Of course, it's my hometown."

He says this as if he has never considered the alternative.

"So Ulcinj is mostly Albanian?"

"Ninety-nine per cent," Gëzim says.

"I feel bad, then, for thanking everyone in Serbian," I say, suddenly recalling the strange looks I received at restaurants and hotels.

Gëzim and Etrit laugh.

"So all the schools are taught in Albanian."

"Of course," Gëzim says. "We learn some Serbian too, but all classes are taught in Shqipëri. There is power in speaking your own language. When Milošević tried to prevent Albanian Kosovar independence, the first thing he did was target the language. Speaking Albanian was seen as treasonous."

That point arrives again when my eyes shine and sparkle with tipsiness, and I desire to know the stories of other folks. I rarely stop to ask myself, though, whether my appetite for their history has more to do with my cultural nakedness than a genuine desire to listen.

"Tell me about Skanderbeg," I ask, Albania's national hero.

Gëzim's eyes widen, and he jumps at the chance. Skanderbeg was born in the northern Albanian mountains, he says, in the early fifteenth century, the son of a prince, a child born from nobility. He was raised among lakes and forests and rock. He learned discipline, the importance of tradition. As a form of taxation, however, he was handed to the Ottomans as a teenager, given away as if he were a little present with a big, bright bow. The Turks gave him a sword and a Qur'an and taught him how to fight. He joined the Janissary corps, an elite section of the Ottoman army, composed of kidnapped Christian youth from the ransacked Balkans. He followed the Ottomans as they burned further through the Balkan Peninsula and conquered more and more territory. At the Ottoman defeat at Niš, however, young Skanderbeg defected, returned to Albania, and joined his countrymen in resisting the Ottoman yoke. They elected him commander-in-chief and, under his leadership, Albanian forces successfully repelled each and every Ottoman advance for decades. He became a hero in the Western Hemisphere and garnered support from Christian kingdoms. Within a decade of his death, however, the Ottomans had subdued the Albanians, who would remain under the Ottoman Empire for centuries.

"The area Skanderbeg carved out, is that what's referred to as Greater Albania?" I ask.

"No," Gëzim says. "Greater Albania is an idea from the nineteenth century. It was a dream to unite all Albanians into one country."

It was the dream of the Albanian League, a nationalist organization born in 1878 in the dying embers of the Ottoman Empire. They met in Prizren to discuss what a future Albania might look like and to press for the rights of Albanians throughout the Balkans. They dreamed of a country encompassing the Albanians of Kosovo, southern Montenegro, western Macedonia, northern Greece, and Albania proper, all living together in the same, self-contained house.

"It never included southern Montenegro, did it?" Etrit asks.

Gëzim's eyes turn fiery and shine with rage. He suddenly towers over Etrit, his body taut and wound. His flexed muscles push through his shirt, his frame wrought with a sense of historic injustice.

"Of course, it did!" he shouts.

He switches to Albanian and further yells at Etrit, and the two exchange argumentative bursts, before they both eventually calm down amid bouts of laughter and finger pointing. I am reminded of my Turkish-Canadian ex-girlfriend, whose nationalism bubbled underneath a rather reflective and compassionate exterior. At a local university bar, a hotbed of exaggerated university speak, full of nouns and isms, we would talk about this and that, but her ears would always be tuned to the conversations around us, waiting for the magic word to draw her attention: Türkiye. If anyone were foolish enough to utter the word without decorum or with denigration, her face would frown, flash, and freeze into an image of anger. She would even, at times, depart our table and join the others to correct them about whichever topic they were incorrect about. She would defend her great homeland. Yet she was empathetic to the minorities who had run afoul of Türkiye's great nationalistic and modernizing push in the first half of the twentieth century, who found themselves living in a republic that viewed them as outsiders and incipient threats. She was sympathetic to the Armenian cries of genocide, just as she was concerned about the persecuted Kurdish population. But whenever we argued about each—I, of course, suddenly became an expert on Armenian and Kurdish issues—she could not envision a solution to either because to acknowledge them would be to sign Türkiye's execution order, to admit wrongdoing would leave her country accountable to reparations and vulnerable to claims of justice demanding atonement. And whenever we hung out with our Armenian and Kurdish friends, there was a whiff of animosity between them, not as people, but as representatives of their various communities. Or that's what I sensed.

Inside, Etrit hands out cups full of beer and rakia. He's in his element pouring out drinks and laughing. The alcohol has suppressed my normal inhibitions and lessened my usual anxiety. I feel so young again. So full of words and opinions. The room flows in an uninterrupted orchestra of sound and movement. The conversations drift in an unstructured and improvised fashion. Soup talks about his bartending job in Turku, Finland, about his distaste of Finnish life and culture; Gëzim regales us with his adventures driving foreigners through the back roads of Albania, Kosovo, and Montenegro. Etrit speaks briefly about his job leading tourists around Prizren and how he loves teaching newcomers about his city. Katerina tells about her experiences in America, about working odd jobs in Montana and Ohio, about her love of Newport, Rhode Island, the best city she has ever visited.

"Newport seems a random city to fall in love with," I say. "Why did you like it so much?"

"The water, I guess," she says.

Gëzim takes another shot and tells us about his best sexual experience. No one asked him. No one wanted to know. Yet I've noticed this among some men, regardless of their country, a certain desire to disclose the intimate, and it is never intimate in the sense of some deep-seated turmoil, some moral or ethical conundrum. They are always tales of conquest, always stories of submission, as if they speak about hunting animals, the thrill of the track, the pleasure of the kill.

"She was the hottest woman I had ever seen. Supermodel hot. And it didn't matter if I was in a relationship. I had to do it. I felt compelled."

Once, I was in a bar in Busan, South Korea, among fellow English teachers in a packed haunt along Gwangalli Beach and listened to an African American man and a white South African man compare the physiology of Korean women to other women of the world. They rated their pros and cons and discussed the best methods for approaching them based on cultural traits. What was remarkable throughout their conversation was how their words, their ability to classify and dissect, seemed to collapse all difference between them. They became citizens of the country of men. Of course, I did not ask the African American man about his experiences of prejudice in South Korea, the stares and gawking, the times when taxi drivers refused to pick him up, nor did I ask the South African about the white professional exodus from his country, about the problems he may have encountered in Busan because of the Korean Education Ministry's desire for North American accents, or about why so few Black South African teachers were present in the country. I did not need to. All difference between them lived; all the subtleties of lived experience seemed to vanish in their appraisal of Korean women. They became men of the world.

I take another shot and watch Soup shuffle on his feet. His stomach hangs over his jeans; blood flushes his shapeless face. His glasses perch on his nose. Soup chats about his time in Thailand, about the country's low cost of travel, about the sense of freedom, about the country's sensuality, its palpable feeling of desire. I stop listening, sip my beer, and remember a time in Quebec City with my Turkish-Canadian girlfriend. Walking through the enchanting Old Québec, the street lights illuminating the charming townhouses painted in light pastels, we fought. I told her about a time in Innsbruck, Austria, before we had officially gotten together, when I sat in a bar with a Romanian woman who looked like Kate Hudson. She drank straight whisky and talked about her experience living and studying in Austria. She got drunk. Her words started to slur, and her eyes sparkled. Outside the bar, on a wintry night, she wanted me to follow her home, but I said I couldn't. She wanted me to at least kiss her good night, but I said I couldn't. And when she walked away in the falling snow, she said I would regret my decision. My girlfriend wanted to know why I didn't kiss her, and I told her because she was too drunk, and it would have been wrong. She glared at me while we climbed Rue Sainte-Famille. She said I had no right to judge the Romanian woman as without choice. She said I had no right to see her as a wilted flower in need of the benevolence of some stranger. She said I had no right to render her actions insignificant just because she had drunk one too many whiskies for my liking, just because I had seen her as a girl in need of protection, not as a woman who makes choices and evaluates risks in a world that would rather she be dead than an agent operating with imperfect means. She said I had no right to become her father. And as we further debated the line between agency and structure, between consent and intoxication, I knew my real reason had little to do with her apparent drunkenness and everything to do with responsibility. What is owed another human being during a one-night stand? When you enter someone's home, place your coat on a chair, have a glass of water, and then warm a cold body, what bonds are sewn? What promises are silently made? What connections linger after you have departed the home, the city, the country? What doors have you forever closed? I left the Romanian woman in the snow because I did not want the work. I did not kiss her, because I wanted to kiss everyone and no one. How can you kiss an entire world?

Soup has finished his story, and when Katerina gets up and exits the building, cigarette in hand, I follow her. We sit on the front step and stare at the forlorn street.

"When I was coming here by bus from Veliko," she says, "I had an eight-hour layover in Skopje, Macedonia."

"Did you like it?" I ask and light a cigarette.

"No." she says, and I laugh.

"Why not?"

"Everything is so fake there. They try to make everything Macedonian. You've got the statues of Alexander the Great, the great

Greek warrior. You've got statues of Saints Cyril and Methodius, creators of the Cyrillic alphabet, Byzantine Greeks both of them."

"Are Macedonian and Bulgarian similar?"

"Almost exactly the same. I understand Macedonian. Yet in the National Museum, in Skopje, they say Macedonian is its unique language, has its own unique culture. Both Macedonians and Bulgarians descend from Bulgars and Slavs. We were once part of the same empire."

"And you want it back?" I say and grin.

"It should be ours," she says, grinning too. "They have no right to invent history."

"Every country invents its past or forgets it. It's amazing what one can accomplish if you only tell certain stories."

She looks at me softly, unsure whether it's a question she should ask.

"Do you know the etymology of *buggery*?"

I shake my head.

"Bulgars," she says.

She stares at me, her eyes thick with a mixture of melancholy and malice.

"The Bulgars are one of the ancestors of modern-day Bulgarians. They established Bulgaria as the literary centre of Slavic Europe and carved out a Bulgarian culture from the Byzantine Empire."

She turns away from me, her anger barely contained, on edge of saying something drastic, important, something she hates to utter, which makes it all the more necessary.

"*Bulgar* became *buggery*."

"Why?" I ask.

"There was a medieval Bulgarian sect, the Bogomils, I believe, who challenged traditional Christian teachings. They rejected all of the church's most important sacraments and were hunted as heretics."

She looks at me, her face hidden behind a cloud of smoke.

"*Bogomil* became *Bulgar*, which became *bugger*."

Her eyes flash and her smile returns. She gives a light chuckle.

"In the western European imagination, we became a synonym for what they saw as a loathsome, bestial act. We became a crime against nature in their minds. We were parasites."

And, again, she shifts from poignant to prideful, and I watch her taste her own anger and own her foreign words, bending and breaking them to her will and liking it. Each word has a vehement flavour; each sound drips in venom. She must grow tired of justifying her country's existence to people from bigger, more boastful ones.

"Do you like leading tourists around your town?" I ask.

"It's a well-paying job. I make more money working a couple of hours a day every week than my parents do in a week."

"Yes, but babysitting the tourists must be a real chore."

"They're not all bad. I like the ones with questions. I don't mind babysitting the children if they're eager to learn."

"I have a question, if you don't mind."

"Go ahead."

"Are there many Turks still living in Bulgaria?"

"In the south, close to the Turkish border."

"And in Veliko?"

"Not too many," she says, her eyes soft with a slight glare, a barely perceptible sheen.

She sips her beer as I do mine, and I wait until she is ready to explain.

"In 1876, there was an uprising in Plovdiv, and the Ottomans, busy fighting in Bosnia, unleashed the bashi-bazouks, a group of ruthless Turkish mercenaries, to put it down. They massacred fifteen thousand Bulgarians."

She goes still. Cigarette smoke lingers above her head. Somewhere a car door slams. Voices burst the silence.

"When the Russians took Veliko from the Ottomans," she continues, "when Gurko entered the city on July 7, 1877, the people rioted and began to burn the mosques. As Bulgaria rose again, won its statehood back, people took their vengeance, took their pride back."

When I returned from Türkiye for the first time in high school, my friends wanted to know all about it. They asked me whether they had cars in Türkiye, whether they had buildings. No one has ever asked me if Canada has buildings, if Canadians drive cars. When I met my Turkish-Canadian girlfriend for the first time, I told her all about my trip to Türkiye, how much I loved the old Roman temples, how much I adored Cappadocia and its weird rock formations made from soft tufa, in which persecuted Christians once hid when Anatolia was pagan, before it was Christian, before it was Muslim. She smiled with great patience, and corrected my pronunciation with delicacy, as a schoolteacher might. And when I told her my friends didn't know Türkiye had cars, she shrugged her shoulders, and said, "You can't know anything about a place you don't think about."

Inside, the music blasts. Etrit says not to worry, as we are the only guests. He lights a cigarette and pours out the last of the beer. He says now we have only rakia to drink, but no one minds. Etrit has handed music control over to us, and each of us takes a turn walking through the "staff only" door and into the main office, which sits in a charming state of disarray—empty beer cans and rakia bottles, piles of unsorted papers, books and binders, crumpled cigarette packages—and selects a song from YouTube. As each unknown voice serenades me in an unknown language, the others discuss its relative position in the great gamut of Balkan singers. They exchange unusual names—famous crooners from Bosnia, Bulgaria, Croatia, Kosovo, and Serbia—and debate their best songs. The voices are wonderfully unfamiliar, and I feel the drunkenness taking over: the hazy lights of unreality, the strange place between sensibility and sleep. Clouds of cigarette smoke hang in the air, the rakia flows, voices rise. The scene reminds me of bars from my youth, before non-smoking signs infiltrated the spaces and robbed them of their atmosphere, where I would sit with my friends and yell to be heard and wait for a song I knew to come over the speakers, so I could feel alive, feel the music inject me with its rhythms and sounds, feel it lift me high with life and purpose.

I ask Etrit if I can play a song, and he says, "Of course." I choose one of my favourites, and I return to my stool and listen as the frantic piano playing fills the room. Its infectious energy transports me to ten years earlier in a basement apartment somewhere in downtown

Toronto. We were saying goodbye to a friend moving to Ireland in the coming days, and before we headed to a local bar, I played this song because it described perfectly, for me, the indescribable qualities of friendship: what it means, how it survives, how it grows. The song speaks to honouring the past without becoming ensnared in it, without drowning in nostalgia, and points to the future, the uncertainty of older age, of taking all those experiences with you into the next and next and next. The song is about aging with dignity, about lasting companionship, about embracing all our little imperfections, all our big mistakes, and taking those memories, cradling them in our arms, and storming into future's darkness. No matter what befalls us, the song says, we will be alright because we have this. We have this. Friends.

My girlfriend glared at me. Outside, we shared a cigarette, and she said I had no right to play the song or to claim the room as my own. "This is her night, not yours. She decides the music, not you. You talk about friendship, yet you cannot let her choose the music on her final night out with us. It's not about you."

"It's not about you."

My anger rose not because she was wrong but because she was right. My discontent intensified because I couldn't see it, because I had to be taught something, because I possessed an answer that was incomplete, inadequate. Soon after, she threw a party at her apartment, and her Kurdish and Armenian friends arrived. On her balcony, she sat between them, her arms flung over their shoulders. She asked me to take a picture. They were all smiling when I pressed the button. Later, she posted the photo on Facebook with a caption expressing love for her friends. And I commented, in a failed attempt at wit, that I don't understand what the big deal is, since you all look the same to me. I suppose I wanted to show how silly the antagonism existing between their respective communities was, how on the individual level they have more in common than history would suggest. I only wanted to say how similar we all are underneath our purported differences, differences often highlighted by self-serving politicians looking to rouse the support of nationalists, nationalists who have little interest in uncovering shared characteristics between people, who desire to separate the world into spheres of family and strangers.

My girlfriend said she did not like what I wrote. She said at best, I sound like one of those universalists who try to erase difference in the name of some ill-defined human solidarity and, at worst, I sounded racist. She said the remarkable thing about the photo is it shows how they became friends, differences in tow. "Difference is good," she said. "We honour our differences in the name of friendship." I did not respond because I was defeated, but in my mind, the conversation continued. *But,* I imagined saying, *that's unlike how many Turkish nationalists think wherein they use difference to construct borders, wherein they mould history to suit a particular narrative.*

"Do you think I am my country?" she asked. "Do you think I am only my flag? I am free to define what my Turkish identity means to me and no one else. Not you. Not Erdoğan. I can love my country without being enslaved to it. My idea of Türkiye is mine. And other people may have their own ideas, more closed ones, but the wonderful thing about ideas is that they can change. They are not fixed. They are not rooted. In any event, Jesse, you cannot ask people to sacrifice their national identity in the name of friendship or solidarity, especially for those people who have experienced dispossession, who have experienced the humiliation of colonialism, who have languished under the foot of another. Tell me, Jesse, have you experienced any of that?"

My song ends with a whimper, and the group begins to disperse. Gëzim wishes us goodnight. In a few hours, he will be wishing his clients a good morning and driving them around Prizren's surrounding mountains and then depositing them here for Etrit's tour.

"Good night, mysterious Katerina," he says. "One day, I will discover your age."

They shake hands.

"Never," Katerina says.

I thank Gëzim for the history lesson, and he says goodbye to Etrit and Soup. Soon Katerina and Soup, too, after taking their final shots, bid their good nights and stumble up to their rooms.

I stand with a cup in my hand as Gëzim holds his. I thank him for his hospitality and give praise for his generosity. Never in all my travels, I tell him, have I met a more affable host. And we down our final gulps of rakia as the 4:00 a.m. muezzin call to prayer rings out from the nearby mosque.

We shake hands and, as he grips mine in a forceful hold, he asks, "So is Kosovo a country?"

What can I say? What is a country?

"Is it?" he asks again.

"Absolutely," I say. "Absolutely."

The following afternoon, I am hungover and in church. Katerina and I and the elderly English gentlemen have been following Etrit around Prizren for the last hour as he teaches us about Kosovar history. The Serbian Cathedral of Saint George, tucked just behind the Sinan Pasha Mosque, is our last stop. Inside, the nave is austere and abstaining, its walls painted in a piercing white. No seats criss-cross the church's floor, an unfortunate occurrence as I would kill for a bench to sit.

Etrit shakes the hand of a hefty man adorned with a flowing beard and dressed in an equally flowing robe. The priest welcomes us and speaks a little about the church's history, a little about the importance of Kosovo to Serb spirituality and identity, about how in 1389, the Serbs lost their independence to the Ottomans here in Prizren, and remained under their control for the next five hundred years. He talks about how the church remained a source of pride and solace through those difficult times. He tells us about how challenging life is for Serbs in Prizren, about how only two dozen remain after the violence in 2004, about the destruction, the looting, the deaths. He says Serbs are slow to return. He says his church has been restored with the help from the international community. He is a humble man and speaks delicately, as if each word were a privilege that could be revoked at any time. He thanks us for visiting, shakes Etrit's hand, and returns to the interior chamber from where he came.

Outside, I ask Etrit about the violence the priest spoke of, about what happened in 2004. He tells me that in mid-March of that year, rumours began circulating that some Albanian boys had been chased by a group of Serbians and their dogs across a bridge in the central Kosovo town of Čaglavica, whereupon one boy slipped, fell into the river, and drowned. The rumour turned out to be false, Etrit says, but that did not prevent Albanian mobs in Prizren from attacking anything Serbian. The vandals killed eight Serbs, injured 170, and displaced hundreds more. About eight hundred Serb houses were burned along with eighteen cultural monuments and thirty-five religious buildings. The Albanians, Etrit says, were not just rioting against the rumoured drowning, but they used it as a pretext to settle old scores. They desecrated symbols of the Serbian soul, for which they had little reverence after decades of debasing treatment from the bearers of those same symbols, after years of fighting Milošević's nationalistic madness.

Etrit thanks us for coming on the tour and reminds everyone about the barbecue he is preparing tonight—meat, salad and, of course, rakia. The thought of alcohol makes me sick.

I leave the group and hike to the fortress. I pass children, kicking a red ball along the steep streets, who wave at me with big, bright smiles. I pass another Serbian church standing desolate and silent, ensconced in a mountain crevice. The breeze picks up and dries some of the sweat pooling on my skin, my body trying to rid itself of the last drops of rakia. The weather is cool and lovely. On the fortress ruins, a few teenagers sit and talk. The sun has begun its descent, and the light is soft and welcoming. I walk to one of the crumbling walls and see Prizren lying in front of me. A dozen or so minarets point to the sky. The stream cuts the city into halves and travels out beyond the buildings and roads to the mountains that look so lazy and tranquil from here, so nonthreatening. Maybe it's the sun breaking through the clouds, or the breeze, or the ancient bridges connecting each side of the stream, but I feel so relaxed and grateful. For what specifically, I cannot say.

I try to picture the advancing Ottoman army, cutting and killing its way through the town seven hundred years ago, but I cannot see it. I try to imagine the Serbian army terrorizing and belittling the ethnic Albanian population, but my mind stays in the present. I try to envision those Albanian mobs burning Serbian churches but cannot hold the image. Instead, I look at the terra cotta roof tiles resembling the crimson sands of heat-beaten desert. But the city is not barren as a desert is. On the contrary, even from this height, it is easy to tell that Prizren beats with life on this Saturday afternoon. I wonder what each person below will discuss this evening when they meet with friends and family. Maybe the continued poverty. Maybe the high levels of unemployment. Maybe the threat of renewed ethnic tension. Maybe they will discuss what their new country will look like in fifty years, for despite the history, a history that should not be forgotten, Kosovo is still at the beginning. And the best thing about beginnings is the endless possibilities.

7

God in Blue Trainers: An Afternoon in Albania

May 2016

Skanderbeg sits on his horse, an emblem of power, the magnificent animal drawn to halt. The equine's front-right knee bends at a right angle while its breast shoulder twitches in exertion. The head and jowl fold towards the neck, the mouth opens, the nostrils flare from discomfort. Its eyes gaze at the ground. The rope tightens in Skanderbeg's left hand; his forearm flexes, and muscles ripple across the skin like water touched by wind. The general controls his animal and has adorned it with an elegant halter, necklace, and saddle, on which he sits thick and powerful as an oak trunk. He has dressed for war. Iron covers his entire body, except his arms, which are the size of babies; his hands could crush bone. A thorny flail lies secured to his thigh; his chest expands, puffed and inflated, as if he had just swallowed a child whole. He has a straight, gently trimmed, beard that points sharply ahead. Everything about the man pushes forwards through whatever thing foolish enough to stand in his way. His stern face commandeers men and inspires hope and fear in equal measure. Men and beast bow for him. What terror he must have evoked in the Ottoman army for decades—this former Janissary turned Albanian national hero, the pride of Europe, the man who protected Christian Europe from southern Islamic incursions, the man who united all the disparate Albanian tribes into one whole—Skanderbeg, the father of Albanian identity, a symbol of unity.

Below Skanderbeg's statue, I look through my camera's viewfinder and wait for the perfect shot. To the left, a pole rises above the statue, and from its top hangs the red Albanian flag. I wait for a breeze so to pull the flag taut and reveal the black, double-headed eagle. Legend says that, at Krujë Castle, north of Tirana, Skanderbeg flew the flag in defiance of the Turks, even when they eventually swarmed and overwhelmed him and his forces in 1468. The flag would not fly again in an independent Albania until 1912.

When the wind does come and lifts the flag from its slumber, the crimson red evokes a stream of blood while the eagles and their feathers resemble a burnt, blackened ribcage. The flag now ruffles over Skanderbeg's helmet—a perfect image that marries man and his symbol. But after I snap the release of the shutter and capture the picture, I analyze the frame for composition and placement of elements and notice that in between flag and statue climbs the minaret of Et'hem Bey Mosque, and it climbs higher than both Skanderbeg and his eagles.

I follow Skanderbeg's gaze across his square to a rectangular building sitting on the other side of the busy boulevard. The concrete building strikes me as lifeless, a rather perfunctory, functional, and brutal design—a fortress or a cage used to intimidate and humble the beings strolling under its watch. But I notice atop the entrance a patchwork of colours brightens the grey and sombre building. It is the National Museum, and the colours are a mural.

Thirteen figures grace it. Each one acts; each one looks determined. At the mural's centre, a woman and two men march towards the viewer, as if about to break the plane, stride into the world, and shout at the people taking their photo. They appear confident with much to say. The woman wears a billowing white dress decorated with tiny stars around the bottom and secured at her waist with a bright belt adorned with a golden two-headed eagle. She raises a rifle in her right hand and extends her left high into the air in triumph, in victory, in defiance. Yet her face is serene, emotionless, bloodless. She expects conquest. She expects to vanquish her foes. And with her arms held high, she says, *Behold, we have arrived as we said we would.* The two men stroll beside her. One wears basic brown trousers and an apron over a white dress shirt. His sleeves are rolled up, exposing his defined forearms, and he has flung his jacket over his shoulder. The second dresses much more regally. He wears boots and a long, flowing jacket while a military cap balances on his head, and he has tied and knotted a red bandana around his neck and, behind him, the red flag unfolds in the wind and above his cap are the two black eagles of prey.

The figures on either side of the three stand in an eclectic mix of clothing and stances. A woman in a white headdress and green dress holds a musket and stares across her body with malice. A man coated in iron aims a bow and arrow at an unseen foe. Another man with a brown beard readies a spear and holds a shield. Another blows a horn while brandishing a sword above his head. Another poses and holds a rolled piece of paper and flaunts a well-sewn suit. Others still raise fists and more rifles.

The painting has a message. These men and women in the background have acted like a barricade or shield throughout history and have protected their homeland from every conceivable enemy. The mural tells a story of development, of a progressive evolution from then to now along a defined line running straight across history's annals. Despite the invasions and conquering, the cultural upheaval and rearranging, these characters know where they come from. They can trace their origins, it seems, to a period before Rome, before Greece, to a time when Europe was merely rock and water, when there were only mountains, and those mountains were ruled by the most skilful archers. But now, the mural says, a modern people have emerged from the work of the ancestors, the progenitors; their preservation has produced the new Albanians, a woman and two men—different, yes—but they still remember the work of those behind them. They have come from their history.

Inside, the museum itself confirms as much. Consisting of nine pavilions, the National Museum charts the evolution of the Albanian people. Although the displays have largely been written in Albanian, and the small English summaries read awkwardly in cumbersome syntax, the nine sections, with their statues, relics, and objects, remain surprisingly readable. All museums are inherently political, all are contested spaces; yet in most, especially in those places where questions linger—of identity, of self in relation to the world—the museum becomes a temple of truth, a guarantor of a particular story. It promises stability in a history that undulates like the Accursed Mountains in the country's north.

The first pavilion, Antiquity, showcases the Illyrian people. The Illyrian culture emerged in the western Balkans near the middle of the Bronze Age, 2000 BCE, and flowered in areas now called Montenegro, Macedonia, and Greece. Authors from antiquity have recounted how the Illyrians were hospitable people yet skilled warriors, known for their archery, their skill at hitting moving targets. Display cases from this period hold painted ceramics and other prehistoric pottery. Artistic ornaments and weaponry buried with women show how much respect Illyrian cultures bestowed upon women. During the Iron Age, the panels continue to tell the visitor, the ragtag group of Illyrian tribes and confederacies was further consolidated. Illyrian urban centres emerged in the fourth and third centuries, and little boxes hold bronze coins indicating that these cities conducted trade and commerce with the growing Hellenistic world around them.

This thread—Albanians are direct descendants of Illyrians, and the Illyrians are original inhabitants of the western Balkans—runs through the entire museum. It argues that Albanians have forever struggled to maintain a vestige of that identity whether submerged under the Greeks, Romans, Byzantines, Slavs, Bulgarians, Serbians, Ottomans, or Italians. It contends they are the region's true autochthons, the original inhabitants, and what was once taken from them should be returned.

In the entrance foyer, I sip from a cup of instant coffee. On a bench next to the ticket counter sits a sturdy man with long brown hair. When he sees me idling by the doorway, he leaps to his feet, and extends his hand. I take it in mine.

"Are you a tourist?" he asks.

"Yes, I am."

"Oh good. I am an Albanian tour guide myself. I am actually waiting for my two German clients who are visiting the museum. The museum doesn't allow independent guides to lead groups around. Where are you from?"

"Canada," I say.

"Wonderful. I love Canadians. They fall nicely between Americans and British. They possess the intelligence of the Brits but none of their relentless seriousness, and they possess the carefreeness of Americans but none of their ignorance. Not too serious and not too dumb."

He comes closer and his jovial face suddenly clouds.

"Will you do me a favour? Tell your country about us."

"Tell them what?" I ask.

"That Albanians are like your Native Americans. We are discriminated against on our old land. We are suffering."

"Will you tell them about us?" He asks again. "Will you tell them about us?"

I have arranged a day tour to Berat, two hours south of Tirana, with a local tour company. The owner has told me over email that he has a man who can take me, but he is not an official tour guide and cannot provide the information a more schooled one could. He says that this inconvenience will affect the tour's price in my favour, and I agree to be taken to Berat, city of windows, by a man named Afrim.

He drives through Tirana, manoeuvring us through its dizzying roundabouts and swollen streets and onto the highway leading to the coastal city of Durrës. Afrim is the second Albanian I have ever met, and he is a gentleman. He speaks English in a flowing, lyrical way, peppered with a slight London accent developed from his years working construction along the Thames. His demeanour emits a softness, a willingness to listen to and answer even the most simple of questions. His body relaxes behind the wheel; each movement, whether changing lanes or driving in reverse, is done in a calm and collected way. He is courteous and well-mannered, empty of any pretension or posturing, free of any conceit.

I met my first Albanian eleven years earlier at a university party in Copenhagen. An exchange student, I was led through the crowds by my student mentor Marcus, a Dane of Pakistani origin. He seemed to know everyone, greeting tall men and women with hair the colour of hay and skin the colour of snow, and introduced me to each with a polite smile. When I asked him if he minded answering a personal question, he said only if it's not about his ex-girlfriend, whom I accidently met fifteen minutes earlier while looking for Marcus. A woman pouring and distributing beer from silver kegs pointed to a tall man in glasses and said, "There he is." Handing me the plastic cup, she seemed cold and joyless, whereas Marcus, thin and tall, had the friendliness and playfulness of a puppy.

"Have you suffered any discrimination based on your immigrant status?" I asked, and Marcus replied, "Not really," before grabbing and shaking the hand of a short, thick man in blue jeans and leather jacket. The man manifested bravado in his every motion. He was aggression incarnate. Because of the piercing, deafening music, a distasteful example of uninspired techno, the man leaned into Marcus to make himself heard, and each time he did, I thought that every one of his sudden, jerky movements forwards would be followed by a right hook or an uppercut. An incipient, menacing violence lurked within him, I felt, and lived within his marrow and cells.

"This is Besnik, from Tirana," Marcus said, and the man immediately lunged towards me and placed his lips under my right ear. "A motherfucker wanted my shoes!" he shouted, and then pointed to his blue trainers standing atop the chipped, wooden floor. "He offered one hundred kroner for them," Besnik said. "Can you believe that? I paid three times that much. Disrespectful. He disrespected me." "What did you do?" I asked. "I told him to go fuck himself," Besnik said, staring at me with his unblinking eyes. "Nothing more?" I asked. "A man disrespects you like that, and you only give him a warning? Why didn't you make him give you that respect back?"

I was drunk and loved Besnik for the clown he was. Not a man, only a bucket of undiluted testosterone. His was the comically tragic character—the macho man. You take a bunch of insecurity, throw in a dash of bellicosity, and you get the masculine man-child thick with rage, so much to prove to the world. I always had a fondness for the excessively virile male, the man who communicates with clenched fists and flexed biceps. I had studied him the way an anthropologist studies the inner workings of alien cultures. I had watched him in his natural habitat—bars, clubs, gyms—marvelled at his ability to become enraged at the slightest provocation and wondered how it was he had become so one-dimensional, so fixed. And although I knew that men like him could snap at any moment, he did not scare me in any tangible sense. I merely enjoyed the show and egged on the performer as one would at a wrestling match.

"Next time," I said to Besnik, barely containing my laughter, "you make that man offer you a decent amount for what is yours; you make him respect your blue trainers." Besnik raised his plastic cup, and I brought mine to meet his. I watched him interact with Marcus and the few others who came and went, entering and departing the conversation as seamlessly as the wind, and I noticed that they all, including Marcus, gave Besnik a wide birth and studied his movement, his shuffling feet, how he turned his body, where he placed his hands, the ways he spoke so closely, so intimately. They all feared him, all dreaded the violence prawning under his skin, and now, sitting next to Afrim, I wonder whether it was the man or the country they feared. Did the descriptive phrase "from Albania" affect their reception of Besnik? And I, who never ceases to be amused by the tantrums of masculine men, I suddenly wonder if an occasion ever exists to warrant fighting over blue trainers. Just because I have never felt the need to exchange blows over shoes does not mean there are not places in the world where trainer ownership may not be so trivial.

"Have you heard of the pyramid crisis?" Afrim asks me as we drive along the highway.

"No."

"It's why I left Albania in 1997."

"What happened?"

"Albania had just transitioned from the dark years of Enver Hoxha. Democracy came in 1992, and people were ready to make money. Markets had been liberalized. Capitalism had arrived. New companies popped up promising fast cash, big money, and people invested and invested and invested. And, of course, all those companies soon collapsed."

Afrim checks his blind spot and flicks his indicator before he changes lanes, gliding effortlessly to the left, and passes a slower-moving vehicle. After allowing for a safe distance to pass, he repeats the process, only this time moves to the right.

"People lost everything. The country squandered over a billion dollars. Gangs controlled cities, the government was toppled, and violence was everywhere. Over two thousand people were killed. People ran, and I went to England. Those were tough times. No one was spared."

Afrim says that *Albanian* became a bad word in Europe. Adjectives such as "shattered," "lawless," "wrecked" filled newspapers worldwide and ruffled the brows of curious readers, who could not remember whether Albania was real or not, but soon it became very real. Albanians suddenly arrived in all corners of Europe from an unknown, corrupt country—part Christian, part Muslim. They were viewed suspiciously and were not welcomed. Italy declared them undesirables. Greece locked its borders. They became dark cosmopolitans, disavowed global citizens, with families and feet in many lands.

"In London, I worked in construction. Long, hard days. We did the work that no Englishman would do. It was secure, paid okay, but there was no life. Work every day. I returned to Albania last year to find more of a life. Life in the West is too mechanical, too soulless."

Afrim has done undignified work in numerous countries. He speaks several languages well and adapts to any milieu. He finds calmness and purpose everywhere. He is a member of the paperless proletariat, globalization's bastard children—the shuffling masses of displaced persons hungry for the chances they find under cool western skies.

"Westerners do not understand that their economies would end overnight if all migrants or illegals were suddenly rounded up and deported. We are the unseen, the engine. We are the invisible muscle. And no walls, no matter how thick or high, can stop us."

I nod and tell Afrim about seasonal migrant workers in Canada, the Mexicans and the Jamaicans, imported to plant and pick onions, carrots, and cauliflower. I tell him I see them every spring and summer working the fields near my house, backs bent in labour, their jeans blackened from dirt, their hands striking the soil, their faces somewhat covered by wide-brimmed hats, somewhat shielded from the sun that inches above the farmlands, black and green, cut into long crop rows, over the sprinklers, and over the signs reading "Farmers Feed Cities." I tell him they can claim few benefits, cannot unionize, can rarely leave the farms, except to buy groceries and other supplies. They feed Canadians, their work fills fridges, and facilitates the entire agricultural and service industries, yet they enjoy few of their rights and privileges.

Afrim nods as if all this sound familiar. "And still people view migrants as lazy, as criminals. *Albanian* means 'dishonest' for many. It is difficult to swim against the stereotype."

Yes, stereotype. The power to take a complex thing and reduce it to something simple and standard and reoccurring, and to take that simple thing and make it applicable to an entire group, to stick it and plant it deep inside the skin, into the blood and bone, until it becomes stuck and permanent, of the soul and temperament, natural and unchanging.

Not long after meeting Besnik, I was watching Spike Lee's *Inside Man* on my computer, about a band of unorthodox bank robbers. To create confusion about their intentions for the negotiators and officers camped outside the Wall Street bank, the thieves play a recording of Enver Hoxha—Albania's eccentric dictator, who ruled the country in a haze of paranoia and violence for forty years—whose fiery and unrecognizable tongue confuses the cops. In a moment of brilliance and knowing they live in New York City, a modern-day Babel, the detectives play the speech over a loudspeaker hoping it will attract someone familiar with this curious language. Soon a muscled officer approaches and says he recognizes the language.

"The man is speaking Albanian," he says. "Albanian?" one detective repeats, befuddled, the word feeling unusual on his lips and tongue and sounding obscure to his ears, as if it were some place he had associated only with myth and legend. "What does it say?" the other detective asks. The man laughs: "I have no idea. My ex-wife is Albanian." And he looks at the detectives with enlarged eyes suggesting an unspoken language among men with untamed and unruly ex-wives. The film cuts to a black-haired woman in a tight green dress and push-up bra. She wears an array of golden rings, necklaces, and bracelets. She hands the detectives a blue bag full of loose paper and demands that they take care of her parking tickets in exchange for translation. The detectives reluctantly agree while she opens a fine case, removes a thin cigarette, and is about to light it when one detective reminds her that she cannot smoke in the police trailer. She playfully pouts; her eyes droop while her bottom lip trembles. Her face bargains and negotiates, and the detective eventually acquiesces to her demand. The recording plays, and when she exhales, the smoke drifts across the detectives' faces, and she giggles and giggles, not at the smoke but at the voice. She says she knows to whom the voice belongs but will not disclose the name until they take care of her tickets. The detectives again agree. "It's Enver Hoxha," she says. "He was the president of Albania." One detective becomes annoyed and wants to know how the former president of Albania could be robbing a bank in New York City. "It is a tape of him," she says, "discussing how Albanian people are great people. How they are immortal people." She says she had to listen to all this propaganda in school, about the virtues of communism, the evils of capitalism, the greatest of Lenin, Marx. She seems proud that knowing Albanian has finally brought her some benefit outside of the country, saving her hundreds of dollars in parking tickets. Yet beneath her comic and sexy and dangerous exterior, a subtle subtext of melancholia is perceptible in her bravado and boldness. She seems sad that she, maybe, once believed it, once believed that Albania was immortal, that the small European country was the centre of the universe. In any event, the detectives do not care and quickly usher

her out the door, never to return to the script, she a handy stereotype to move the plot forwards, to show the ingenuity of the robbers, how novel it is to use Albanian history to cover their true motives.

Afrim laughs when I recount the scene.

"Yes, Albanians are horrible drivers," he says sarcastically.

He shakes his head and smoothly passes a transport truck.

"Have you seen the *Taken* movies?" he asks. "Those films have set Albanians back a generation."

I have always had a soft spot for the simplicity of revenge fables. I have always silently cheered when the wronged person, through many trials and tribulations, cuts down the parties who have hurt her, demeaned her, when, in the end, covered in blood and bruises, she savours an antiquated form of justice: a limb for a limb, an eye for an eye. So in *Taken*, when Liam Neeson tells his antagonist, an Albanian, over the phone, after listening to his daughter's kidnapping, that he will pursue him, will find him, and will kill him, I feel my skin tingle with excitement and righteousness. These people will pay. These people will suffer. The viewer rejoices as Neeson hunts down these hyenas, packs of trafficking Albanians, on Parisian streets, as he murders a dozen of these savages with his bare hands, and as he electrocutes another beast for information. Neeson fights not only for his daughter's return but for Europe's future, the film suggests. He has the resolution to do what the French authorities will not: he takes back Europe from the darkness creeping over its borders. These people, the film shows, come uninvited to Europe's warmer corners from darker and colder places with unsavoury and un-European histories. They stay here illegally. They deal drugs and traffic in weapons and women. They prey on the dreams of lily-white girls. Watching Neeson return a measure of justice to the world, the audience participates in the collective bloodletting, and applauds and claps as Albanian goats are paraded through a French town and slaughtered for their sins, the mutton served to a ravenous French populace.

But looking at Afrim now driving over a highway, surrounded by sparkling green fields, I wonder why Albanians were chosen as the traffickers, why them over any other nationality?

"How many Albanians did Neeson kill?" Afrim asks.

"I lost count," I say.

"I suppose it doesn't make sense to keep count after ten. The point has been made."

I remember the Albanians in the film and how they wore leather jackets, had their hair combed back, slick and shiny, and smoked incessantly. I remember how I knew they were criminals before they even spoke, before they even did anything. I just knew.

Outside, arrows of light drop and slide through the dissolving clouds and onto the fertile grounds washing the landscape in richness. I think of Besnik again, all tough and tenacious, railing against the insult done to his blue trainers. And I wonder how much of him I actually saw, how much was my reaction predetermined by unexamined images or untranslated messages I devoured every day. Was he one of the many who had fled Albania during the pyramid crisis seeking refuge in northern European countries? Would I have responded the same way to another male acting in a similarly foolish macho way, or was there something about Besnik specifically that stirred my mockery?

"Did you know that Albania was the only European country to defeat the Axis forces singlehandedly? We overthrew both the German and Italian forces." Afrim says this with little emotion; he relays only a fact.

"I did not," I say.

We arrive in Durrës, the port city and newest vacation spot for Tirana's well-moneyed. The Greeks founded the city in the seventh century BCE and, ever since, Durrës has seen no shortage of marauders who sacked and then rebuilt the city, only then to watch the next wave of invaders sack and rebuild it again. Afrim also tells me about the oil production happening offshore, about the apartment blocks appearing overnight, about the hordes of vacationers descending on the city in July and August, about the rush of development that has overstepped the demand, leaving many apartments in these shiny blocks empty and dark.

On this late-May afternoon, however, a drowsiness floats throughout the city, the streets are quiet, but the evidence of boom is ubiquitous.

Yellow construction cranes stretch and extend towards the sky. Along the pier, brown and grey cargo containers lie stacked on top of one another in neat rows. Buildings rise half-finished: only the bottom halves are covered in windows; the tops appear exposed, unprotected, gutted.

Afrim says in August, red and blue beach chairs, and multicoloured umbrellas blanket the sands and, from above, the umbrellas remind one of mushroom patches. Hawkers atop donkeys prowl the beach, traversing its multi-kilometre limits, and sell various treats and refreshments so that the beachgoers need not move at all. Discotheques blast music from their sound systems until the sun rises, until the young families with shovels and pails replace those revellers who now stumble home drunk and happy. "Durrës has many faces," he says, "and each negotiates with the other for time and space to create a happy equilibrium among the diverse guests' intentions and desires." He says he would never buy property constructed on sand. "Sands shift," he says. Sand is unreliable. He does not trust quickly built things

Driving along Durrës's main boulevard, I cannot see the Aegean, as a barricade of ochre-coloured buildings blocks its view. I can only assume its presence. I imagine the oil rigs nestled out in the water, floating and undulating in the waves, their pipes pounding the seabed and pulling up petroleum. I imagine the wondrous views from the highest apartments and the new windows and metals sparkling in the light and the new families up there cooing and sighing as they watch the sun disappear into the sea. When I open my eyes, however, clouds still cover the sky, and the sidewalks are deserted, the buildings half-built.

"Welcome to the new Albania," Afrim says.

Outside of Durrës, a team of tourists pedal along a highway that has cut communities into two, with no crosswalks or traffic stops available. I see a man on the shoulder waiting to cross four lanes of traffic to visit the other side of his community. "Capitalism and development," Afrim says, "have little time for community." We drive past wheat fields, vineyards, and fig farms. Cattle and mules plod along the sides of the road chased by trim men in grey wool sweaters and holding whips and scythes and pitchforks. Agriculture still beats in Albania's economic heart, despite the opened markers, foreign investment, nouveau riche, and aid packages.

I gaze out the window at the nearing mountains poking the clouds that have gone from grey to blue, getting heavier and plumper. Mountains have always inspired me. Growing up in Ontario's rural flatlands, among its puny hills and knolls, I always longed for British Columbia's craggy and bold Rocky Mountain peaks, as I adored them for their inviolable strength and immobile power. I had seen nothing so elemental, so primal as a mountain range, the perfect blockade from the outside world's threats. When I was in high school, my mother and I went to Alaska, where we visited Denali National Park, home of North America's highest peak. After an hour's hike, we stood atop a mount and stared across rolling green hills to Denali standing serene in the distance, covered in snow. I told my mom I could live here, build a nice little log cabin, and spend forever admiring the mountain's elegance and poetry, thinking of words and phrases to describe its shape, power, and beauty. My mother laughed, touched my shoulder, and said I would get bored quickly.

Approaching southern Albania's mountaintops, I believe my mother: I do not possess the mental resiliency or psychological creativity to withstand decades living in the mountains' crevices. Mountains are best enjoyed sparingly for a bracketed period of time before the enjoyers retreat to the comforts of their abodes, refreshed and cleansed of the desire to live more in tune with nature's vagaries. The ancient Albanians, however, called the mountains home and lived within them separately in their own distinct clans, with their own particular traditions, isolated and hidden, until Skanderbeg called them together in the fifteenth century. In the northern Alps, the Ghegs lived by their set of rules and regulations, an ancient constitution called the *kanun*, inherited from the Illyrians themselves. The kanun outlined all acceptable social interactions, all taboos and offences, taxations, and obligations. The series of laws, more importantly, tried to regulate the *hakmarrje*, or blood feud, which was endemic in the more remote communities and ravaged its members. The hakmarrje sought to bring some semblance of justice to secluded communities living far away from more lawful centres. In the name of retribution, the code sanctioned revenge killings. If you kill a member of my family, I kill a member of yours. In its words, the oath sounded so brutally simple, so viciously fair. But in its popularity, in its deadly efficiency, the code cut down entire groups of men, depriving the area of a young workforce. Scores of young men went into hiding, deeper into the forests and mountains, hoping the feud could be resolved without their blood spilling. For this reason, many northern Albanian houses became fortresses built in stone, ancient bunkers, with a few slots serving as windows. There, imprisoned, young men waited and hoped they could one day leave and rejoin the world.

"The practice still happens in some northern parts of the country," Afrim says.

I think of the isolation those young men must experience confined in their prisons, how fascinated yet terrified they would be of the world outside. How paranoid they would be of any rustling pine branch or scurrying rodent.

"Albania has a rich history in paranoia," Afrim says. "Under Hoxha, the entire country feared what they could not see. They fiercely believed that the world was ready to invade—Yugoslavia, Russia, the United States. Everyone and everything were an enemy. And you can see what the results were."

Afrim points to what appears as a massive grey water lily sprouting atop a green field.

"Hoxha built over seventy-five thousand of those."

Bunkers. Steel and grey bunkers that could withstand a tank. Steel and grey bunkers that appeared on beaches, playgrounds, and hilltops. Steel and grey bunkers with little windows and ledges, on which soldiers secured their sniper rifles, stared out into the world in silence, and waited for the war to come. Steel and grey bunkers that reminded every peasant and intellectual, every schoolteacher and party member, and every man, woman, and child that strife was soon.

"Fear is a powerful unifier," Afrim says. "When you believe everything outside your borders can kill you, when you believe the enemy knocks on the gate."

Afrim tells me about Enver Hoxha and his trust issues. He removed Albania from the Warsaw Pact in 1967, believing it had lost its Marxist ways, and moved closer to China—until he broke off with the red giant in 1978, thinking it had moved too close to the West following Mao's death. Hoxha was infamous not only for his isolationism but for his purges. He murdered anyone he suspected of dissidence: old comrades, party members, intellectuals, priests, heroes, friends, former girlfriends. He crafted his cult of personality with meticulous care and rewrote history books to exaggerate or altogether fabricate his role in Albania's history. And when he finally died in 1985, he left Albania unprepared to finally meet the world in the early 1990s.

Fear has a high political currency and yields wonderful results. I imagine families poisoned by hints of ideological infidelities while they implode in hails of accusations, betrayals, and turncoating: spouse against spouse, sibling against sibling. I imagine schoolchildren at wooden desks scribbling communist commands under Uncle Enver's photograph, he in a smart red tie and simple overcoat, with a fox smile and omniscient eyes, his hand an iron fist punching the sky, the young pupils staring at him, digesting his lesson, his every hint and clue.

When I was a child, I believed our new house in Bradford was haunted. Everything I saw—how the clouds mingled in the sky, how the crumbs on the floor aligned, how a particular door closed, how an old photograph looked under certain light—convinced me that our house had residents not of this realm. Although these signs terrified me, I was secretly excited for having seen them because no one else had, not my sisters, not my parents. I held the key to a secret world. Something had chosen me to reveal its knowledge. And what I began to fear was not those things going bump in the night, the ghost in the closet, the goblin under the bed, but the opposite: I feared their inexistence. Because if they were not true, if they were falsehoods, what did that say about me? What did it say about what I had believed, cherished, revered?

We drive along Osum River under blue-hued clouds whose soft bellies are eviscerated by mountain peaks, and before long the countryside cedes to the streets and boulevards of Berat. Afrim searches for the road leading up to the citadel, Berat's ancient bulwark against the outside world. He stops at a group of gentlemen playing backgammon and asks where we may find the entrance to the citadel. In a flurry of gestures, laughs, and smiles, one man points south to a road bending up towards the sky. Afrim waves in thanks, and we depart.

Berat is nicknamed "the city of a thousand windows," and each one stares at every moving pedestrian as if in a string of eyes shimmering from the whited stone of the old Ottoman houses. Everywhere in Berat, I get the sense of being watched, gawked at, ogled. You note your behaviour more, more aware of your hands and body, more cognizant of your movement, because behind each glass sheet could shine a pair of black eyes hunting for any error or misdeed.

We pass the Muslim quarter, with its ascetic mosques and donor outlets resting beneath the limestone peak of Tomorr, before we circle back through the brutally designed new Berat, an ode to Stalinist architectural precepts, with its bare apartment blocks and wide avenues, and climb the dizzying roadway beside bending pines and rocky bulges to the rusted door that has protected the valley and its citizens for centuries.

"Welcome to Kalaja," Afrim says.

The fortress has stood for centuries and borne to witness to a slew of prowling peoples, a revolving door of swords and shields. Lines of lampposts go unlit along cobblestoned pathways past the stone walls and watchtowers covered in wild grasses. The grounds possess a bygone feel, a sense that Kalaja has passed its prime and has become just a monument to the past—a curious museum in need of a weeding.

"People still live here," Afrim says while we walk past two farmers plying the hills with spades and shovels below a reclusive Orthodox church whose quiet power ruffles the calm. He buys a basket of cherries from a woman selling her produce and offers me one, which I take. I feel the fruit in my fingers, firm yet tender, and note how its cardinal colour contrasts with the deadened and dingy grass, the overwhelming grey daubing the fortress along with the sky, a brownish tinge painting the environs dull and dreary on this dry, late spring day. The cherry holds the day's last remaining colour.

We climb to a viewpoint overlooking the Osum slinking beneath Tomorr and beside Gorica, the old Christian neighbourhood with a smattering of houses resembling copper-coloured pebbles. Other visitors balance along the edge with cameras slung around their necks, trying to capture the best panorama of Berat's mountains, rivers, and houses. I follow suit with my own camera and scan the horizon with my viewfinder, but wherever I look, wherever I settle my lens, Berat refuses to cooperate; it is too unwieldy, too unruly. The city rejects the stable confines of composition.

"Do you know the legend of Tomorr?" Afrim asks. "How the mountains of Tomorr and Shpirag sprang into being?"

I shake my head.

"The two big mountains in this region, Tomorr and Shpirag, were once giants and were once brothers," Afrim begins. One morning, Tomorr was slicing long grass in the fields when a young woman walked barefoot past him. The light cast the entire meadow in glitter while the grass and oak leaves sparkled in early morning dew. Tomorr dropped his scythe, shielded his eyes, and fell in love. Adoration struck him small, as in that moment, he was no giant but a babe in the presence of an angel. She was the most beautiful woman he had ever seen, her loveliness unmatched in all of Illyria. Despite his renowned shyness, his insecurity around anyone except his brother, he approached her that morning and asked her name. "Beauty," she replied in a half-smile. "My name is Beauty." "Beauty," Tomorr replied in shocked reverence, struck still as he was by her eyes shining as round and lustrous and solid as gemstones. "Beauty," he said again. "I love you very much." And he took her hand and led her back to the open meadow, where they sat and talked and laughed.

That same morning, not five kilometres away, Shpirag was working his fields. With his spade, he cut and hacked the black earth, preparing it for planting. He whistled a melody to himself and was generally pleased with how his work was going. The sun warmed his angular face, and his body, despite being in a state of labour, felt limber and loose and young. Of the two brothers, Shpirag was the social one, always saying the right thing, always making the funny joke. So when he saw a young maiden moving beyond his wooden fence, he greeted her naturally but soon realized, as did his brother not three hours earlier, he was in the presence of the divine, because the young maiden was sublime. No words did her beauty justice. She was to be admired, venerated. "Beauty," she said. "My name is Beauty." "Of course, it is," Shpirag said. "Anything else would be an insult." The two talked for hours under the high sun, but when Shpirag whispered "I love you," he did not know that his brother had himself surrendered the same declaration with a similar seriousness and solemnity.

Beauty visited both brothers in secret, and both brothers fell more deeply in love with her. One afternoon, Tomorr was raking and bundling his hay when he spotted Beauty descending a knoll in the distance. He looked harder, squinted his eyes, and then he frowned. She was not alone. A man walked beside her, and he heard her laughter, as musical and melodious as when he made her laugh. Then he heard the man's voice, and it was unmistakable. He dropped his rake, grabbed his scythe, and marched towards them. Shpirag saw his brother approach pointing his scythe at him, and he dropped Beauty's hand and readied his cudgel. Tomorr's eyes were as black as obsidian, his voice thunderous, his words striking like lightning, "Brother, she is mine." Shpirag raised his cudgel to his brother as to an unknown enemy and screamed "You are wrong, Brother. Beauty is mine!" Shpirag swung his cudgel, but Tomorr evaded it, and as Shpirag lifted his bat for another strike, Tomorr sliced his brother's back from shoulder to hip and then again and again and again, leaving long rows of scratches like claw marks. Wounded, Shpirag sank to his knees, but as his brother crept in for the kill, he mustered one last swing and landed it across Tomorr's face, breaking his nose and jaw, and cracking his skull. And there on the grass, the two brothers died together and eventually solidified and hardened into mountains.

After both brothers died, Beauty walked slowly through the meadow before dropping to her knees. From her eyes dropped two tears, which slid down her cheek and fell to the ground. Then dropped two more tears and two more and two more until she was sobbing and shaking. She cried and wept and howled, and her tears saturated and flooded the ground around her. And as she cried, her waters rose and rose until they touched her knees, belly, shoulders, and finally her lips. She could not stop crying, even when she was under water, even when her lungs filled with liquid, even when her heart stopped beating. Her tears created Osum River, which flows under the peaks of Tomorr and Shpirag.

As he finishes his tale, I detect an authenticity in Afrim's words I cannot describe. His words, his story, affect me because they seem unplanned and unpractised. I am not a tour guide, he keeps reminding me, yet I believe him more because of that very fact. Although the typical distance and imbalances within the paid and payee relationship remain intact, Afrim's nebulous position as an unauthoritative, unlicenced escort gives him a flexibility and freedom I have rarely seen among other tour guides, who follow the same script, recast the same jokes, mirror the same itineraries. Afrim has the independence to wonder and to reimagine. At times, I feel he is rediscovering his country along with me.

I study Mount Tomorr across Osum River, which today has few of Beauty's tears, and think about how ugly love can become when it parallels obsession, when it signifies control, when it turns into hatred's twin. I think about how the discourse of love can take a person and transform him into a monstrous, unrecognizable thing.

"Enver loved Berat," Afrim says. "He said it was the prettiest town in all of Albania. He called it a living museum." We follow the stone fence in silence until Afrim points to Mount Shpirag and encourages me to look closely. I squint my eyes and have trouble seeing what Afrim points to. Then, I distinguish faint white lines from the grassy mountainside, and I follow their movement and edges and shape until the word "NEVER" forms in my eyes.

"It used to say 'ENVER'," Afrim says. "The villagers in these parts have long debated Enver's legacy and argued over the virtues of the man who loved their Berat." The surrounding evergreen hills seem calm, but the tranquility hides the unsettled whispers spoken by villagers who have climbed Shpirag's face with buckets of paint three times to debate Enver's history. They first ascended the mountain in 1968, with mules and pails of whitewash, under the explicit instructions to paint in bold one-hundred-metre-high and sixty-metre-wide capitals "ENVER" to remind the countryside of who gave them everything—and they did. In 1994, the post-communist government threw napalm at the mountainside, stripping the name, wiping the memory. But in 1997, true-believing communities urged the villagers to return to the top and repaint the heroic lettering, to recall the man who gave Albania to Albanians, who provided them with a proud life, and who was ready to die defending the sovereign eagle drenched in blood—and they did. In 2012, the villagers returned, ruminated, and resolved to move the N before the E to spell "NEVER," to honour the past, prepare for the future, and recast their unfulfilled demands as citizens of an independent, democratic, multicultural country—and they did.

We pass under the Orthodox church's lonely cupola covered in terra cotta tiles; a small metal crucifix juts out from it.

"Enver did not like competition for his affection," Afrim says. "He made the state officially atheist in 1968." Afrim pauses and looks solemnly at the church, perhaps reflecting on a question he has longed debated. "After that year, Hoxha closed over seven hundred mosques and over six hundred churches and monasteries. He purged the clergy. Some churches were burned to the ground."

I used to daydream about a similar happening. For as long as I can remember, I have disputed God's existence and have disavowed his compassion. I stopped believing in God long before I stopped believing in Santa Claus. Growing up in rural Ontario, I was stuffed with Christian propaganda on a daily basis. Christian morality tenets, as well as allusions to Christian biblical stories and parables, saturated many of the books I was required to read, of which, because of my secular upbringing, I was blithely unaware. People told me to keep Christ in Christmas; people acted offended when I told them I was never baptized. Children told my sister she was going to hell because my parents were not married. The way the Bible could turn seemingly decent people bad disturbed me. I saw classmates advertise their homophobia unreservedly simply because they interpreted certain passages from a thousand-year-old book to condemn love between human beings of the same sex. I saw how the Bible's teachings on gender, the appropriate behaviour for girls and boys, moulded and shaped dispositions and quickly cordoned off acceptable roles and responsibilities for each. I was appalled that I owed the preachers of these religions—whether priest, pastor, reverend, or even rabbi or imam—respect simply because they were men, or sometimes women, of God, as if that in itself justified the reverence, the fawning adulation.

It wasn't atheism's adherence to science that mainly attracted me. Although I admired the attempts of biology and physics to decentre God as an explanation for the origins of the universe and human life, and much preferred descending from an ape than from Adam, it was atheism's willingness to critique the God character, to put Him under the same scrutiny as any other human being, to challenge His ethics and His teachings that inspired me. Nothing is beyond reproach, not even God.

The more I read of this God—a God for whom violence, jealousy, and wrath seemed to come as naturally as oxygen to human lungs—the more I could not understand how He aroused such devotion among His billions of adherents. He did not deserve our love. He did not deserve our adoration. He did not deserve our glorification. I watched Him turn millions of people into judgmental, hate-filled ones. I watched Him take life's complexity, the unbridled confusion of existence, and melt it down into memorizable slogans and chants. I watched Him shrink and suffocate love until it resembled only unquestioned loyalty, until it became something horrible that flattened and straightened any rough edges. God's love strangles.

I became a follower of the new atheists, particularly Christopher Hitchens. He put a language to everything I felt and thought. I watched YouTube videos of him, religiously, in which he massacred some hapless lemming of some ancient belief system. He schooled them with his rhetoric and knowledge, as he cited effortlessly from dozens of texts and quoted scores of philosophers. He embarrassed them and left them speechless and flustered. I loved how he took the sacrosanct, the untouchable, and pinned it to a pad and dissected it, with his sharp, silvery scalpel, like some dead reptile, how he yanked God down from His cloud and cut Him with saws, scissors, and forceps. Hitchens was not afraid to offend.

Nor was I. An acquaintance of mine, a friend of a friend, was a practising Christian, a polite and affable young man whose decorum and decency irked me. I felt him disingenuous, his benevolence a mere performance. I saw his behaviour as a subtle act of proselytizing, an advertisement for the detached tranquility of the Christian life. I understood his enthusiasm for prayer, his love of Christian rock, his zeal for quoting passages from the Gospels as evidence of his simplicity, his superficiality, as proof of his cosmetic intelligence. I despised his assuredness, the inner peace that must come from surrendering all critical thought and directing all doubt to the dictates of a single book. I wondered how he could love a God responsible for so much evil in the world. I pondered how he could ignore his religion's role in sponsoring colonialism and the slave trade, in promoting misogynistic witch hunts, in sanctioning the killing of independent thought, in condoning the worldwide spiritual destruction of alternative viewpoints and cultures. Had he no shame?

In a Toronto bar one night, I sat across from him among a larger group of friends. Soft ambient music played, the pints flowed merrily, the conversations were spirited, and the candle wicks danced in the low light. Through the bouncing and flickering glow, I watched his freckled face laugh and giggle and smile, and I was overcome by revulsion. His grin, his voice disgusted me, and in a moment of blind rage, fuelled by alcohol and my own sense of superiority, I attacked. I accused his religion of being synonymous with hate, his God of being a tyrant, and his flock of being unthinking automatons with a slavish desire to exist only for his glory, to live only to please him. My legs shook and my voice elevated. I demanded he apologize for his church's role in history's long river of blood. I told him to take responsibility for what his fellow worshippers have done in his God's name. I wanted him to own his church's history, and I wanted him, here and now, to beg for forgiveness, not for original sin, not for the slaughtering of the son, but for the slaughtering of us, of human beings, residents of this world, the only world, who have had to live with his God's merciful madness, His suffocating love, for far too long. He did not rise to my verbal assaults, did not respond in any forceful way; he just sat there and absorbed each blow, his face serene and dutiful. He seemed to grow stronger with every insult, and the calmer he became, the angrier I got. And as my friends screamed at me to shut the fuck up, to stop being so obnoxious, so judgmental, so simplistic, I suddenly felt crude and heavy and cumbersome, simply stupid like a stone that keeps rolling and rolling and rolling.

I revered Hitchens a little less after that, especially after I found he had supported the American invasion of Iraq with great gusto and had layered his arguments with atheistic sentiments. His rhetoric disturbed me in that it mirrored all too easily the thinking he critiqued, the dogmatic kind—thick, rigid, parochial. He stuffed his arguments with childish binaries—good and evil, light and dark, civilized and backwards—and did not allow for any nuance, any grey, any doubt to enter his analysis. In one video, he chastises a rabbi for circumcising his son, equates it to child abuse, and asks the man if he has no shame. As much as I agreed with him about the suspect practice of cutting the genitals of a non-consenting child to solidify a covenant with God above, I could not help but feel embarrassed for Hitchens. He beat the man into stunned silence and piled on the insults and accusations until the rabbi simply cowered in his chair, sullen and defeated, until Hitchens, despite all his talk of atheism's privileging the thinking, of its unquestioned commitment to freedom, began to resemble the autocratic God I had read so much about and come to dislike so greatly. I had become like Hitchens, simply a drunk at the bar, only an arrogant louse who points and shouts and accuses like God Himself with his finger wagging from some distant cloud.

Looking at the forlorn Orthodox church, one that had survived the purge, I think Enver had simply replaced God with himself, had simply placed himself on society's apex, atop some haughty cloud. I picture the churches set alight and imagine flames burning through the naves and pews and desecrating the altars and mosaics. I envision the adherents gathering around the fire and weeping and watching as the grey smoke floats through the black, starless night, listening as the wood crackles and splinters and breaks, and I feel guilty for having thought such an image as a necessary prelude to a freed and dignified existence.

We walk through the web of Ottoman homes whose coppery terra cotta roofs burn the grey skies. White stones rise and round into oval shapes holding closed wooden doors. The neighbourhood appears intimate, as if everyone sips from the other's tea, yet not a sound rings from the interior, no greetings, no conversations, no arguments.

"Some of the homes," Afrim says, "have been abandoned, the families gone to Tirana looking for work and a better life."

The pathways are rocky and unwelcoming. Some flowers have wilted. A cat scurries past. A German tour group sips from soup bowls at an intimate café. Their tour leader barks that this is the last chance to use a restroom for several hundred kilometres. A line forms in front of the solitary toilet. Murmurs of discontent begin. The afternoon humidity arrives, and everything gets heavier and longer. Staff members clear the tables. We walk back towards the car amid the boarded homes, solitary farmers, and scattered tourists.

"Berat has struggled in the democratic transition," Afrim says, as if feeling the need to further explain the atmosphere. "People do not have jobs. Universities have closed. Corruption is widespread."

"Do people often long for the old times?" I ask.

"Some," he replies.

He takes a moment to adjust his thoughts, deciding how best to describe Albania to an outsider who knows nothing of its textures, hues, and gradients.

"Albania has an identity crisis. We are some of the earliest settlers in Europe, yet we have been conquered by so many people that we do not know what is ours anymore."

He gazes towards the distant mountains, the warring brothers at peace, their bodies still scarred from their ancient battle.

"Christianity. Islam. Communism. Capitalism. These are all alien things."

I see a minaret below reaching to the sky.

"Nowadays, some Albanians want to see the Ottomans, the Turks, as our brothers in Allah. They want to view the Ottoman period as a rosy one. They forget that the Albanian language was banned. They forget that Albanian children were conscripted into the Ottoman army. They forget the taxation. They forget the humiliation."

In the distance, sunrays sever the plump clouds before they explode in light.

"The Ottomans were not our brothers but our occupiers."

Back in the car, we descend through the narrow path over cobblestones and past rusted and broken cars.

"We must choose the right path ahead, a path grounded in our realities and in our needs. We can be anything, so as long as we choose."

By the river, we park the car. A shepherd herds his goats over the dry embankments. Under the Gorica Bridge, they chew on long grass. Afrim and I stroll in silence towards the city's heart. I spot a kiosk that stands in front of a large concrete space on which stand the Lead Mosque on one side and Shen Dimitri Orthodox Church on the other. They face each other and release their respective worshippers onto the world.

I ask Afrim if he can buy me just a single cigarette from the kiosk, as I am trying to quit. He asks me if I smoke a particular brand. I do not.

He explains the situation to the woman, who produces a single smoke and a few words that make Afrim laugh.

"She says you have a made a wise decision. Smoking is bad for you and any less of it helps."

I nod my head and smile in thanks.

At the car, before our journey back to Tirana, I smoke my cigarette and ask Afrim about his life back in Albania.

"I enjoy my life in Albania. I don't need to work so many hours to have a good life. I do odd jobs here and there. Maybe one day I will become an official tour guide."

"Maybe you should," I say. "You're good at it."

He smiles.

"These days, more and more people are returning to Albania from abroad. Some of them are experiencing their country for the first time."

He is silent for a moment.

"There is a lot of uncertainty about the future," Afrim says. "But it is good to know that a future exists, and we Albanians can shape it."

On the drive to Tirana, the highway winds through fields of green warmed by soft sunlight. Women and men work the land. Just beyond their working bodies, in the distance, Durrës rises in opulence, the shimmering buildings standing half full on shifting sands. Democratic Albania is only twenty-six years old, still so young, yet so robust and vibrant as well. Energy is here, yet in which direction, for what cause, such human creativity will fly remains the unanswered question.

In the heart of downtown Tirana sits a rather ugly concrete pyramid. The structure often catches visitors by surprise, as it appears incongruent with the surrounding architecture and infrastructure. It sits just north of the Park on the Artificial Lake, where children ride tricycles and frolic in the shallows, where young lovers walk hand in hand through passageways under canopies of green leaves, and where young, muscled men challenge one another to pull-up competitions on red bars. It sits just east of Blloku, the city's trendy upscale neighbourhood—former residence block of the communist elite— where the wealthy sample burritos and savour cappuccinos and party until dawn. It sits south of the massive roundabout, the National Historical Museum, and Et'hem Bey Mosque, and west of sprawling roadways lined with student housing.

From whichever way one happens across the pyramid, its sudden appearance, as if some kind of spaceship had landed, shocks the senses. Party loyalists built the pyramid after the death of Enver Hoxha in 1985. The pyramid would both serve as a museum, a secular temple to the late leader's greatness and gently remind citizens that his work, the communist revolution, was an always-in-progress event, never safe, never finished, never satisfied. The pyramid took three years to build, but two years after it opened in 1988, communism fell, and the country's history was about to be rewritten.

Since Albania's emergence from its isolation, the pyramid has served a myriad of purposes and has undergone something of a transformation in meaning. In its early days, it served as a memorial for persecuted and killed activists; during the 1999 Kosovo crisis, it operated as a humanitarian centre. News channels also have operated from it. Nowadays, it is vaguely described as a conference centre. The state, however, has long debated destroying it, razing it, and using the prime real estate for more modern purposes. Yet the pyramid has become a rallying cry for the citizens, a site of protest and solidarity, a symbol of the past's brutality as well as the future's hope.

Standing in front of this monstrosity, I am awed by its ugliness. It is undoubtedly the work of megalomania, befitting a man who considered himself God among men. But in its dilapidated state—its chipped concrete, broken windows, graffiti-sprayed slopes—the old pyramid casts a melancholy pall. It reminds me Ozymandias's fate, the inevitable destiny of all those who think themselves above time or immune to the universe's awesome indifference. In Hoxha's memory, teenagers now race up the slopes, skateboards underarm, pause near the top to absorb their city's fine views, its ever-evolving state, before skating down the concrete, balancing on their boards and directing their energy to new and exciting places.

Afterword

COVID-19

In January 2020, I submitted my thesis for my master's degree in refugee protection and forced migration studies—a two-year distance education program offered by the University of London. My thesis examined the 1972 decision of the Pierre Elliott Trudeau government to accept thousands of Ugandan Asians who had been expelled by Idi Amin in August of that year. I argued that despite Trudeau's rhetoric that Canada had a humanitarian obligation to help these people and that such a noble gesture would follow in the country's proud humanitarian tradition, the decision to resettle these expellees was ultimately self-serving. Since many of these Ugandan Asians were university educated, had highly skilled jobs, and could speak English, the Trudeau government decided to intervene in the Ugandan crisis because the decision ultimately benefitted the Canadian state; it represented nothing less than a transfer of skilled labour from a developing country to a developed one under the guise of humanitarianism.

I had enjoyed researching the project, especially poring over the documents and files from the National Archives in Ottawa. I liked reading about how different government officials thought about these expellees, how they weighed the positives and negatives of their resettlement, and how they could frame the Ugandan Asians' acceptance in such a way that the Trudeau government and Canadian state ultimately benefitted. Yet I had felt my time spent in the archives shielded me from the real-world experience of actually working with displaced persons. From the second-floor reference room, I would take a break from photographing pertinent documents and gaze out the large windows to the Ottawa River and Gatineau in the distance, and I'd think about that world outside. The windows felt like a barrier, or a border, between the historical research I was conducting and the lives of displaced persons I had read so much about.

So when I handed in my thesis in January, I decided I would spend a few months volunteering with displaced persons somewhere in the world. For most of February, I researched different volunteer opportunities in Calais, Athens, Lesbos, and Kuala Lumpur, but decided on Lebanon because I had spent some time researching the situation there as part of one of my courses. I applied to an NGO working in the Beqaa Valley close to the Syrian border and was accepted to start volunteering there in April. In the interim, I would travel for a few months in Southeast Asia—Taiwan, Myanmar, Laos, Malaysia, Singapore—countries I had never been to before. At this point, I had travelled to 103 countries and was desperate to add to my list. I felt excited, ready for the next step. I had lived with my parents for the last few years so that I could focus on finishing my studies. But now I was finally prepared to stand on my own two feet.

The novel coronavirus 2019-nCoV did not at first concern me. I thought after an initial scare, the illness would eventually fade away and be no more a concern than the coronaviruses that preceded it, such as SARS or MERS. The Wuhan lockdown had successfully contained the virus, I reasoned, and those few cases that did manage to escape the Chinese government were no more harmful than the common cold, especially for younger people like me. Even when the first case arrived in Canada, I felt safe, since the Canadian government assured its citizens that the 2003 SARS outbreak had taught it some tough lessons about coronaviruses and how they spread, and that the country's health-care system was better prepared this time around. And I would not let a virus stop me from taking this next important step to re-enter the world of movement. So despite the swirling uncertainties about this virus and its potential threat, I left Canada for Taiwan on February 26, confident that COVID-19, as the virus was now called, would have little or no impact on me.

On the flight from Vancouver to Taipei, about half the passengers wore masks, which I thought an overreaction, a capitulation to the increasing hysteria around the virus. In Taipei, authorities took COVID-19 seriously, requiring people to have their temperature checked whenever they entered a museum or a hotel. Flights from China had been banned. On the streets, everyone wore masks. Hand sanitizers were everywhere. Gradually, my thinking changed. Given Taiwan's success in curtailing the virus's spread, especially given its proximity to China, I thought the virus's worst excesses could be avoided by simple precautionary measures; life could continue as before with only the slightest of modifications.

At Chiang Mai airport, officials handed out masks to arriving passengers and, for the first time, I felt the polypropylene on my skin. I snapped a selfie of myself, with my mask and backpack firmly on, and thought that I could handle the mask's annoyance if it meant I could still travel. I still had dreams of circumventing the globe with a pack on my back and a mask on my face. Yet the virus's effect on tourism in Thailand became quickly evident. Guides told me about the dwindling numbers arriving and about the steady increase of COVID-19 cases in the country. Horror stories began to emerge from Iran, Spain, and Italy about the awful toll the virus had taken there— the skyrocketing number of dead as well as the communities left in complete lockdown. But I still believed I could outrun the virus.

In Laos, officials had recorded no COVID-19 cases, but commentators doubted the veracity of these government claims and argued it was only a matter of time before cases could no longer be hidden. More and more research was published about asymptomatic spreaders and the scary reality that even if one did not present any symptoms, one could be infected and spread the virus. Much to my disappointment, I decided to postpone my volunteer placement in Lebanon because I felt a refugee camp would be an ideal place for the virus to spread, and I did not want to be responsible for importing it.

In Myanmar, officials there, too, reported no cases, which was particularly suspicious considering the country's long and unpatrolled northern border with China. Outside Myanmar, the virus was spreading like a bush fire. On March 11, WHO declared COVID-19 a pandemic. The virus had established itself in western Europe and the United States. States of emergencies had been called. Hospitals were overflowing with people. Makeshift field hospitals were erected. More PPE equipment was needed. Health-care systems were breaking under the virus's weight. The football, basketball, and hockey seasons had all been postponed. Stay-at-home orders were issued. Concerts and theatres were indefinitely closed. Borders were closing. Countries were falling like dominoes. The world was locking down.

As I travelled through Myanmar, I swayed between denial and acceptance. Part of me argued that the most sensible and responsible thing to do was return to Canada, since I did not want to get sick abroad and potentially burden the health-care system of an already struggling country. Another part, however, railed against the idea of returning home, where I would have to hunker down with my parents for God knows how long, waiting out the COVID-19 storm. I would not accept the notion that I had to return, not after I had invested so much emotionally into this trip and its significance, not after it came to represent to me a step towards true independence. No. I could not accept becoming a burden to my parents, yet again, living off their generosity, while the world and its movements stayed outside my window, just out of reach. So I decided I would travel to Kuala Lumpur, rent an Airbnb apartment, and let the worst part of the pandemic pass.

On March 16, however, in my Yangon hotel room, I watched Prime Minister Justin Trudeau give a press conference in which he implored all Canadians abroad to return home in an effort to combat the worsening pandemic. Just after that announcement, I read that Malaysia would close its borders to foreigners. I could no longer hide in denial. COVID-19 was real and was here to stay. I got online and went to work cancelling flights, searching for new ones. And just a few days after I had promised myself I would not return to Canada, I was in a taxi driving to the airport, the first part of my journey from Yangon to Tokyo to Montreal to Toronto.

I had to self-isolate upon my return to my parents' cottage deep in rural Ontario. It could have been worse. The cottage was isolated, yes, hidden deep in a forest on a lake, but its seclusion made staying away from other people rather easy and effortless. And from the safety of our sanctuary, we watched on television as the world fell apart.

Staying at my parents' cottage, I was privileged in many ways. I worked as an editor, so I could easily edit from home. I could go for a run or a walk and not have to worry about meeting another person. There was the lake, and when spring turned into summer, I could go swimming or canoeing every day. There was space and lots of it. There was the reassurance that I did not have to risk my life to make ends meet.

Yet for a person accustomed to movement, lockdown and quarantines were anathema to my identity. Every time I heard a car in the distance or saw a plane drift across the sky, I was reminded that a world still existed out there. Running kept me sane. Running kept me moving. Every day I searched online about when the world might open again, when countries might welcome visitors again, when we might be able to move again. I needed something to look forward to, something to hope for, to work towards. A goal. A finish line. A destination. I happened across an MA program in photography in Barcelona starting in October. That was something. That was a plan. Studying photography in Barcelona sounded great; it rolled off the tongue. Living and studying in Barcelona, what a dream, what an opportunity, what an idea!

I got in.

The rest of the summer was spent basking in the glow from the light at the end of the tunnel. The days no longer seemed so monotonous, so opaque; they were now decorated with the reality of future movement. The European Union once again allowed Canadian tourists to visit. I searched for apartments in Barcelona; I arranged all the documents required for my student visa. I brushed up on my Spanish, started thinking about photographic projects I could undertake, researched and then applied to various NGOs working with refugees in Barcelona, and imagined completing the Camino de Santiago.

And even as my departure date approached and I read about an increasing number of COVID-19 cases in Spain and about the likelihood of a second wave, I did not let such negative news dissuade me because I believed that the western world would never go back into lockdown, would never impose stay-at-home orders, would never enforce curfews, and would never again imprison their citizens in their homes. I believed that the world had learned how to live with the virus, at least until a safe vaccine was developed and widely distributed, and that life could resume with some level of normalcy.

In any event, I convinced myself that I had done my time. I came home when called upon. I adhered to the quarantine protocols. I stayed home to flatten the curve. I followed all public health guidelines. I acted responsibly, and I believed I could continue to act responsibly while travelling, while living abroad. My life was ready to resume. I could wait no longer. It was time to step back into the world. Since the virus was to be with us for some time still, I was prepared to make some sacrifices and suffer through some inconvenience if it meant I could set my eyes on a city I had never seen before.

Once I arrived in Barcelona at the beginning of October, little time passed before those ideas were revealed as the fantasy they were. The number of cases continued to rise in Catalonia. Restaurants and bars closed. Schools went back to remote learning. A curfew was called. Internal travel was restricted. And finally, a state of emergency was called lasting till May.

My design school decided to keep in-person classes running, even though members of the larger community had become stricken with COVID-19, even though the city around it was getting sicker and sicker by the day. The administration did not want to go remote because many of the in-studio classes could not be done online. They reasoned that our class's small number would protect us against the virus as long as we wore masks and followed the other protocols.

They did not convince me. And because of the steep price tag attached to the year-long program—eleven thousand euros—I did not want to commit to a program that seemed to stand on such unsteady ground. There were far too many question marks around whether the program could continue, whether the classes would be forced online, whether Barcelona would drift further and further into lockdown. I did not think the school took the situation as seriously as they could have, especially considering not only the worsening situation around them but also what the country had gone through the previous spring. And what if I got COVID-19? I had insurance, yes, but practically I was not sure what that bought me.

So after only a month in Barcelona, I decided to leave the program and then the country. I travelled for a month or so after— Türkiye, Iraq, and Egypt—but with each PCR test I needed to enter the country and new worries surrounding what would happen if I tested positive, my anxiety grew and spread, and I decided to return a bit earlier than anticipated, even though I had always originally planned to return home for Christmas.

I did my second two-week quarantine at my cottage, with my parents. We celebrated Christmas together and looked forward to finally putting 2020 behind us. Yet news of a growing second wave in Ontario and another lockdown and stay-at-home order issued for Boxing Day dampened my spirit and made me realize that the first half of 2021 was likely to feel similar to 2020. I had still planned to go abroad again in January, somewhere, anywhere, but reports of new and more highly transmissible variants popping up in the United Kingdom, Brazil, and South Africa again gave me a moment of pause. And then the Canadian government issued more rules and regulations making it more difficult and less appealing for Canadians to travel abroad. They first made it necessary for returning Canadians to have a negative PCR test before boarding a flight to Canada. The government then cancelled flights to Mexico and Caribbean destinations. And a few weeks later, they required returning Canadians arriving by air to get tested upon arrival and then quarantine in a hotel for three days while awaiting the test's results.

The news angered me, as I felt governments at all levels were scapegoating travellers, while the real cause of community spread was factories and warehouses full of workers who could not work from home and who had to put themselves in harm's way every day just to get a paycheque. If leaders were seriously concerned about rising case numbers and increased hospitalizations, I reasoned, they would find ways to make these work sites less combustible and ways to support and protect workers who did not have the luxury of working over Zoom—including more paid sick days, more rapid testing, more benefits, more financial assistance—but instead they zeroed in on the border and portrayed travellers of all stripes as selfish and privileged people who did not care about the safety and well-being of others and were not prepared to make sacrifices for the sake of others. It angered me how travel became associated only with beaches and leisure, cocktails and swimming pools. It angered me that something I held in reverence was paraded across media outlets as nothing but holidaying or vacationing. And it angered me that while the government was telling Canadians that now was not the time to travel, that same government had recommenced deportations the previous November, had recommenced the violent act of removing undesirables in the middle of the pandemic. Why was it unsafe for Canadians to travel abroad but perfectly acceptable to put a deportee on a plane and send them to a location whose COVID-19 situation may be worse than Canada's?

Despite my frustration, I soon realized there was little I could do to change the situation, so I gradually accepted it: I would not be travelling for the foreseeable future. So I focused on the day at hand and tried to fill it with meaningful activities. I wrote and ran and read. I worked. I paid back some student loans and managed to put some money in a savings account. I took an online photography class, which forced me to search for interesting subjects to shoot in my day-to-day life. Most of my photography to that point had been of the travel variety: beautiful landscapes, interesting architecture, busy city streets. Now, I had to look for subjects in familiar surroundings, within scenes I had taken for granted. I had to look for beauty in the commonplace. I shot a fairground that I frequented as a child, blanketed in snow. A marsh I had run through countless times but had never considered its photographic potential. A Walmart parking lot, full of unreturned shopping carts. My old public school, which now looked so small and vulnerable compared to how I remembered it. A movie theatre where I had seen some of my favourite movies, which now sat closed and unused—abandoned. The Bradford GO train station, which sat emptied of cars and activity yet whose existence still reminded me of a world outside of my own sequestered one. A green canoe sitting atop a frozen lake, which served for me as an apt metaphor for travelling during COVID-19 times.

Photography became my way of travelling in the pandemic. It made the familiar strange. It opened my eyes to scenes I had never noticed before. It forced me to stop and look around. To look more closely at things I had considered just there, as mere background, only decoration. Nothing of substance or value or interest. With my camera in hand, absolutely everything became fascinating. Every photo became a thousand little decisions. What if I angled my camera this way? What if I shot the scene from ground level? What if I blurred the foreground but left the background in focus? What if I put my subject in the left of the frame instead of centring it? What if I darkened the exposure? What mood am I trying to convey? What's my story? Photography forced me to look again and then again. It made me take my time, to stay still for a moment or two longer than I would, and simply watch. And every time I pressed the shutter and examined the result on the screen, I saw something new.

Yet photography itself still couldn't prevent me from religiously following the news about Canada's slow vaccine rollout or about when I would be eligible for the shot or about when I could travel again. I looked on envy as the United States and the United Kingdom vaccinated their population with incredible speed and looked set to return to a degree of normalcy in the not-too-distant future. I looked on in despair as new variants took hold in Ontario, ICU admissions increased to record highs, and the government ordered another lockdown and another stay-at-home order to flatten the curve and lessen the burden on the health-care system, which was on the brink of collapse. I looked on in concern as the people who were now ending up in hospital and lying on a bed attached to a ventilator began to look a lot more like me, as it now seemed that young age and good health were not the shield against the virus they once were.

It is now May 2021 as I write this. The pandemic is close to fourteen months old and has killed over three million people. The vaccine rollout has picked up pace in Canada, in Europe, and a few other countries, but large swaths of the world's population, particularly those living in poorer countries, have not yet received their first shot and do not appear likely to anytime soon. Nationalism has reared its ugly head again, this time in the form of vaccine distribution, as the rich countries have prioritized vaccinating their populations and hoarding vaccines instead of engaging in a more equitable delivery of inoculation. Rich countries have even taken vaccines earmarked for poorer ones. In March, for example, Canada announced that it would receive 1.9 million vaccines from the COVAX Facility, which is a global initiative to ensure equal vaccination access among richer and poorer countries. As reported on CBC News, when asked whether it was right for a wealthy nation like Canada to take vaccines from such a program, Public Services and Procurement Minister Anita Anand replied, "We are going to make sure that all Canadians have access to vaccines. That's our priority, that's the role of the federal government." Canada would not share any doses with other countries until all Canadians were vaccinated.

In a cruel twist of irony, the COVAX AstraZeneca vaccines Canada did receive were manufactured by the Serum Institute of India, and now India is on fire. There's no need to recount here the list of horrors the country is experiencing on a daily basis; suffice it to say, India is now the epicentre of the pandemic, and its daily COVID-related deaths are in the thousands. The point is that the vaccines Canada accepted from India could have been better used vaccinating Indians themselves. The point is that no one is safe until everyone is safe. As vaccinated westerners look forward to a potential maskless summer with fewer and fewer restrictions, the majority of the world will lurch into July and August still unprotected, still providing a warm body for the virus to evolve, adapt, and find ways to circumvent the antibodies produced by the vaccines. No one is safe until everyone is safe.

Despite the pandemic's global reach, its distaste for borders, and its non-discriminatory nature—infecting everyone regardless of sex, gender, race, creed, sexual orientation—the world's outlook has remained parochial, fastened to the nation-state. And as the world builds back better and fixes the many cracks to our collective security and well-being that the pandemic has laid bare, I would like to think that travel can play a small but important role in setting fire to borders, if not in reality than at least in our minds. As global travel restarts, it must escape the logics that had previously defined it: capitalism and narcissism. To have any relevance in a post pandemic world, travel must become more than simply an expensive mirror for our own vanity. Travel must become cosmopolitan in its outlook and focus on communities of people, not communities of states. It must bear witness and stand in solidarity with the world of people. Travel must surpass the level of policy, the parliaments and assembly halls of states the world over, and instead foster new relationships between the self and the world. It must demand that we see ourselves as connected, as part of the same web of relations, part of the same ecosystem. Travel must resurrect notions of hospitality from the service industry and must ask communities how they may support people on the move, out of place, or in need of protection. It must demand that communities open their doors to the world without demanding gratitude or thanks, without asking for anything in return. It must reject ideas of altruism and idealism and instead replace them with notions of being in the world, the radical potential of merely thinking about other people.

Last January, in a moment of both creativity and desperation, I dug out our canoe from its winter resting place, dragged it from the dock, and pulled it across the frozen lake until it was a good fifteen metres from shore. I wiped the snow from its exterior so that its green colour could shine in the wintry sun. I looked at the canoe sitting atop a sheet of thick ice and liked the absurdity of it, the silliness of thinking that this would be an effective mode of transportation in such conditions. It looked so wonderfully out of place. I removed my camera from my backpack and took over a hundred photos of that green canoe resting in the middle of a frozen lake. I wanted to photograph it from every angle. I crouched. I sat cross-legged. I got down on my belly and positioned myself like a snake. I stood on my tiptoes. I liked what I saw. I like what it represented—that even though travel was almost impossible at the moment, its idea and possibility still existed, that even though its actualization at the moment was absurd, its idea certainly was not. Hope. It was something like hope.

I grabbed a paddle, sat down in the canoe, and tried to paddle myself back to shore. And even though I knew it would not budge, I still imagined that the ice had melted into water under my effort and that I was free to explore the lake as I had always done. And in my mind, bass swam underneath my canoe, a beaver slapped its tail in the distance, and a heron flew overhead. No wind disturbed the lake's surface. No waves, not even a ripple. The surface was like a mirror reflecting to me the lazy clouds hanging in the sky and the curvy pine trees standing on the shoreline. Everything was so still and quiet. The only sound came from my paddle cutting gently through the water calmed like the way mother would run her fingers through my hair as a child. The sound was peaceful, rhythmic. It was the sound of movement, of propulsion, of going forwards and forwards.

In my mind, the sun had risen above the pine trees, and its light danced and sparkled across the lake's clear blue surface. I canoed towards a rocky outcrop, a place my father has long called the Secret Spot, stepped upon the shore, and tied the canoe to a tree. Without thinking, without stopping, I walked right into the water and felt its coldness against my feet, then my legs, my stomach and chest, and finally my neck. Under water, the world was familiar yet strange. The outline of a fallen tree or a boulder, likely dating back to prehistoric times, was smudged, blurry. Nothing was in focus. Streams of light broke through the surface to reveal the darker areas that my eyes could not catch, inviting me to visit a world so unlike my own.

I lay flat on my back, used my hands to steady myself, and let the water support me. I floated there in the middle of the lake with my eyes closed, arms by my side, and my breath controlled. I heard the occasional loon call or human voice from a distant cottage. Every now and then, my ears would dip below the surface, and my drums would fill with water, creating an intriguing pressure. Sometimes, water would roll over my mouth and leave my nose as oxygen's only entrance. I would float there without aim or purpose, letting the water and slight breeze push me in whichever direction they pleased. Even with my eyes shut, I felt the sunrays push through my eyelids and explode into a million different shiny stars. I focused on my breathing and the sounds my arms made through the water. I felt the cool liquid on my fingertips, the water's gentle touch massaging my muscles. I felt at peace, calm. Everything felt hazy and easy. I was freed from reality's incessant noise. I only had to close my eyes and float. Close my eyes and move.

Acknowledgments

The publication of this work would not have been possible without the support of my parents, Andrea O'Reilly and Terry Conlin, as well as the generous contributions of Karen Shimoda, Jennifer O'Reilly, Christine Conlin, Yudum Yonak, Jason Brennan, Matthew Carlson, Dawn Lane, and Steve Lane.

Thank you all!

www.ingramcontent.com/pod-product-compliance
Lightning Source LLC
Chambersburg PA
CBHW030302100426
42812CB00002B/536